IMAGES
*of America*

# POQUOSON

**On the Cover:** The fishing boat *Elsie Jane* is tied up at Carroll's Dock, which was part of the Poquoson Seafood Company, managed by Carroll Thomas Forrest. The small boat tied up next to it is the *Cecil*, the Freeman family's pleasure boat. The *Elsie Jane*, named for Jane Freeman Bunting, was originally an Army T-boat during World War II, patrolling the area harbors. The boat was converted to a trawl boat in 1948 or 1949. Capt. Herbert "Fuzzy" Freeman ran the boat until it went down off the Eastern Shore while traveling to Chincoteague. (Courtesy of Henry Freeman.)

IMAGES
*of America*

# POQUOSON

Poquoson Museum and
Poquoson Historical Society

ARCADIA
PUBLISHING

ISBN 978-0-7385-9835-2

Published by Arcadia Publishing
Charleston, South Carolina

Printed in the United States of America

Library of Congress Control Number: 2012947788

For all general information, please contact Arcadia Publishing:
Telephone 843-853-2070
Fax 843-853-0044
E-mail sales@arcadiapublishing.com
For customer service and orders:
Toll-Free 1-888-313-2665

Visit us on the Internet at www.arcadiapublishing.com

*This book is dedicated to Thomas Vincent Watkins,*
*Jessie F. Forrest, Ura Bradshaw, and Harold Shaw*
*and to all past, present, and future caretakers of the past.*

# Contents

# ACKNOWLEDGMENTS

Many of the photographs in this book are housed at the Poquoson Museum and at the Poquoson Historical Society. Barbara Hudgins Whitlow and Mary Bradshaw Clemons are most grateful to the following: the City of Poquoson, the Poquoson Fire Department, the Poquoson Masonic Lodge, Claytor Rollins Funeral Home, Trinity United Methodist Church, and the Poquoson Kiwanis.

We also thank the members of our small community that allowed us to scan photographs from their personal collections and gave us invaluable information: Patricia Smith Apelt, Katie Evans Arredondo, Edna Mae Insley Barr, the family of William Bradshaw, Mr. Clary, Bethany Forrest Diggs, Nannie White Diggs, Phyllis A. Firth, Carleton P. Forrest, Carrie B. Forrest, Harold Freeman, Henry Freeman, Manfred Freeman, Melissa Forrest Gardy, Phoebe Harcum, Susan Downs Herring, Jackie Insley Holloway, Joyce Butler Holloway, the family of Thomas C. Hudgins Jr., Dr. Robert Huggett, the family of Rose Ward Huggett, George Hunt, Edith Wade Insley, Robert V. Insley Jr., Sonny Insley, Bonnie Karwac, Carol Ann Winder Mann, Charles McDaniel, Georgia McDaniel, Carroll Watkins Martin, Sid Pauls Jr., Frances Evans Potts, the family of Mary Quinn, Hunter Riggins Jr., Roman Rollins, Will Rollins, Tim Smith, Maresa Firth Spangler, Leroy Wade, Durwood Watkins, the family of Nelson C. Watkins Jr., Myrna Gail Forrest Wechsler, Jane Smith White, and Paul A. Whitlow Sr. Special thanks go to Tim Smith for his invaluable assistance with the cover.

# INTRODUCTION

Poquoson was originally hunted and fished by the Virginia Indians before it was settled by the English. The name Poquoson is an Indian word that describes elevated land between the boundaries of creeks or streams with their marshes. Poquoson holds the distinction of being the oldest continuously named town in Virginia.

In 1631, Christopher Calthrope was granted a 500-acre land patent in New Poquoson. The land patent was one of many granted by royal governor Sir John Harvey in order to extend the English settlement from the James River across the peninsula to the York River. After the restoration of Charles II to the throne of England, land again began to be patented in Poquoson, starting with Black Walnut Neck and parts of the Great Marsh in 1663. The time of the large patents had begun, and plantations dominated the area during the Colonial period.

After the American Revolution, in the late 1700s, new residents, watermen, and farmers migrated from the Eastern Shore of Virginia and Maryland and began settling in Poquoson. The continued presence of the British on the Eastern Shore and the rising tensions between England and the United States led in part to the mass exodus. One of the first to venture to Poquoson was Zaddock Messick, who came to the area around 1800. He purchased a portion of the 17th-century Boar Quarter land patent, which he used for commercial and residential purposes. This area became known as Messick. Another area, Moore's, got its name from the Moore family, who had substantial land holdings in the northwestern part of Poquoson.

The Union army was encamped in Poquoson during the Civil War. A famous ghost story from the time, known as Dolly's Mammy, detailed a mother who took revenge on her disobedient daughter from the grave and was documented by the Union army. Residents were under military rule until after the war, and the suffering of the locals caused by the Union raids made the population weary of outsiders.

In the late 1800s, the community of Odd was established, named after the Independent Order of Odd Fellows Lodge. In the 1800s and the early 1900s, the communities of Odd, Messick, Jeff's, Moore's, and Poquoson were defined by their post offices. These distinct communities, though in close proximity to each other, had their own stores and post offices. In fact, five separate post offices served these communities.

A sixth post office, Earnest, was a shipping address established by local businessman George W. Amory. The post office, on Amory's Wharf in the Back River, was used for shipping freight by shallow draft steamers to the wharf. Later, the post office served several residences in southern Messick.

According to York County records, these distinct areas were considered by the officials in York County as separate communities within the Poquoson Magisterial District. As the 1900s progressed, new families moved into the area after the establishment of Langley Air Force Base and NASA nearby. Poquoson became a town in 1952 after a dispute with York County over moving the high school to another place in the county, and by 1959, all of the post offices merged into the Poquoson Post Office. The City of Poquoson was chartered in 1975. Today, Poquoson schools are on the list of the top 1,000 schools in the United States. Traditions of civic duty and community pride are reflected in the number of civic organizations in the city and in events like workboat races and the Poquoson Seafood Festival, which celebrates the community with food, music, history, and the maritime skills of the local watermen, and have continued to this day.

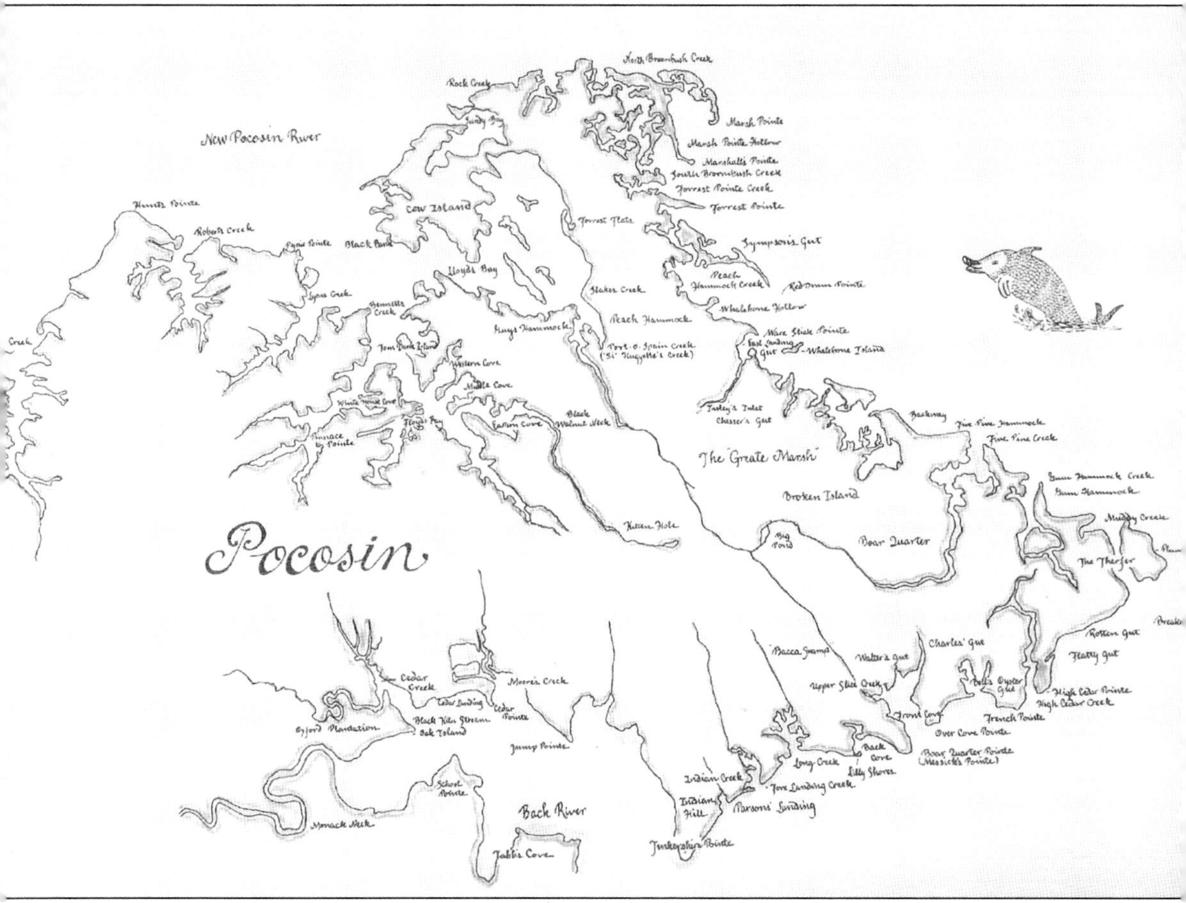


This map of the original land grants in Poquoson shows the names of the patent holders as well as their locations. The map was drawn by hand and hand-colored. Some of the land patents had unique names, such as Boar Quarter, which became Messick, and Oxford Plantation, which became Wythe Creek Road. (Courtesy of Robert Huggett.)

# *One*

# The Poquoson and Moore's Communities

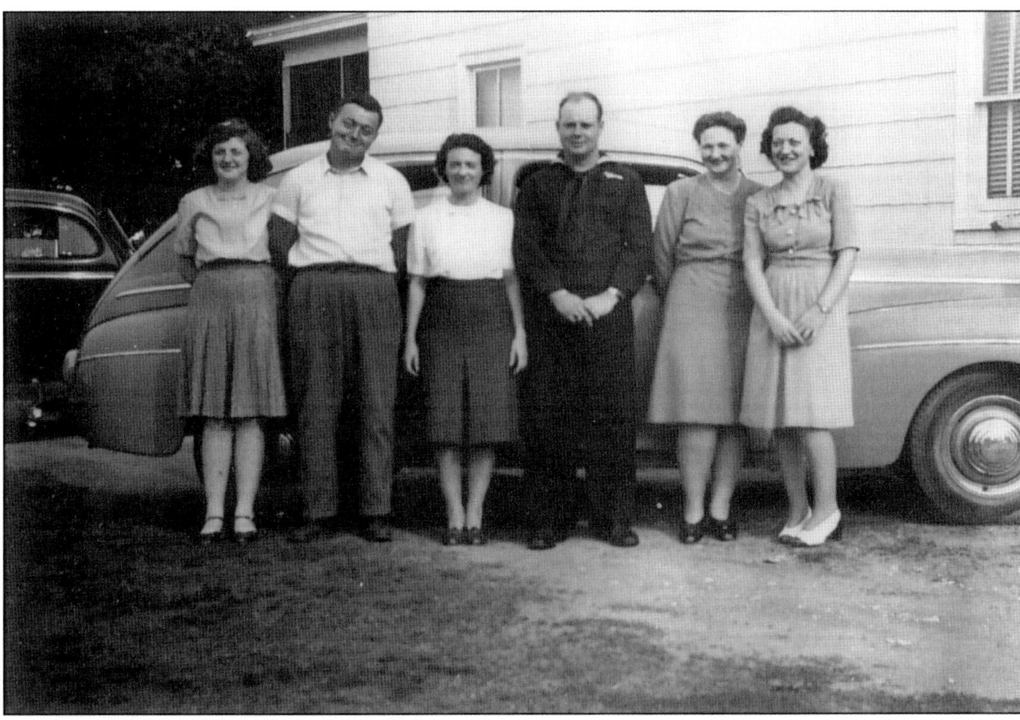

From left to right, Barbara Hunt, George Hunt, Sarah Hunt, Kelsor Hunt, Ruth Hunt, and Lucille Hunt pose for a photograph outside their family home. George Hunt was the last postmaster for the old Poquoson Post Office. (Courtesy of George Hunt.)

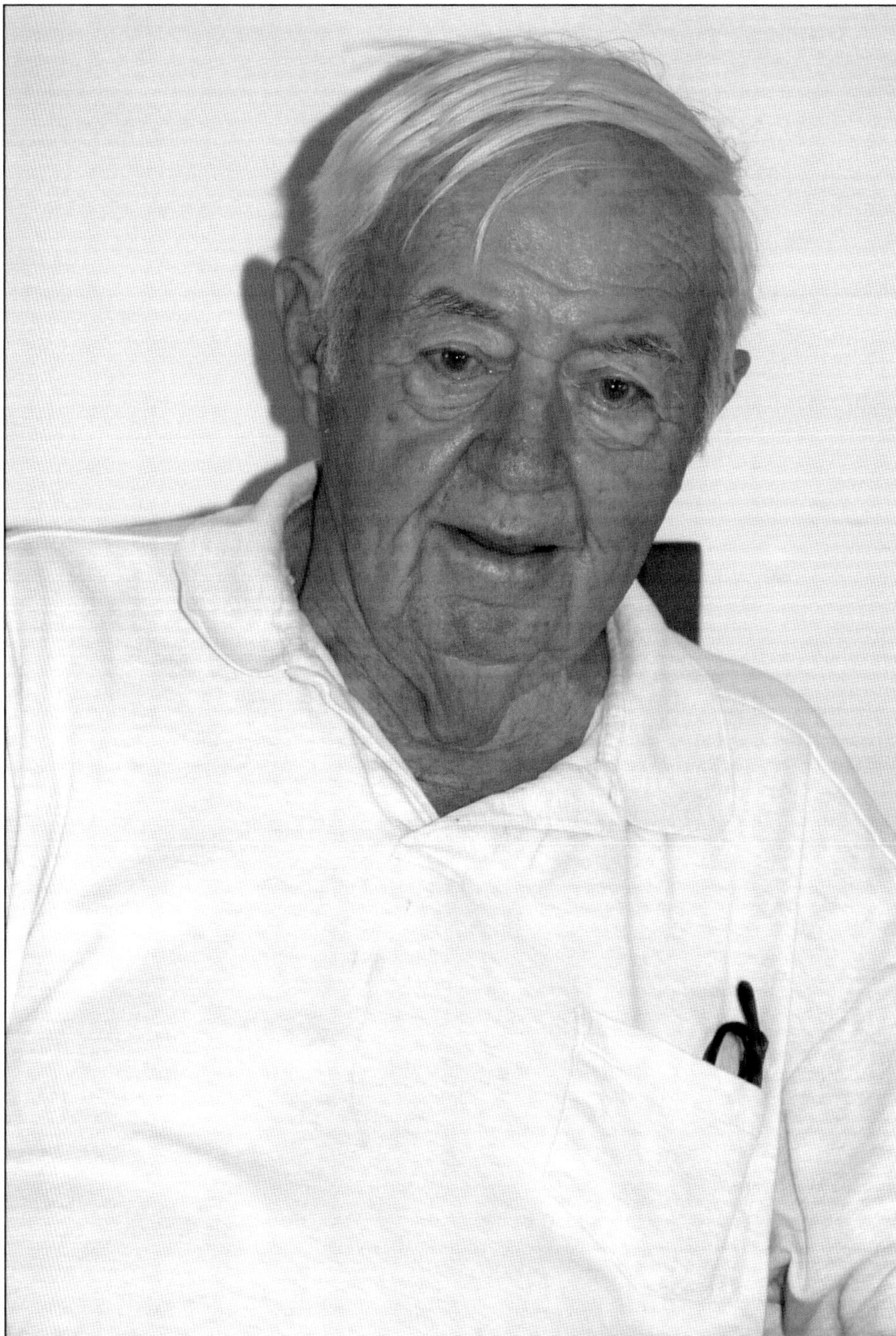

George Hunt was interviewed by members of the Poquoson Historical Society in 2012. He explained how the post office evolved over the years that he worked there and discussed how the area had changed over the last 50 years. He was the last postmaster of the Poquoson community post office before all the post offices were consolidated into one, which was located across Poquoson Avenue from Tabernacle United Methodist Church. Hunt later was in charge of the Hampton area post offices. (Courtesy of Barbara Hudgins Whitlow.)

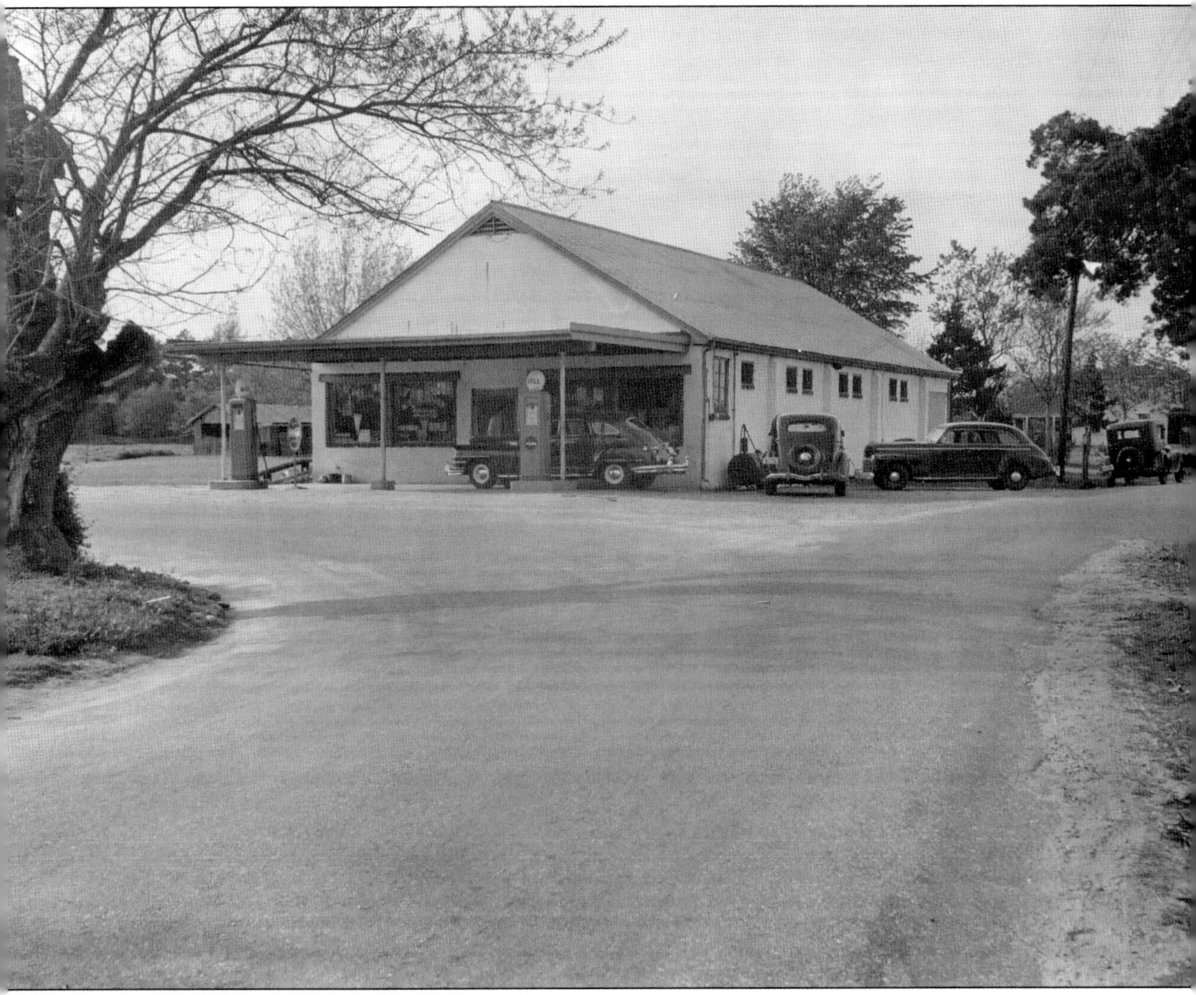

The B.C. Smith store was built by Conway Hudgins and sold to R.F. Jurney, who ran an electrical appliances store and gas station there when this photograph was taken. Bernard Clyde Smith Jr. bought the store at 895 Yorktown Road in Poquoson in 1946. He was known by the nickname of "Rooster," and the store became known as Rooster Smith's store. The store sold everything imaginable to the northern area of Poquoson. The local children bought penny candy at the store, and it was also a local informal meeting place for men to come and discuss politics and events of the day. It was deemed important enough for future Virginia governor and US senator George Allen to use as a whistle stop during his early campaigns for state delegate in the 1980s. At the gas pump in front of the store is a 1946 Ford. (Courtesy of Jane Smith White.)

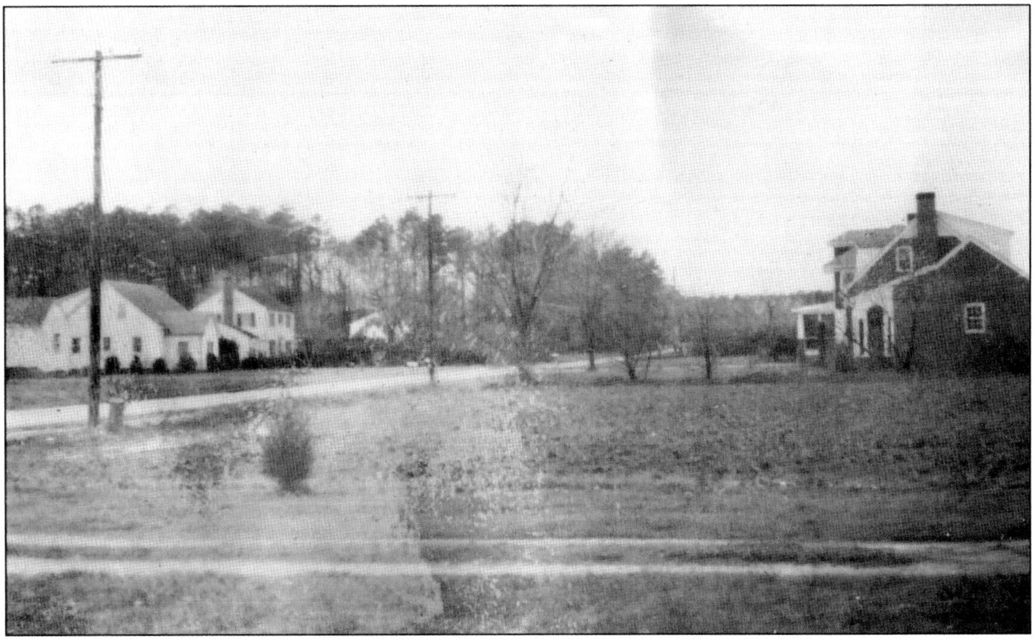

This 1950s photograph looks northwest at houses along Yorktown Road. On the right is the residence of Sara Shields, now owned by her daughter Sally Lindberg. The house on the far left belonged to Alva and Roselyn Hunt and was purchased by James and Mary Lindberg after Roselyn Hunt's death. The adjacent house was owned by Dr. John and Ann Hunt. Their daughter Deborah Sterling currently owns the property. (Courtesy of Jane Smith White.)

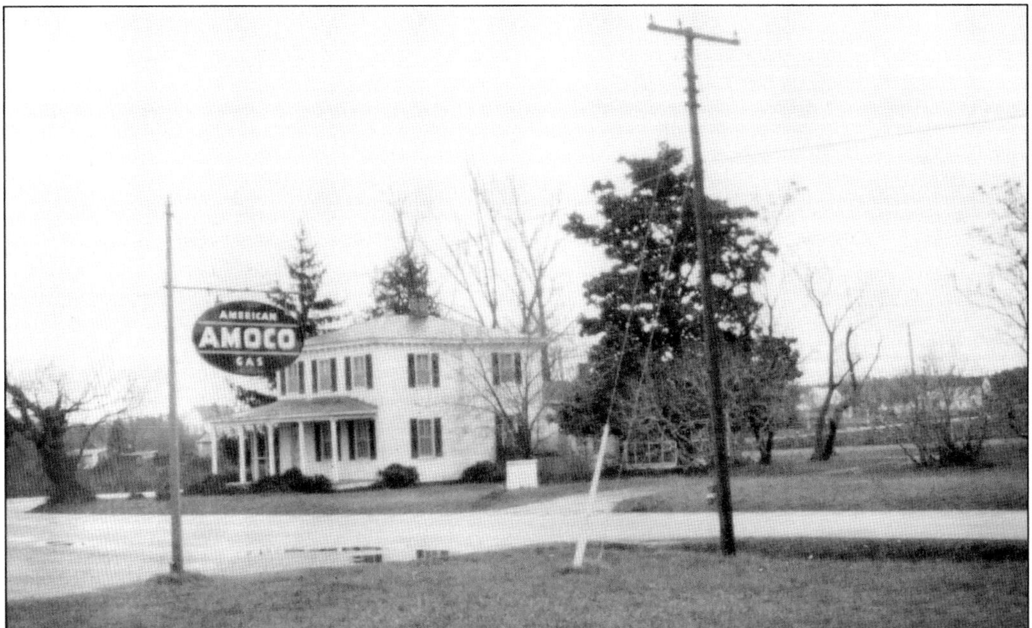


The southern portion of Yorktown Road is seen here in this 1950s photograph, which shows the home of William and Pearl Moore on the corner of Yorktown and Wythe Creek Roads. (Courtesy of Jane Smith White.)

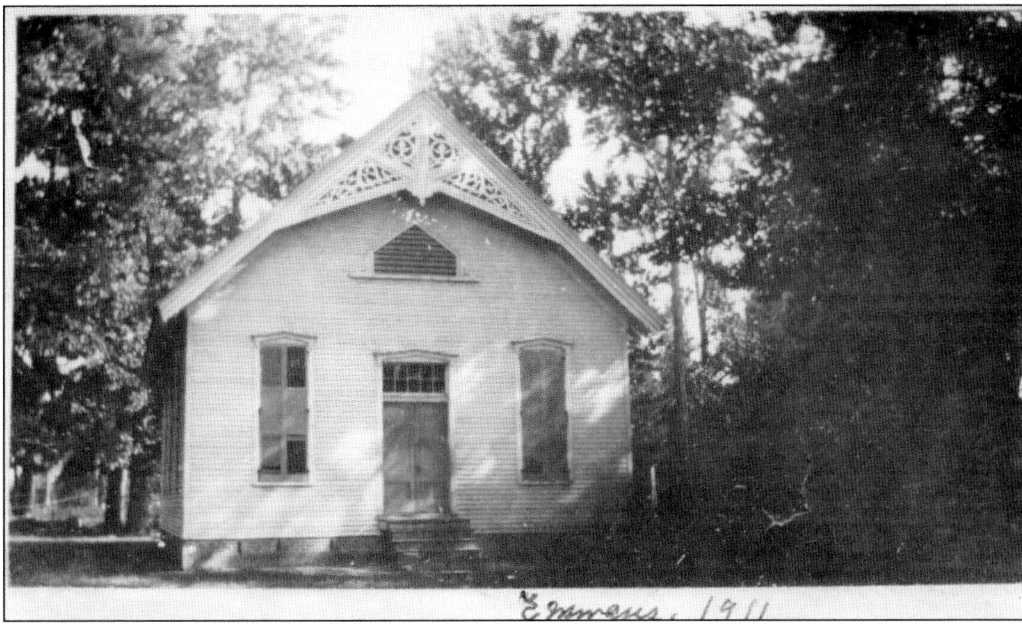


Emmaus Baptist Church was founded on June 21, 1878, with 27 members. It moved to its current location in 1888, when this small chapel was built. Additions to this structure were made in 1925 and 1949. A new brick sanctuary and education building were constructed in 1960. (Courtesy of Edith Wade Insley.)

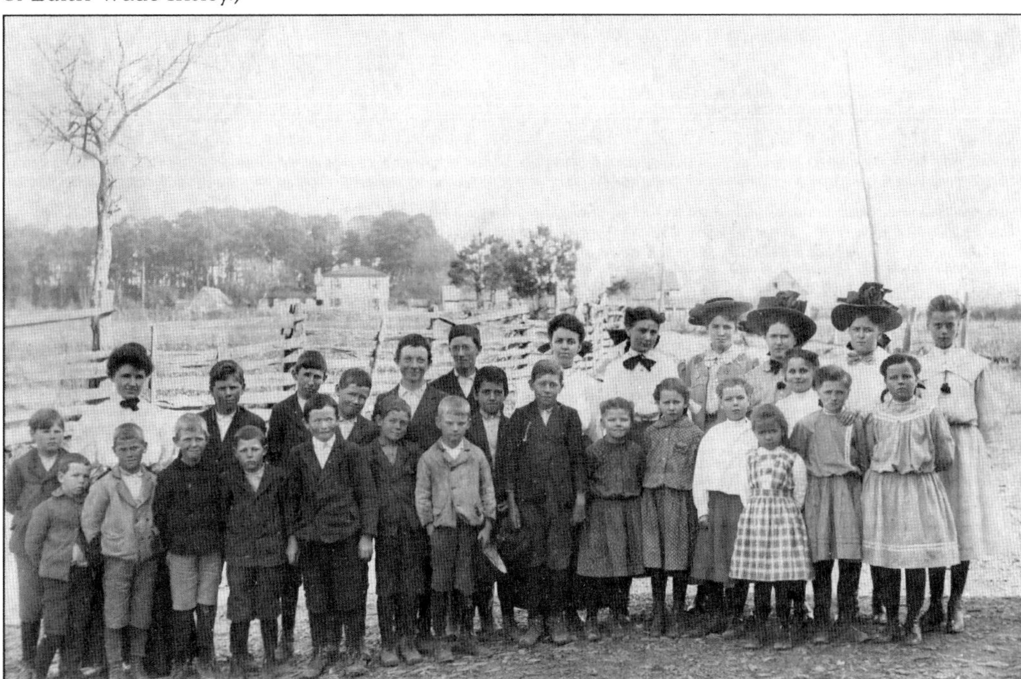

The 1907–1908 Sunday school pupils of Emmaus Baptist Church are seen here on an outing on Hunts Neck Road, which was the original location of the church, near the head of Robert's Creek. (Courtesy of the Poquoson Historical Society.)

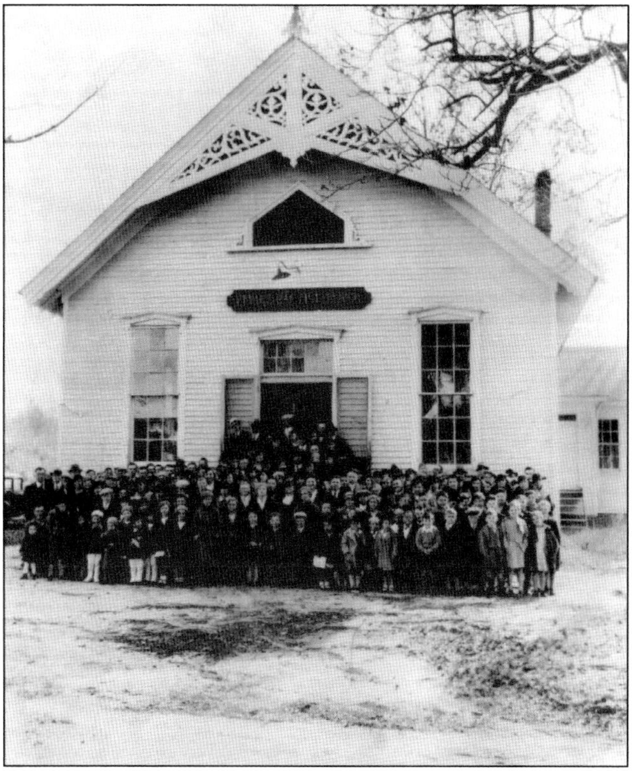

The congregation of Emmaus Baptist Church is seen here outside the original wooden church in the early 1930s. The church continued to grow throughout the 1900s. A new brick sanctuary was constructed in the 1960s, but the old wooden church is still used by the congregation. (Courtesy of the Poquoson Historical Society.)

Below, the Hopkins family poses on the front porch of the family home around 1910. The Hopkinses were a family of local farmers and fishermen who lived in the Moore and Poquoson areas. (Courtesy of Edith Wade Insley.)

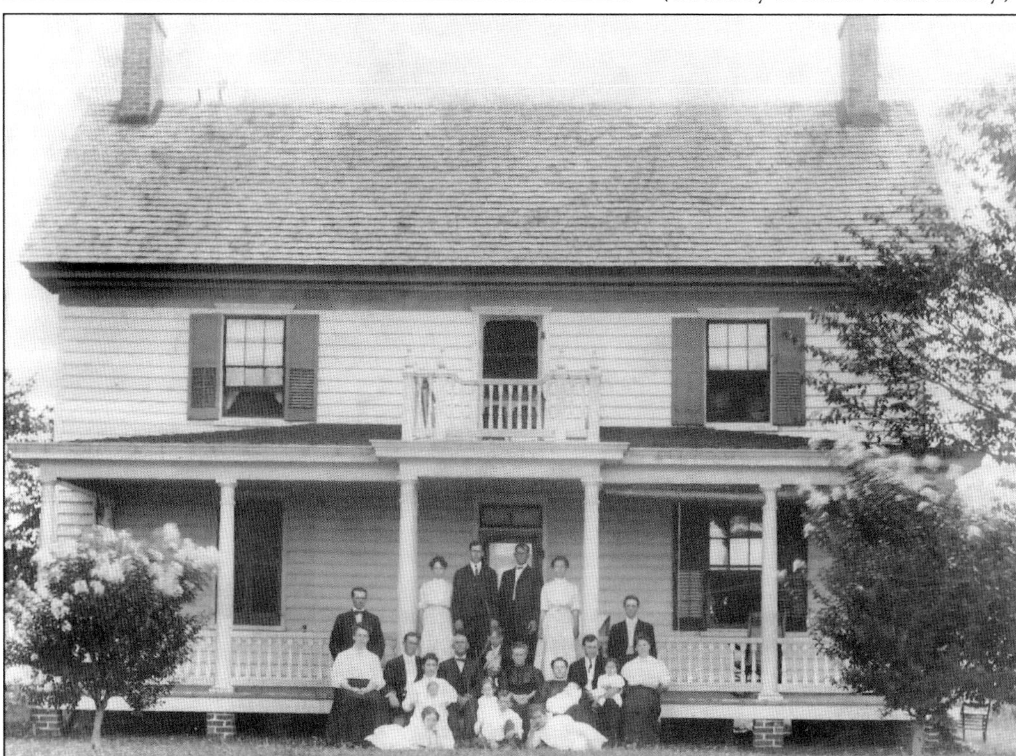

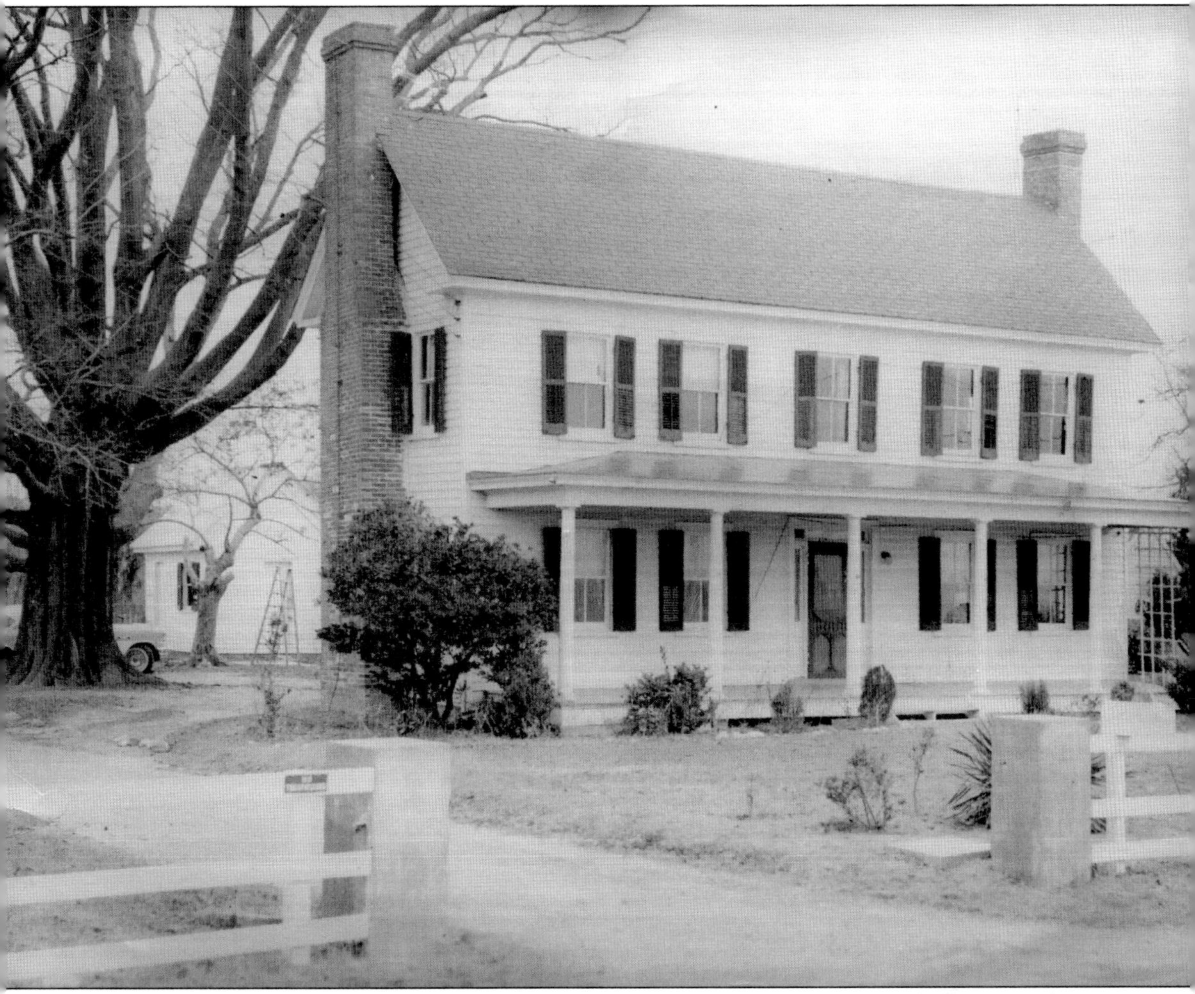

The Wornom family home, built in the 1800s, is seen here in the early 1950s. This property has been extensively renovated with a number of additions that have made it almost unrecognizable today. The Wornoms were among the families that migrated from the Eastern Shore of Virginia in the early 1800s. One of the first recorded documents with the surname of Wornom was the estate sale of Joseph Hopkins's property. (Courtesy of Mr. Clary.)

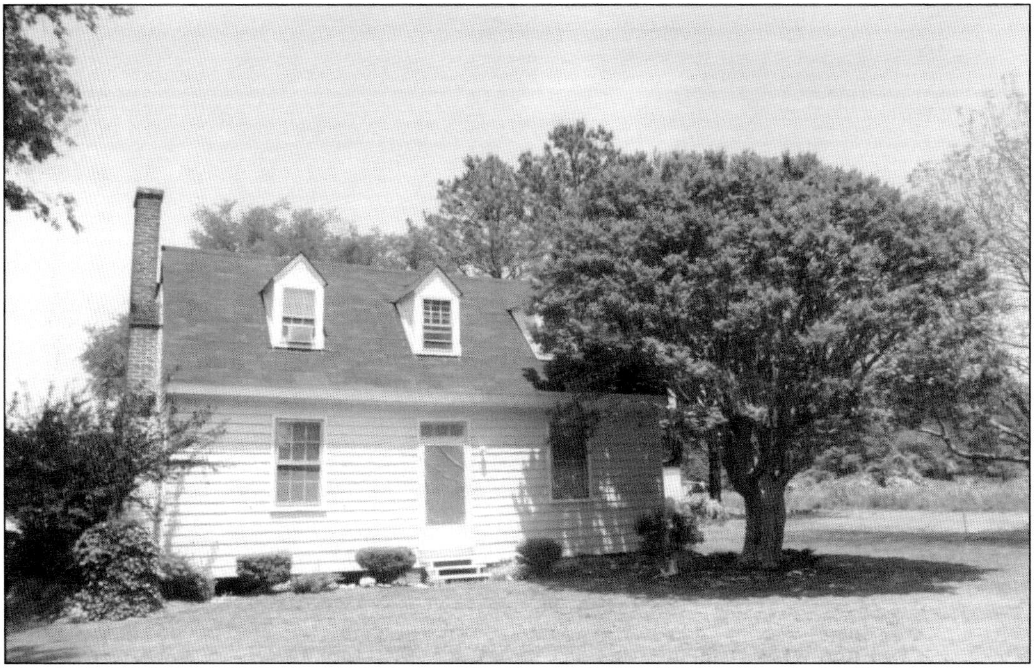

The Smith house, at 175 Smith Street, is thought to be the oldest house in Poquoson. It has been owned by the Smith family since Robert Henry Smith and his wife, Rosanna Bunting, moved there in the 1850s. In the early 1900s, the southern portion of Poquoson, where this house is located, received mail addressed RFD Hampton. (Courtesy of Phoebe Harcum.)

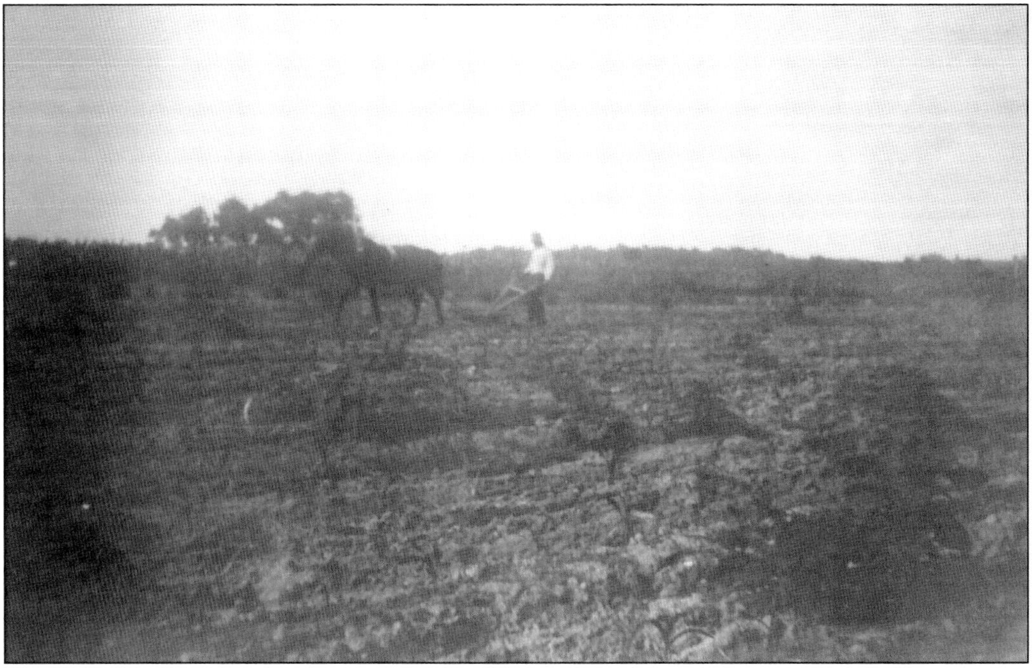

Moses Russell is seen here plowing a field in 1912. He was a hired African American field worker for the Hopkins family. Farming was labor intensive, so hired workers were necessary to maintain large farms. (Courtesy of Edith Wade Insley.)

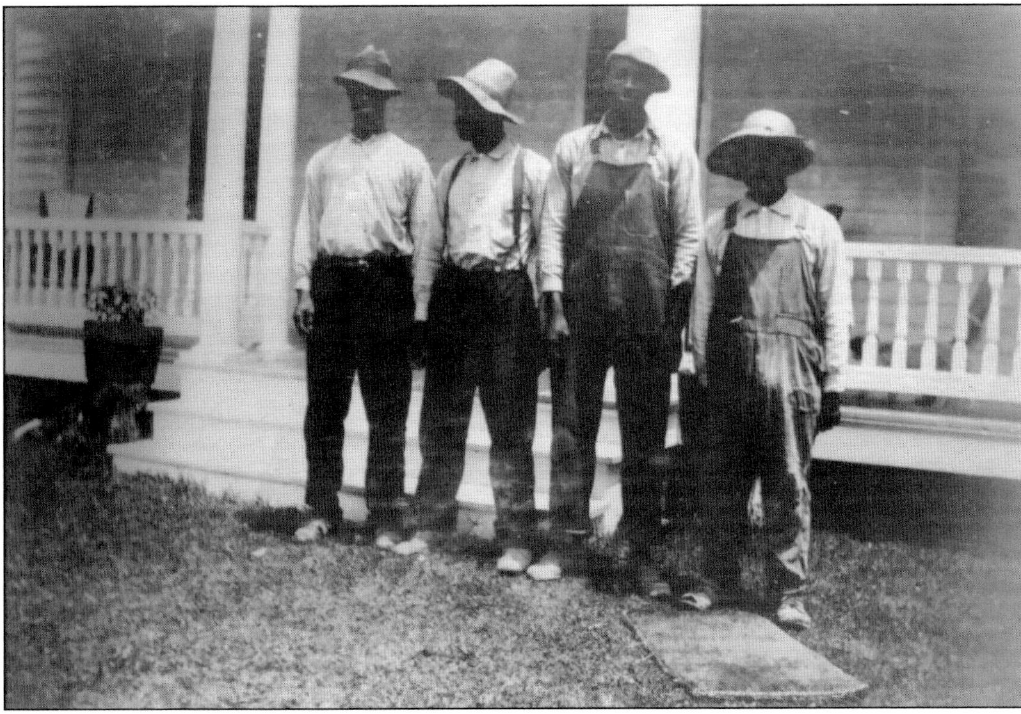

Above, farm workers pose in front of the Hopkins house. From left to right, they are identified as Moses, Shed, Elijah, and Jim. These men performed a wide variety of jobs on the farm, from plowing and planting to harvesting the crops. (Courtesy of Edith Wade Insley.)

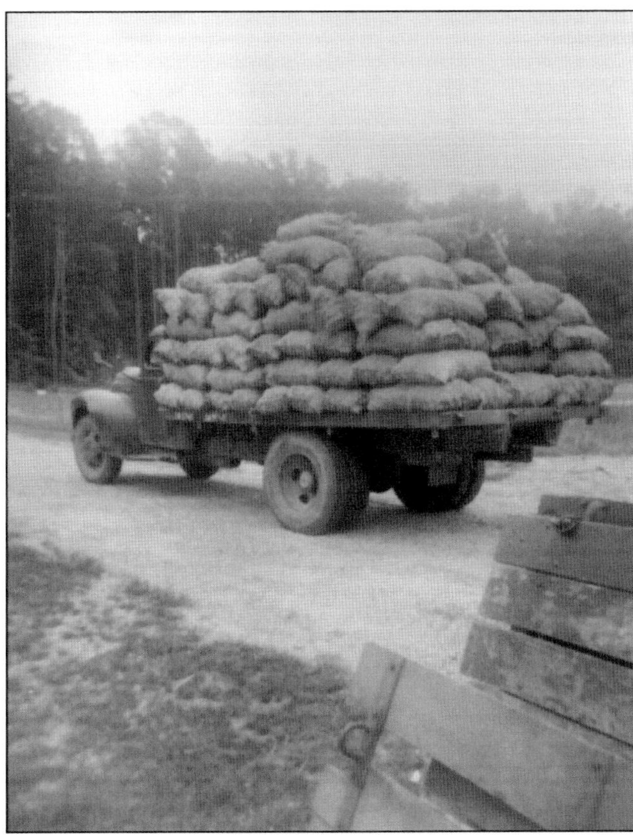

This farm truck is filled with large bags of potatoes to be taken to the market and sold. Potatoes were purchased from local farmers by the military during World War II. (Courtesy of Manfred Freeman.)

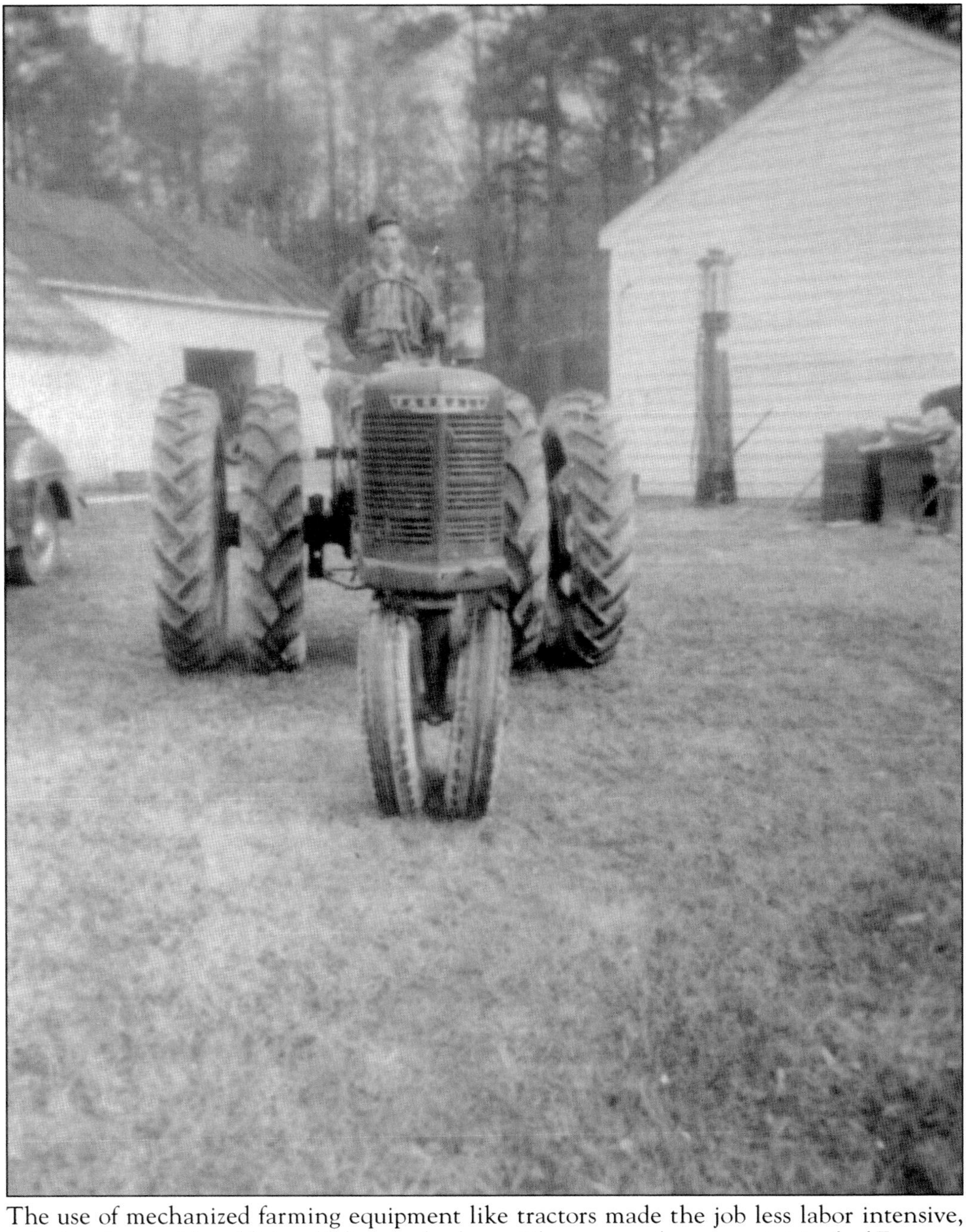

The use of mechanized farming equipment like tractors made the job less labor intensive, reducing the need for additional labor on the farms. The man on the tractor is Manfred Freeman Sr., and the photograph was taken on his farm in the community of Moore's. The gas pump in the background has a glass top that is dated to the 1940s. Many local farmers with larger farms had their own gas pumps, so that they would not have to drive to the local country store to get gasoline. (Courtesy of Manfred Freeman.)

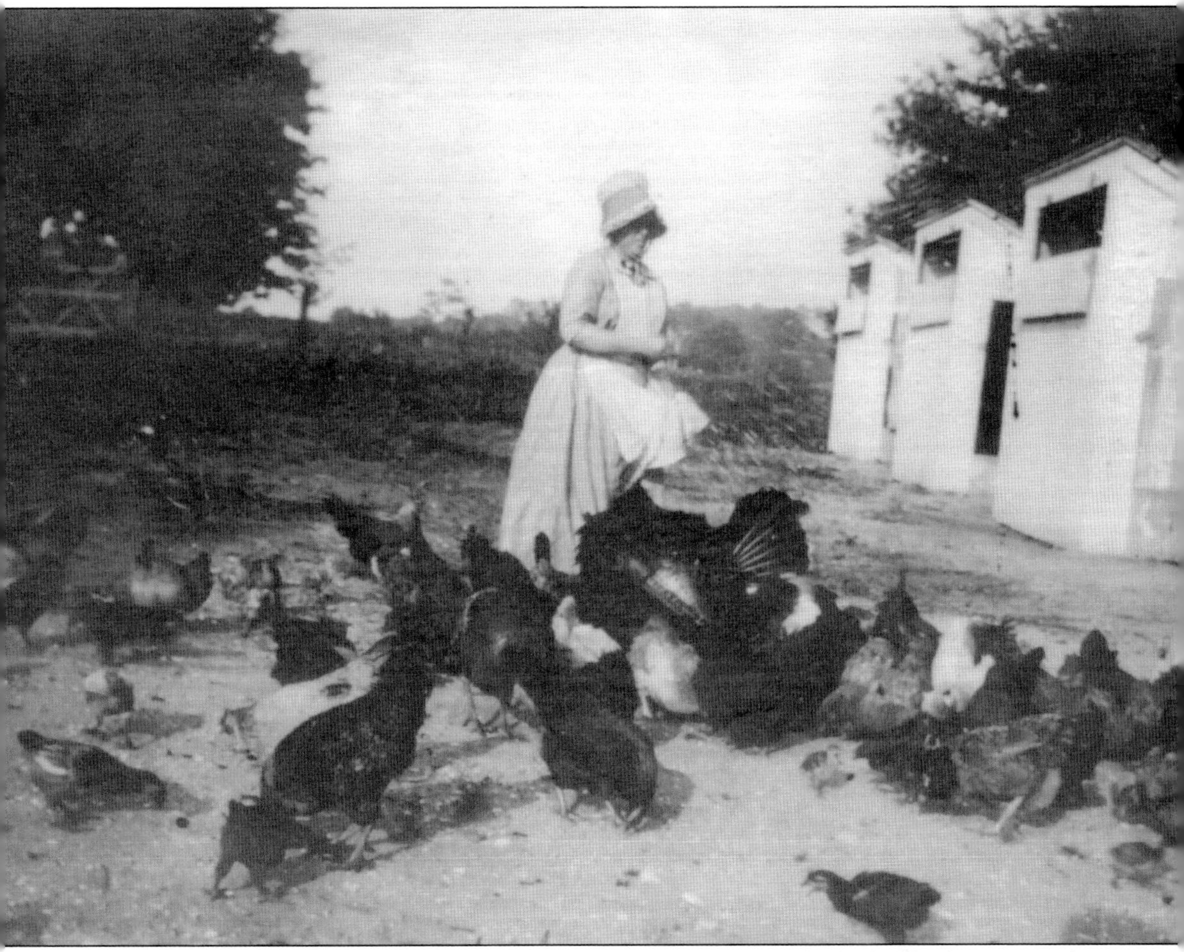

Farm work was not limited to the men. Here, in 1911, Diana Hopkins feeds the chickens, one of many jobs that women did on the farm. The chickens' eggs were sold and also used to feed the family. This farm was near the Poquoson River; Leonard Moore also had an orchard nearby. Some of the local residents that worked in grocery stores in Hampton and Langley Field in the late 1940s and 1950s stopped by this farm to purchase produce. (Courtesy of Edith Wade Insley.)

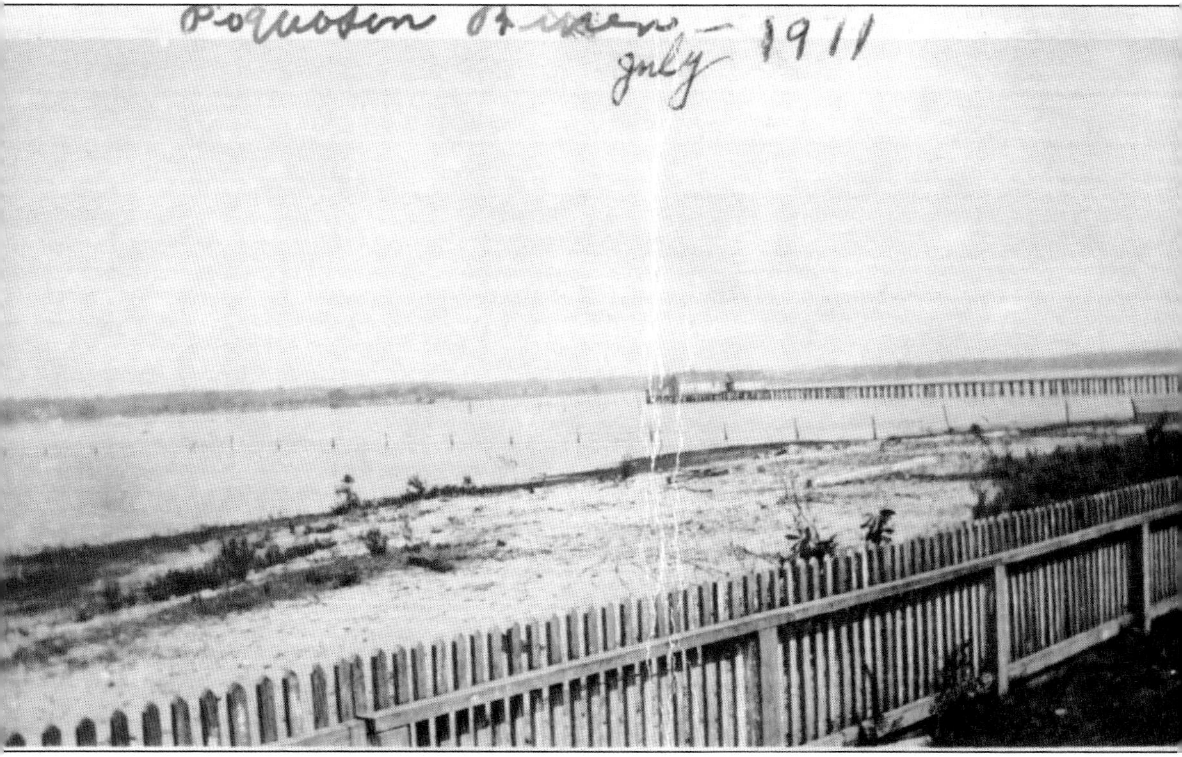


The Poquoson River is seen here from the end of Hunts Neck, in front of the James S. Hopkins house, in July 1911. This rare photograph shows Wornom's wharf in the center. The wharf was at the end of the present Hunts Neck Road. Only a few of the oldest area residents remember the wharf. (Courtesy of Edith Wade Insley.)

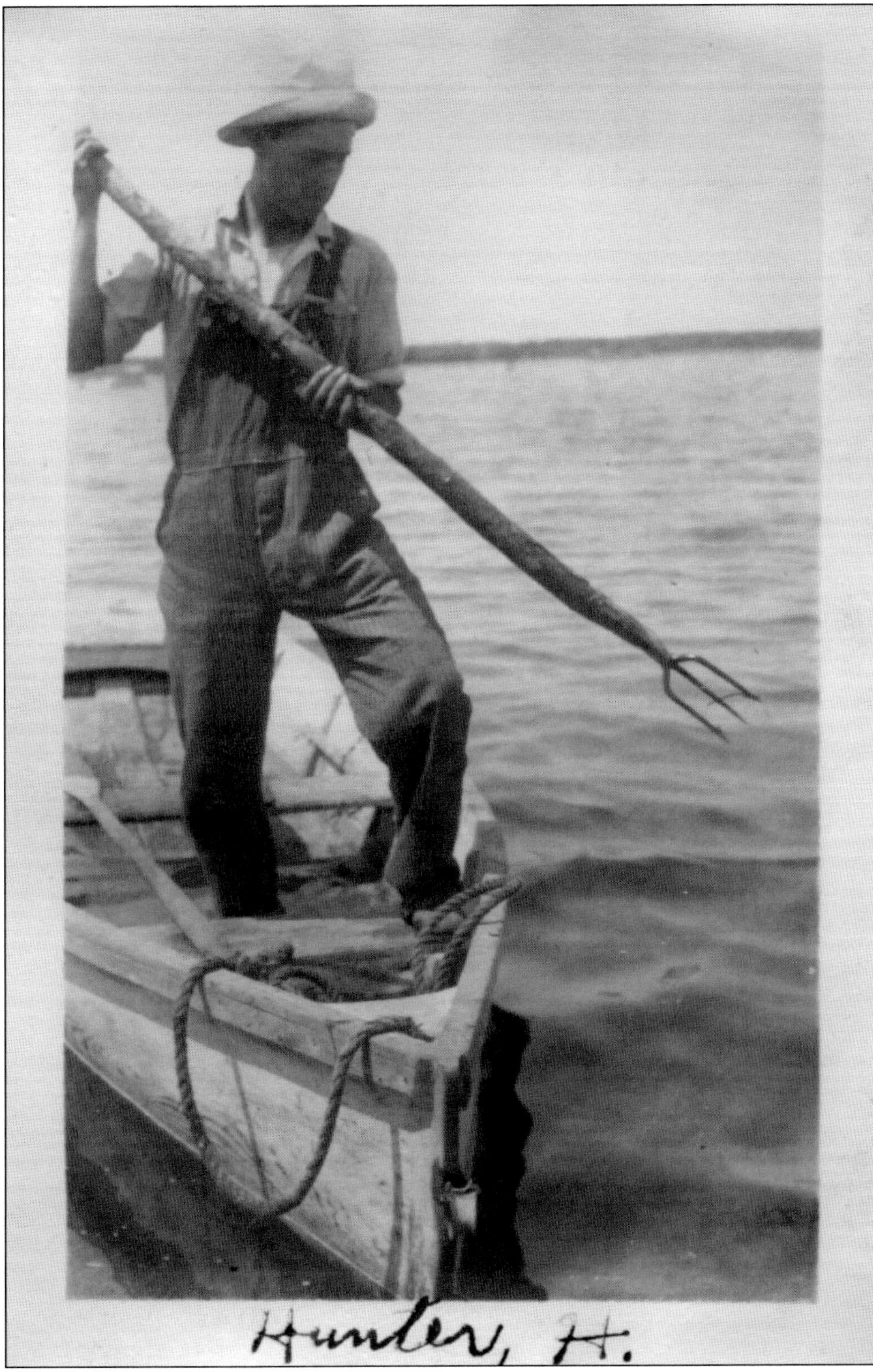


Hunter Hopkins is poised to spear a stingray in the Poquoson River in the early 1900s. Stingrays can sting wading fishermen and cause serious harm, so they have to be removed before nets can be set. (Courtesy of Edith Wade Insley.)

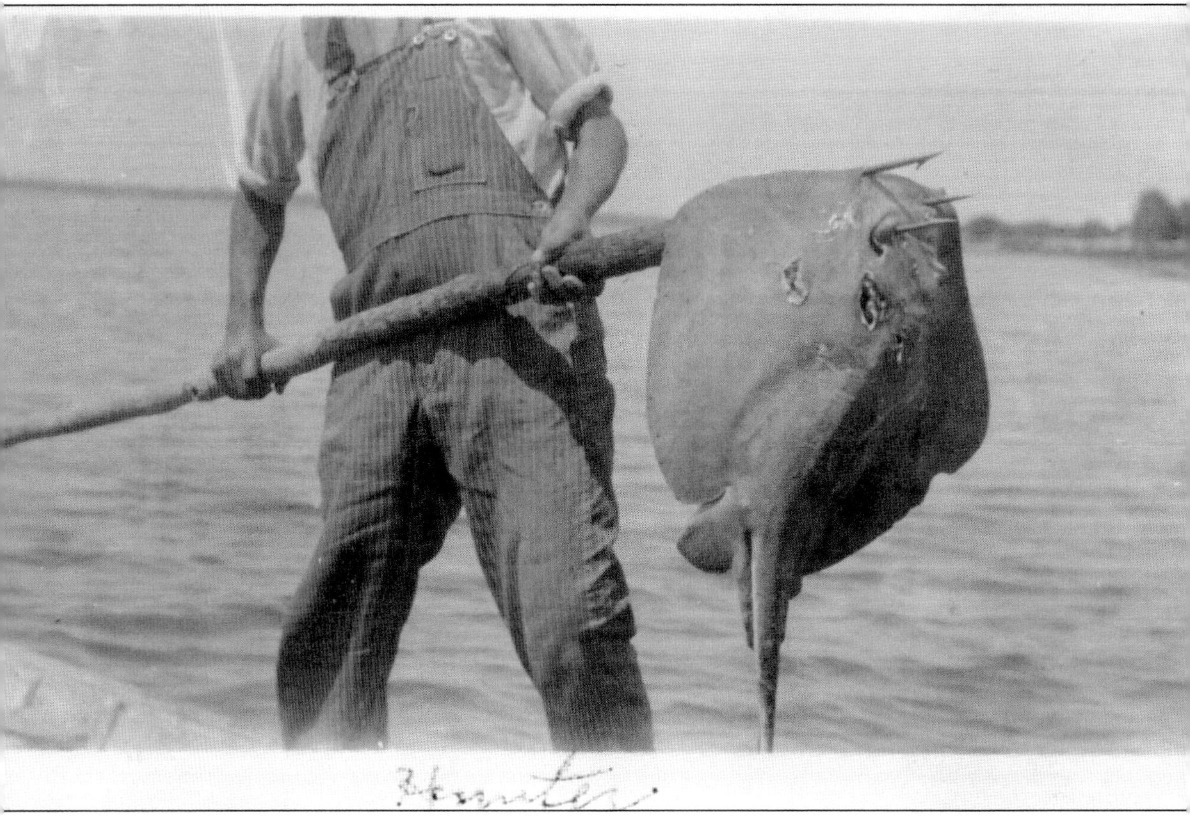


Hunter Hopkins holds up a large stingray that he speared in the Poquoson River. The trident fishing spear, with its barbs, was an ideal instrument for fishing these creatures. Stingrays are an invasive species in the local rivers. (Courtesy of Edith Wade Insley.)

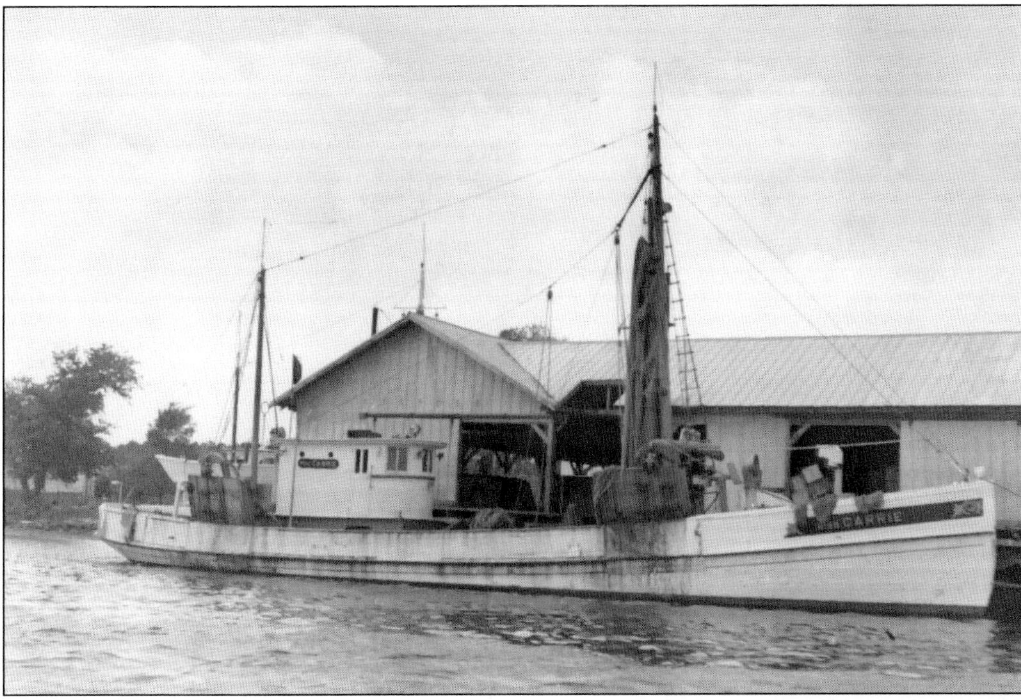

The fishing boat *Miss Carrie* (above) was named after Capt. Henry Leslie "Scoop" Freeman's sister. The boat sank at Little Inlet, about five miles south of where the *Elsie Jane* would sink many years later in 1984. (Courtesy of Henry Freeman.)

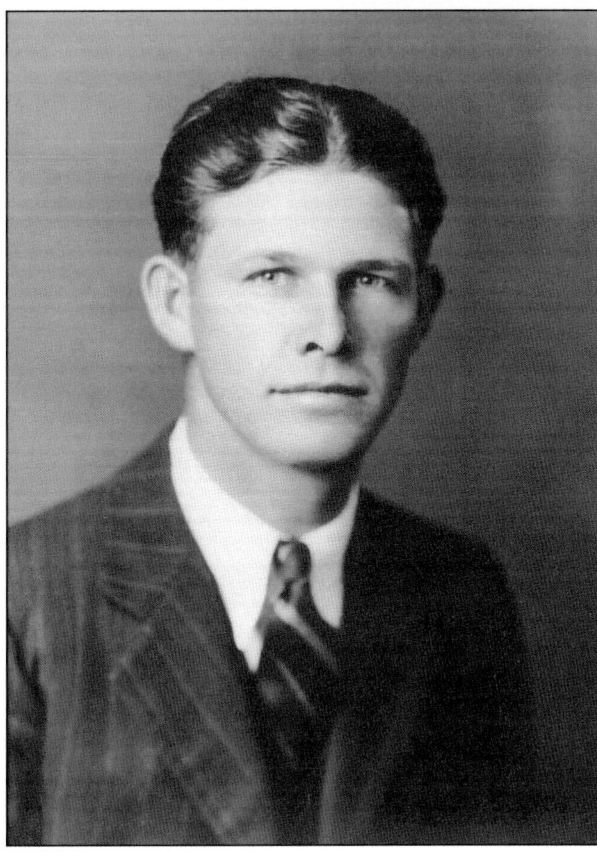

Capt. Henry Leslie "Scoop" Freeman, the captain of the *Miss Carrie*, poses for a portrait around 1940. Captain Freeman was killed in 1950 when his hip bootstrap got caught in a winch during the night. (Courtesy of Henry Freeman.)

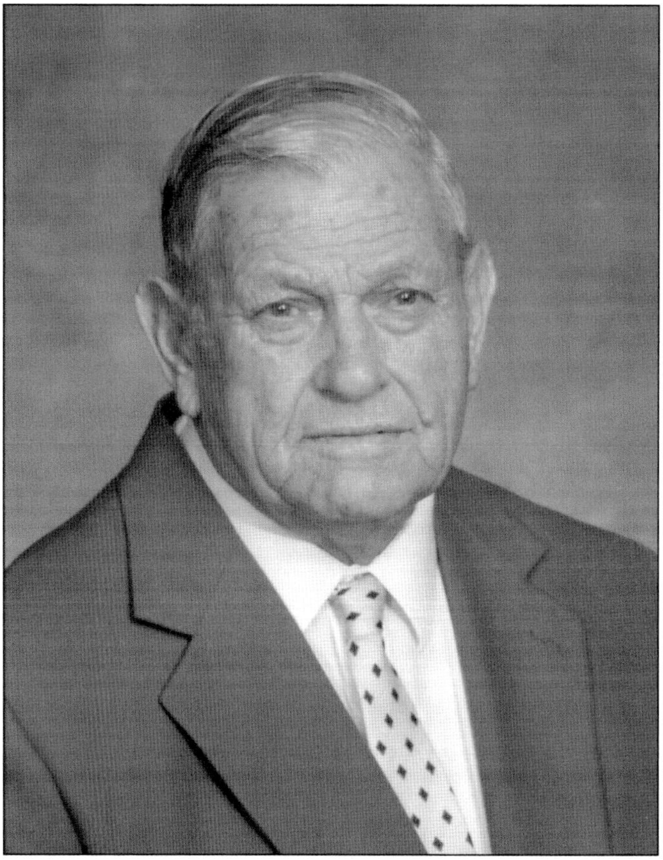

Capt. Herbert "Fuzzy" Freeman, the captain of the *Elsie Jane*, survived the sinking of the boat by holding on to the mast until he could be rescued. Two of his crew died when the boat went down: Francis Freeman, who drowned, and Joe Bailey, who had a fatal heart attack. (Courtesy of Henry Freeman.)

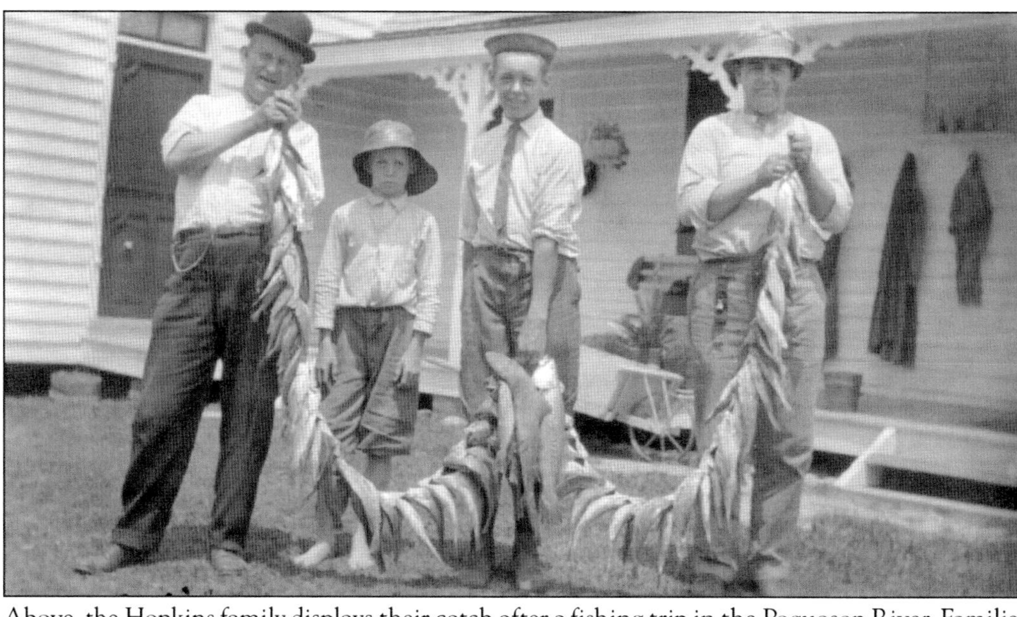

Above, the Hopkins family displays their catch after a fishing trip in the Poquoson River. Families took fishing trips on the weekends, bringing the fish home to fry for dinner. (Courtesy of Edith Wade Insley.)

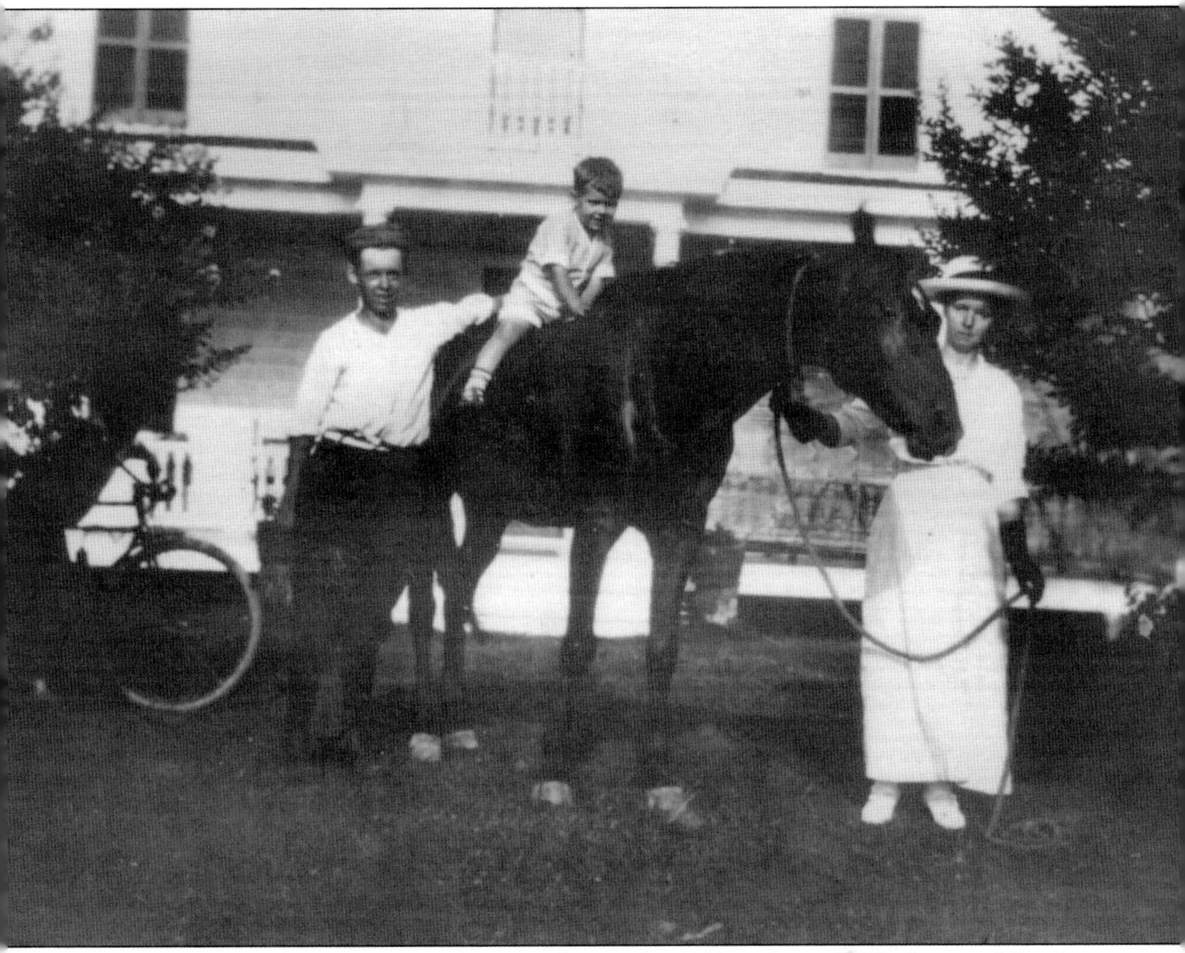

Sarah Elizabeth Hopkins Moore was born on August 31, 1889, to James F. Hopkins and Sarah Elizabeth Hunt Hopkins. She married Leonard Levi Moore, the son of Henry Freeman Moore and Sarah Elizabeth Riggins Moore, in 1917. She is seen here at age 22, standing on the right with her horse Senator, facing the Poquoson River with her home in the background. Standing on the far left is John Hopkins, and seated on the horse is young Charles Hopkins Jr. Sarah Moore once rode sidesaddle on Senator all the way to Yorktown for a celebration. The family still has one of Senator's horseshoes framed, as well as a stirrup, to save that memory. A look at the home behind them shows the full front porch and second-floor balcony, which was not original to the home but was added by the oldest Hopkins son, William James Hopkins. (Courtesy of Edith Wade Insley.)

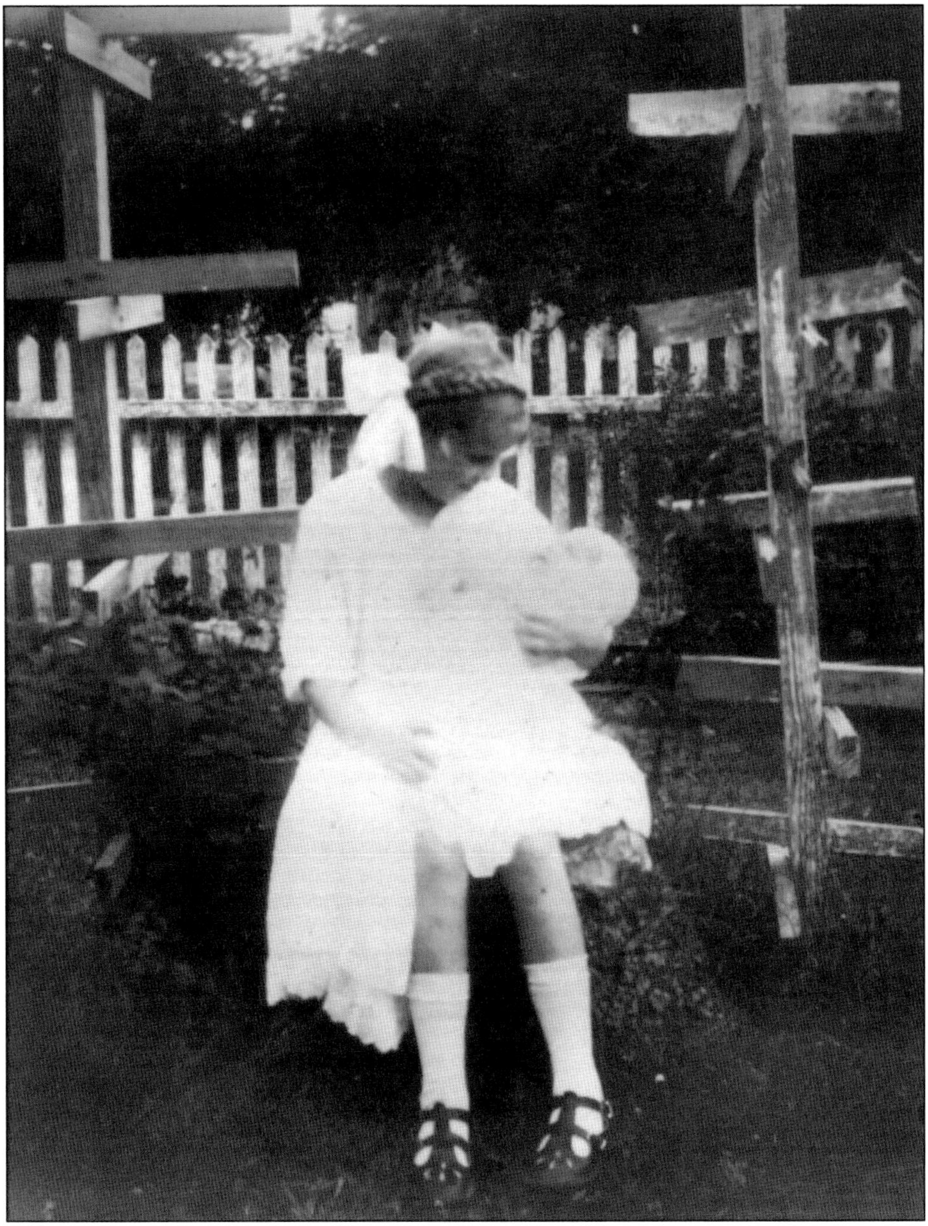

The three-story Hopkins home was built by a 23-year-old James S. Hopkins on a west-facing hill on a very large parcel of farmland. He and his wife, Sara E. Hunt Hopkins, raised 10 children there. They harvested seafood from the river and crops from the fields. Wool was spun from their sheep to make blankets, and there were chickens and hogs on the farm. James Hopkins also built wooden canoes and launched them on the property. For four generations, the home was the gathering place for all the families to come home to. In this photograph, taken in the flower garden, a young visiting niece of James S. and Sarah Hopkins, Marguerite Hunt, is only too happy to hold the Hopkins's new grandson, Charles Hopkins Jr., in 1908. In the background is the fence that surrounded the outer yard of the home. There are two wooden trellises for the climbing roses, which were planted nearby. A note on the photograph says "the little mother," referring to Marguerite's demeanor with the baby. (Courtesy of Edith Wade Insley.)

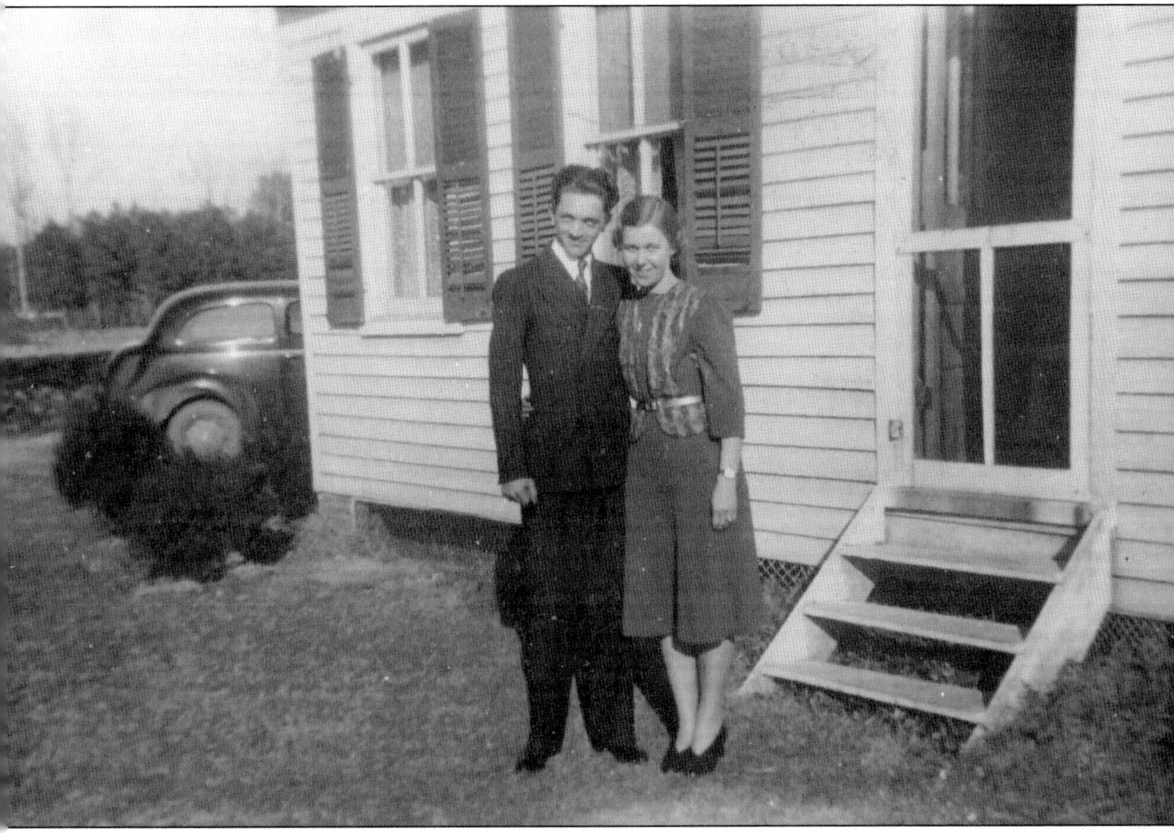

Vincent Watkins and his wife, Emma, are seen here on a visit with relatives in the community of Odd. Vincent was a famous piano teacher in Poquoson. Later in life, he became a noted local historian and was instrumental in the establishment of the Poquoson Historical Society. He was the first historian for the City of Poquoson. He wrote the definitive book on the early history of Poquoson, *A History of Poquoson in Three Parts (1631–1860)*. A portrait of him was dedicated by his wife and daughter to the Poquoson Public Library Roots Cellar after his death. The portrait now hangs in the Poquoson Historical Society Room at the Poquoson Museum. (Courtesy of Charles McDaniels.)

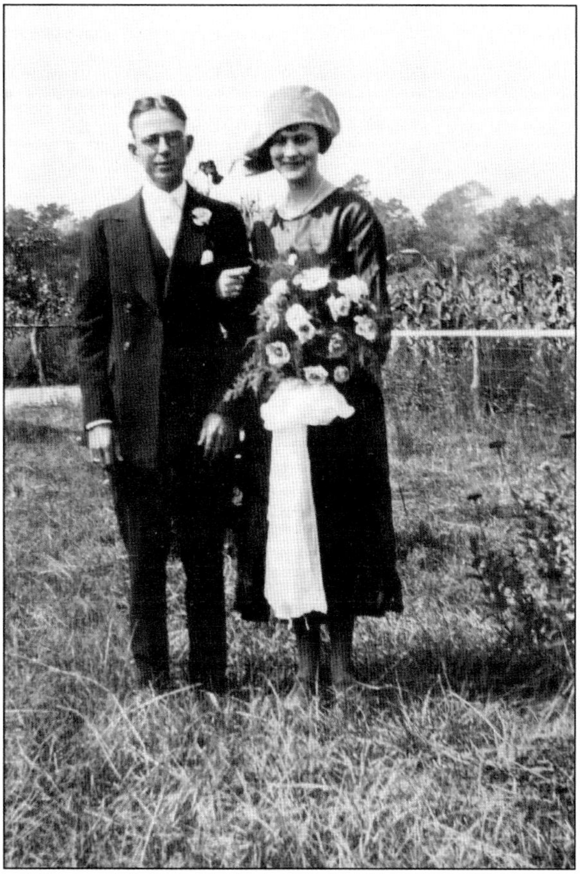

Bernard Clyde Smith Jr. and his bride, Dorothy Freeman, pose for a photograph in their yard on their wedding day. Dorothy is holding a large bouquet of flowers. Bernard Clyde Smith Jr. was born on October 20, 1903, to Bernard Clyde Smith Sr. and Irella Eliza Watkins Smith. Dorothy Russell Freeman was born on November 7, 1906, to William Russell Freeman and Susan Elizabeth Hudgins. (Courtesy of Jane Smith White.)

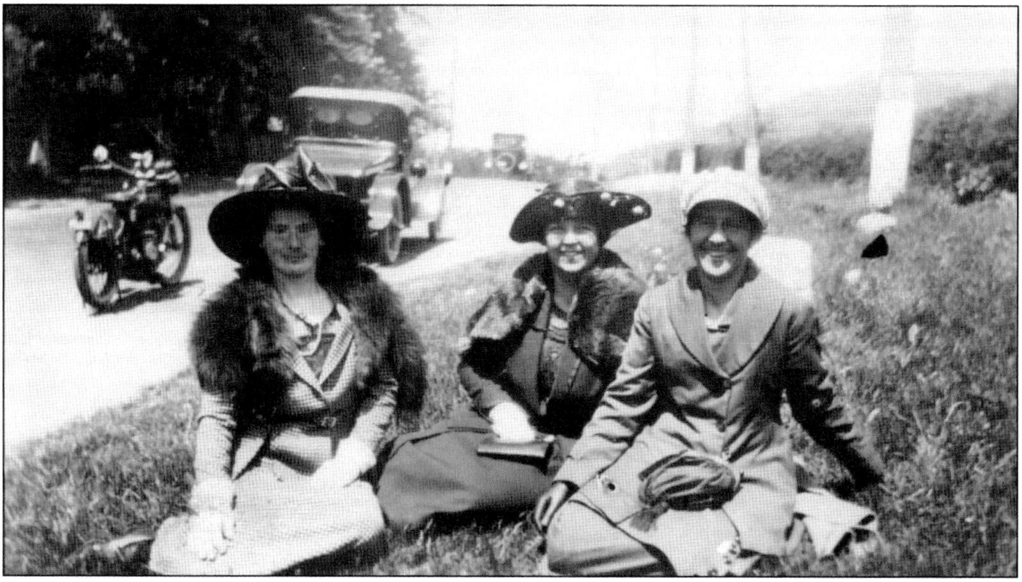

Above, from left to right, Lula Wynne and Nan and Aline Hopkins have a roadside picnic. It was normal to bring lunch on a trip and just stop whenever it was time to eat. (Courtesy of Edith Wade Insley.)

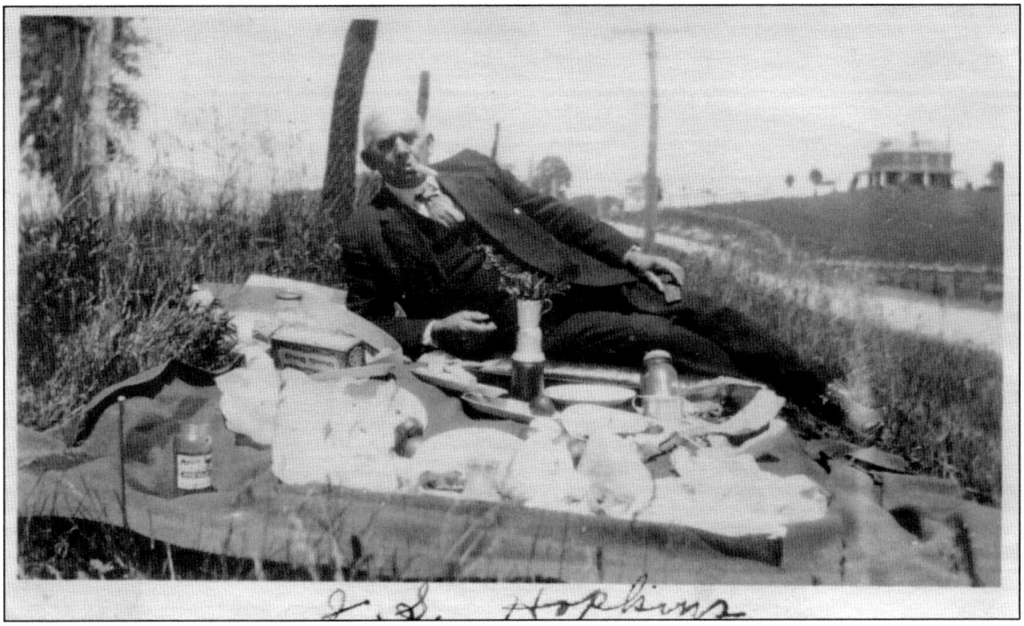


James S. Hopkins Sr. reclines during a picnic lunch on a family trip. A good rest by the roadside after lunch was part of the day's trip for many people in the early 1900s. (Courtesy of Edith Wade Insley.)

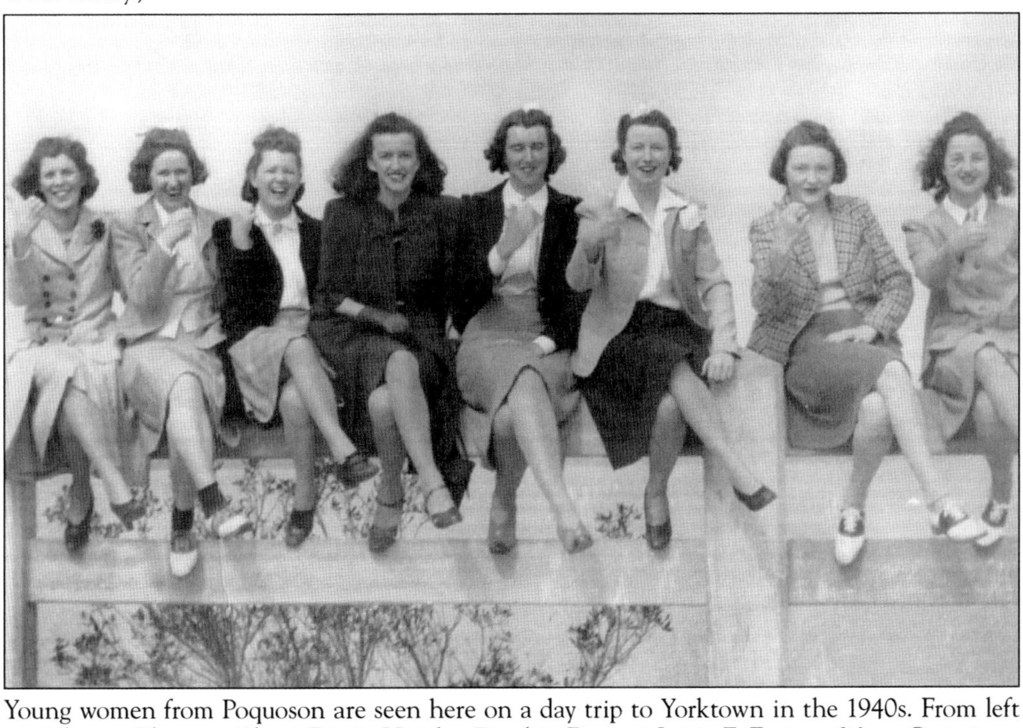

Young women from Poquoson are seen here on a day trip to Yorktown in the 1940s. From left to right are Florence Shaw, Roxie Haight, Peachie Downs, Jessie F. Forrest, Mary Carmines, Caroline Freeman, Sara Virginia Watkins, and Victoria Freeman. Forrest became the first female rescue squad director in Poquoson and was also a noted genealogist and historian. (Courtesy of the Poquoson Historical Society.)

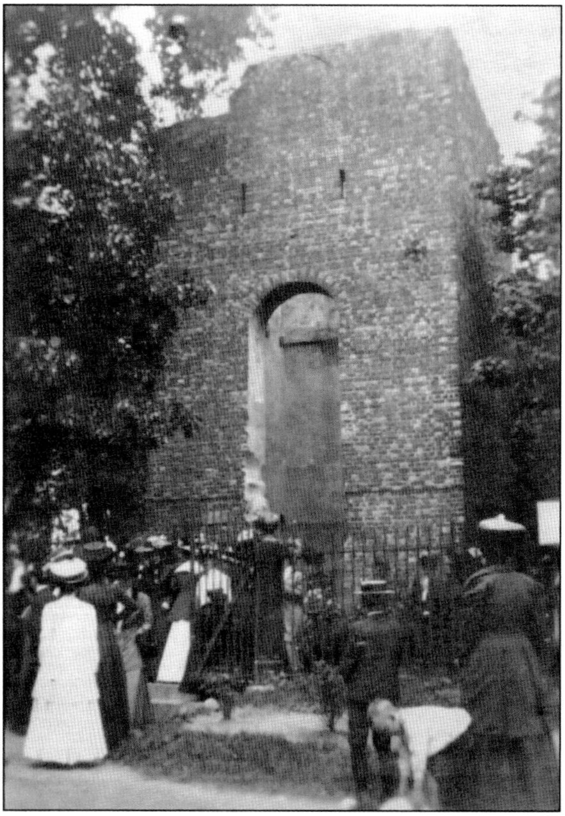

Poquoson residents are seen here in 1907 on a trip to Jamestown to celebrate the 300th anniversary of the settlement. People stand outside the old bell tower at the church on Jamestown Island. (Courtesy of Edith Wade Insley.)

The Hopkins family is seen below on a day trip to Yorktown, standing outside of the Lord Cornwallis Cave, where British general Charles Cornwallis sought refuge from American artillery and infantry fire during the Revolutionary War. Note that the admission price was only 10¢. Trips to Yorktown became popular with tourists during the Jamestown Exposition of 1907, which celebrated the settlement's 300th anniversary. (Courtesy of Edith Wade Insley.)

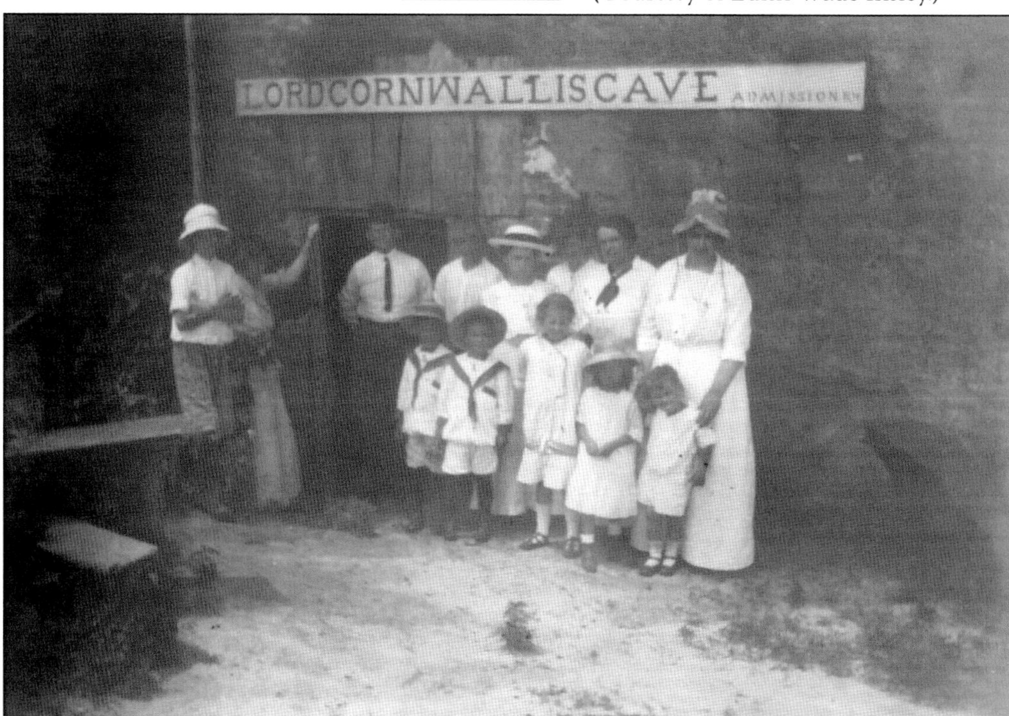

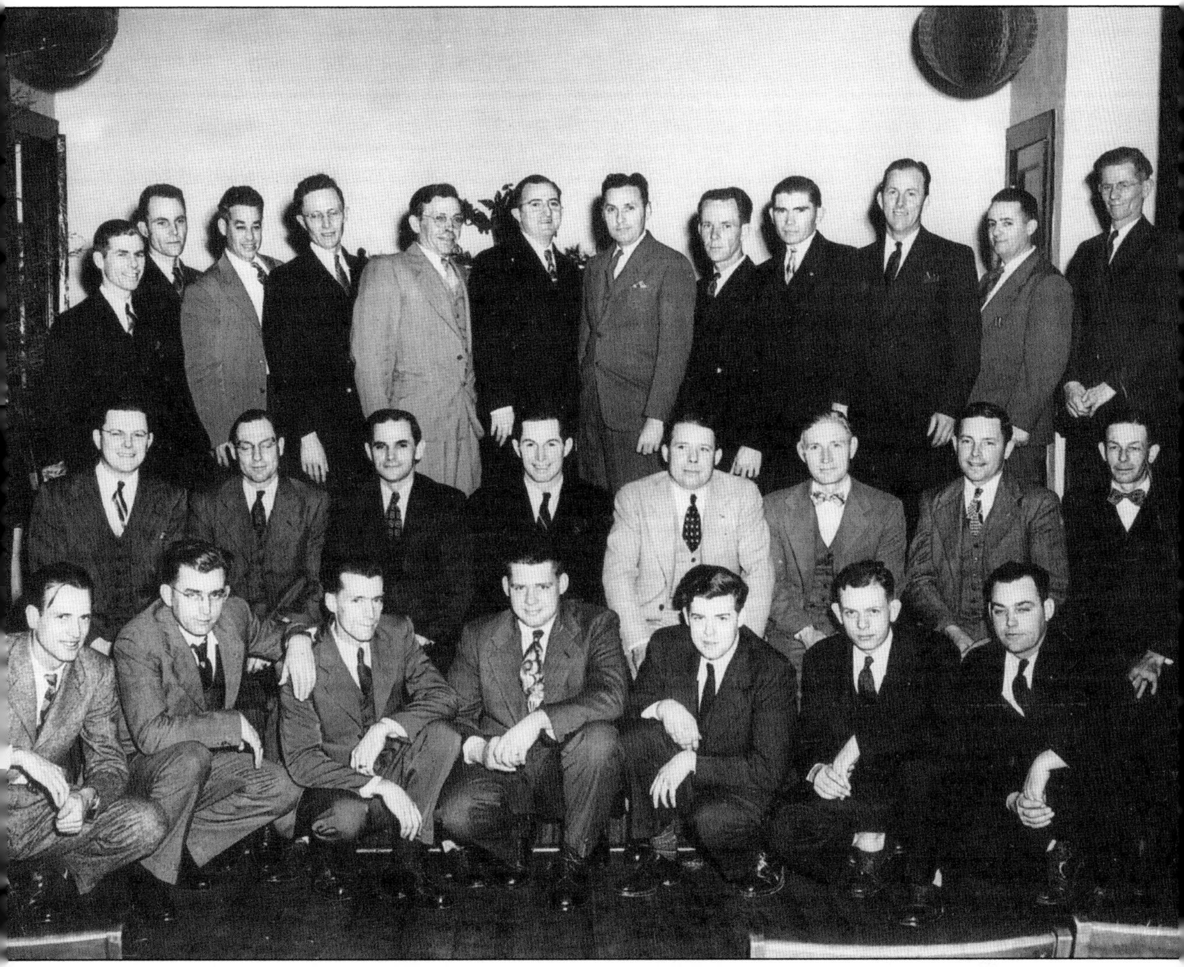

The Virginia Reserve Militia (VRM) was formed during World War II as a civil defense group to help out in the event of a crisis while the military was fighting in Europe and the Pacific. The Virginia National Guard was federalized in 1941, so small state-run militias were formed to help keep the peace by supporting the local police and aiding in natural disasters until the war was over. The local branch of the VRM was named the York Rangers, after the Confederate soldiers from York County. During the Civil War, the York Rangers were members of the 32nd Virginia Infantry and fought in most of the major battles of the Civil War. The World War II–era York Rangers were made up of men who worked in the defense industry in York County, which included Poquoson. The Virginia Reserve Militia was disbanded when the war ended in 1945. (Courtesy of Charles McDaniels and Bonnie Karwac.)

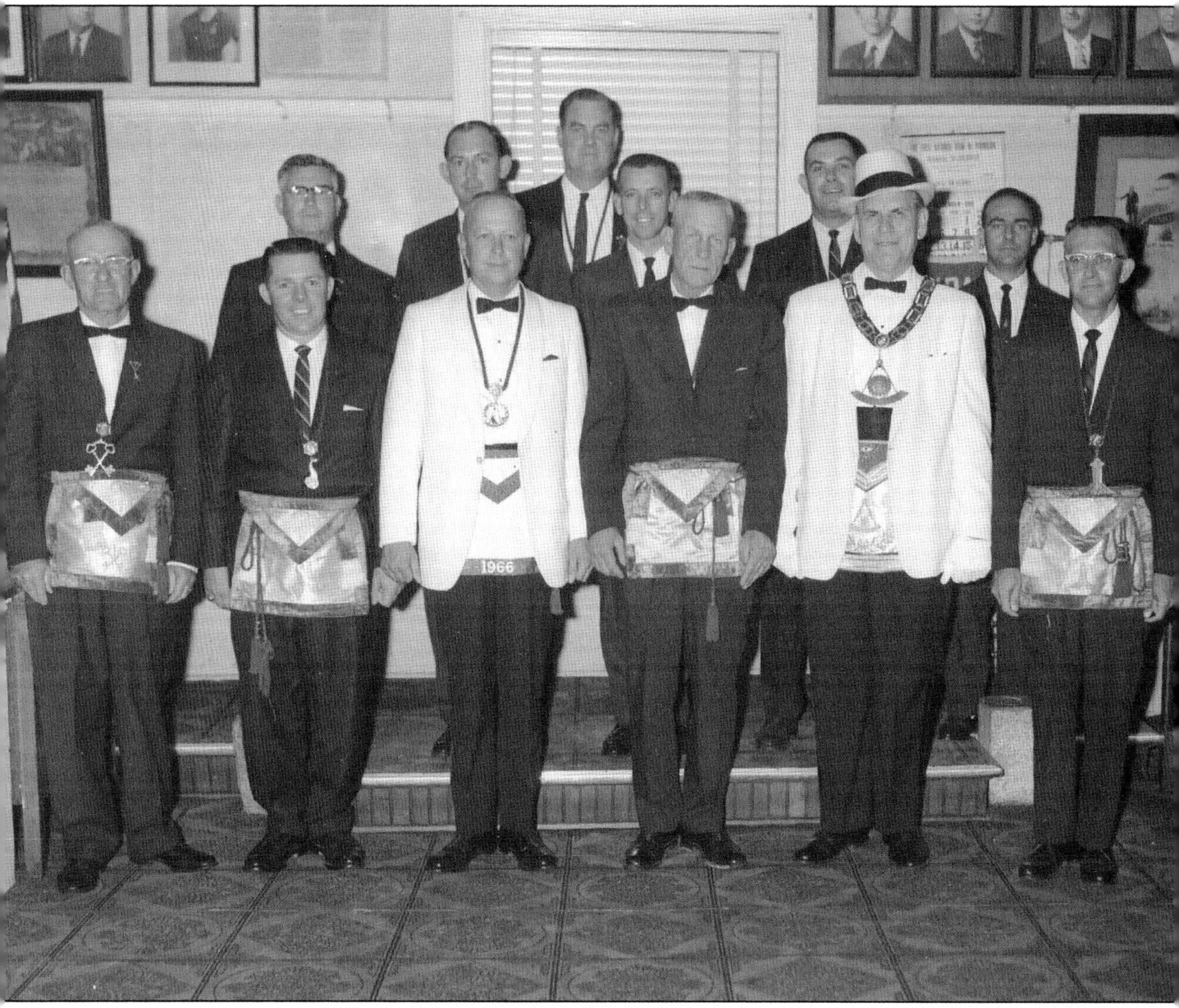


Poquoson Masonic Lodge No. 49 was founded in 1932. The first meeting of the group was at the Odd Fellows hall in the community of Odd. On April 4, 1933, the charter was presented, thereby making the Poquoson lodge a regular Masonic Lodge. Alvah E. Riggins was the first worshipful master, Robert E. Hunt was the senior warden, and John F. Rollins was the junior warden. The meetings were held at the Odd Fellows hall until April 1939, when the meetings were moved to the Juniors' and Redman's Hall in Messick. In 1976, the meetings moved again, to the new Masonic Temple on Hunts Neck Road. This photograph documents the official visit of the Grandmaster. In the white jackets are district deputy Bill Johnson (left) and Williamsburg postmaster George Elderidge Kidd, the Grandmaster of the Masonic Lodge. (Courtesy of Poquoson Masonic Lodge No. 49.)

*Two*

# THE COMMUNITY OF ODD

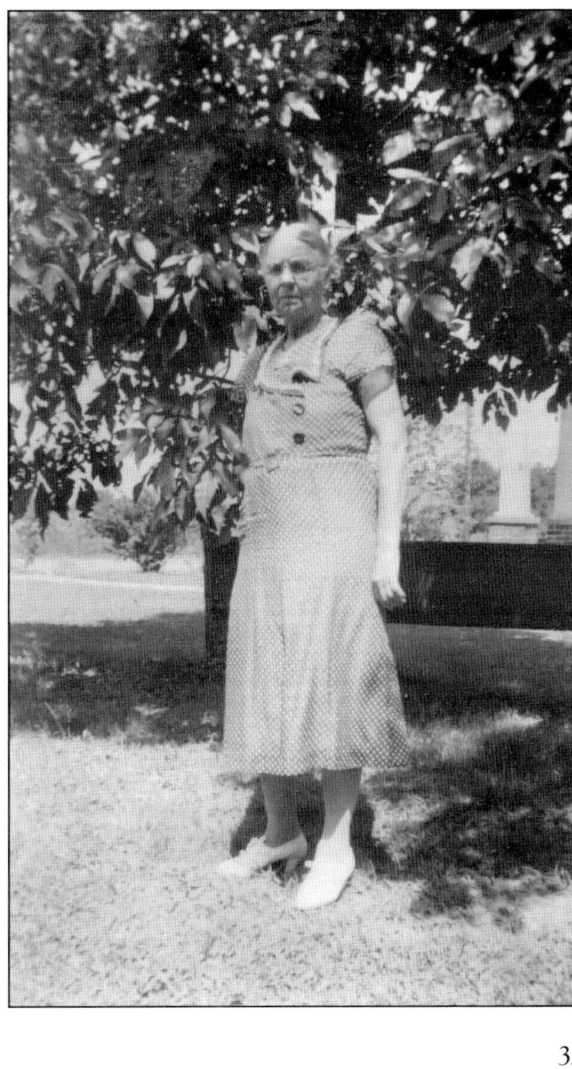

Sarah Elizabeth "Sadie" Carmines, seen here, was married to store owner John Thomas Hunt, the postmaster of Odd. (Courtesy of Charles McDaniel.)

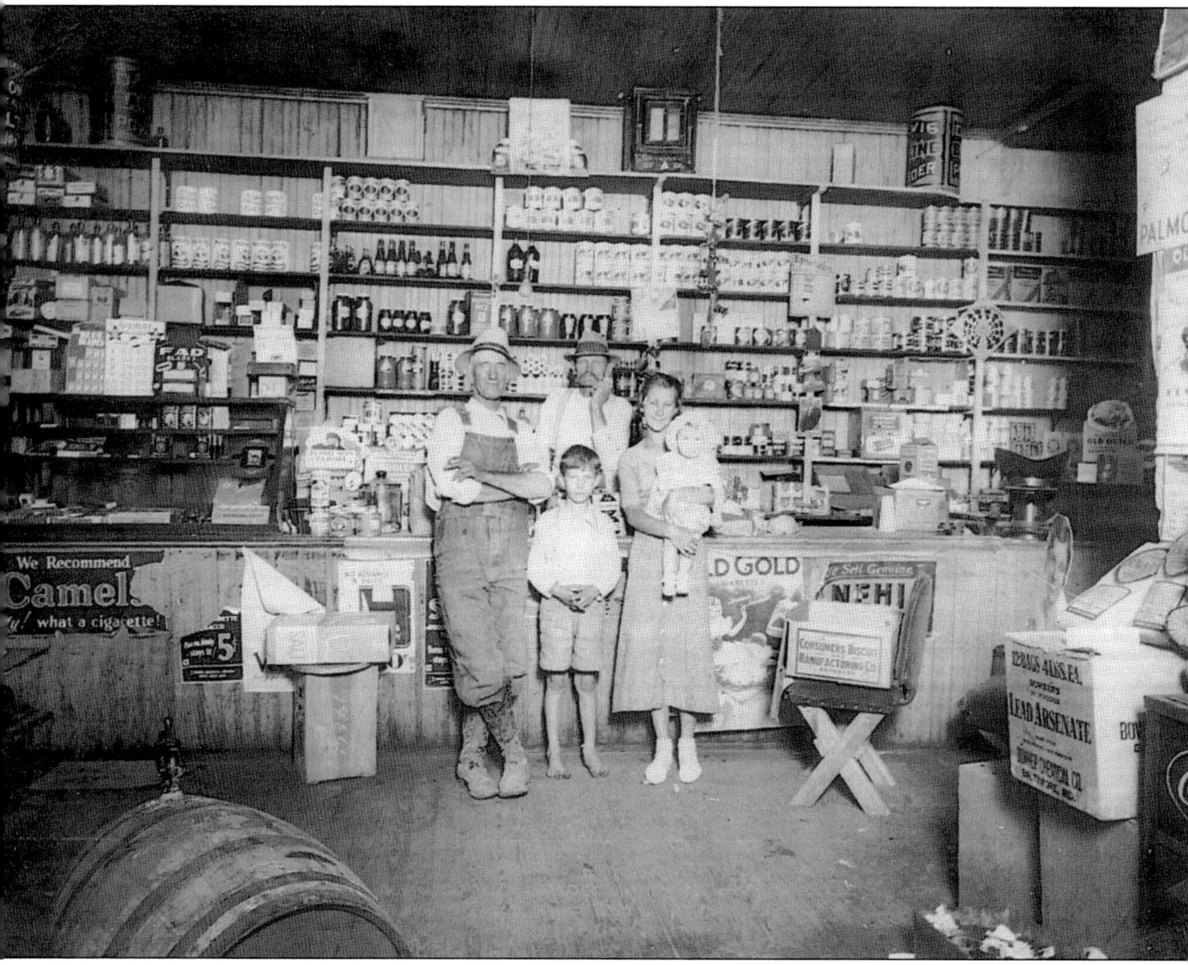


The Odd Post Office was in John Thomas "Tom" Hunt's store. The community of Odd and the post office got their names from the Independent Order of Odd Fellows Lodge, which was next to the post office. This 1930s photograph shows, from left to right, (in front of the counter) Jimmy Dryden, Billy Dryden, and Eva Dryden, holding baby Mamie Dryden; (behind counter) Tom Hunt. Odd Road was part of the Kirby plantation in the early 1800s, and the homesite of the plantation was at the opposite end of Odd Road from the store. The plantation was part of the original 17th-century Football Quarter Creek patent. (Courtesy of Charles McDaniel.)

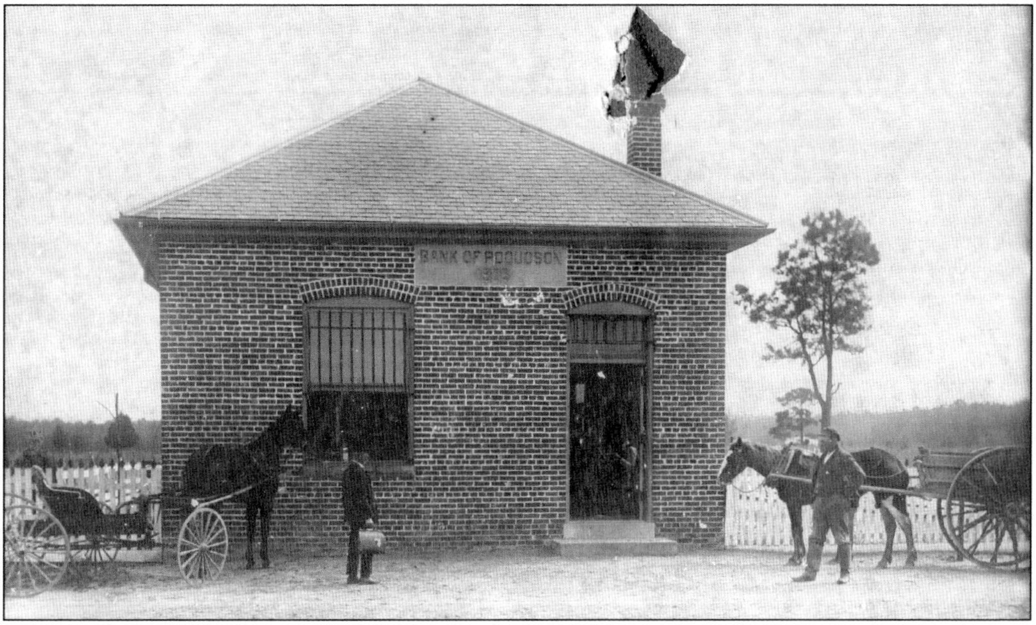


The Bank of Poquoson, on Poquoson Avenue, was established in 1905. It was bought out in 1918 and renamed the First National Bank of Poquoson. It served the entire Poquoson area. The small brick structure was built around the vault. The building was expanded while it was still the bank, and it later became the Poquoson Library. It still stands today and is now home to the Poquoson Police Department. (Courtesy of Charles McDaniel.)

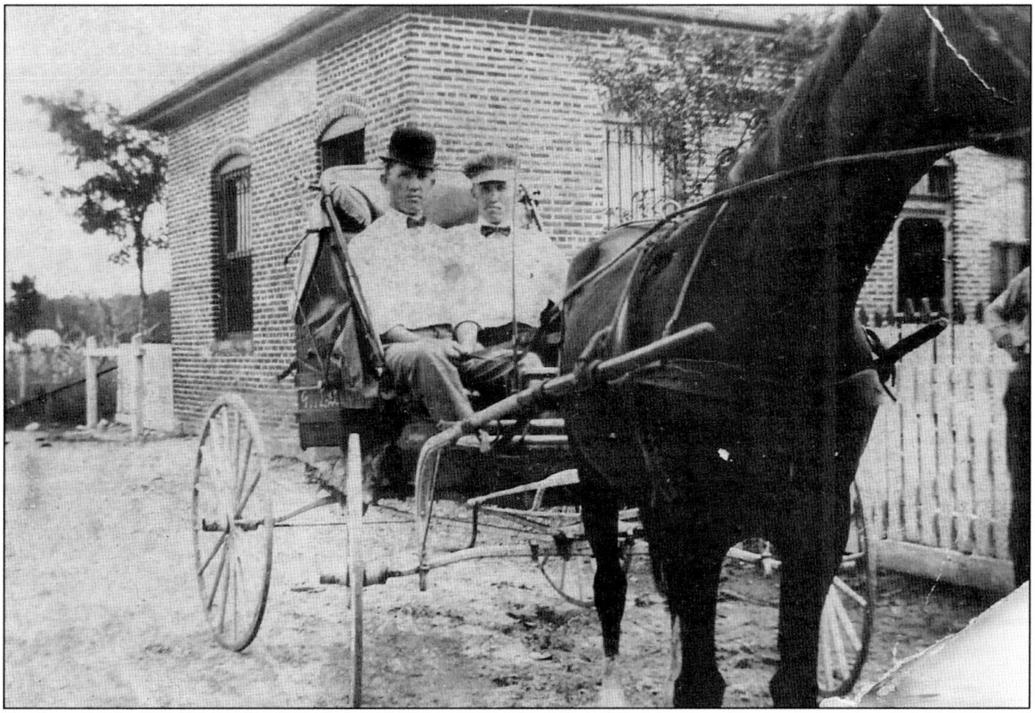

Dr. Estridge Peterson White (left) sits in his buggy outside of the Bank of Poquoson in Odd. The doctor made house calls in the horse and buggy in the early 1900s. (Courtesy of Nannie White Diggs.)

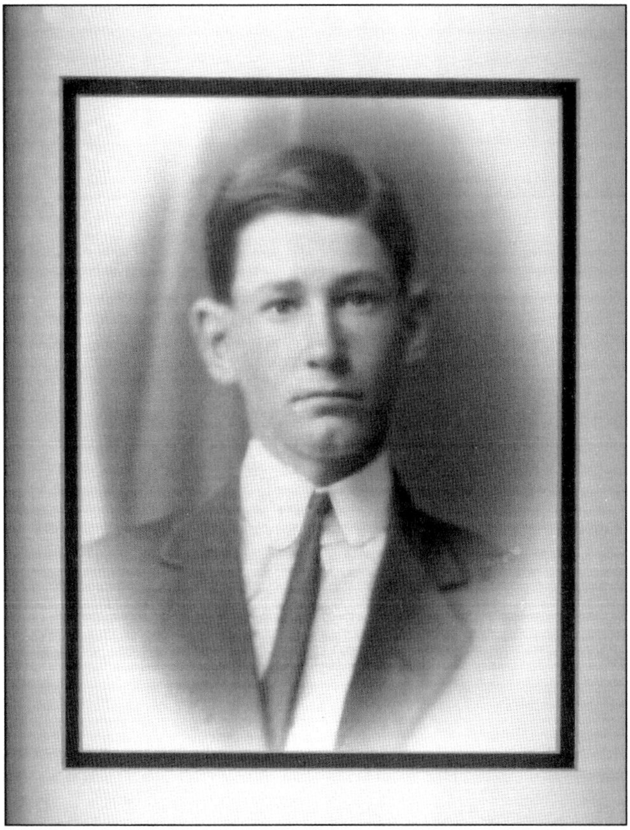

Hunter Riggins Sr. was the founder of Riggins Motor Company, which is still known for its friendly customer service today. (Courtesy of Hunter Riggins Jr.)

The well-stocked interior office of the Riggins Motor Company is seen below in the late 1930s with organized shelves of merchandise. The company is still owned and operated by the Riggins family. (Courtesy of Hunter Riggins Jr. and Charles McDaniel.)

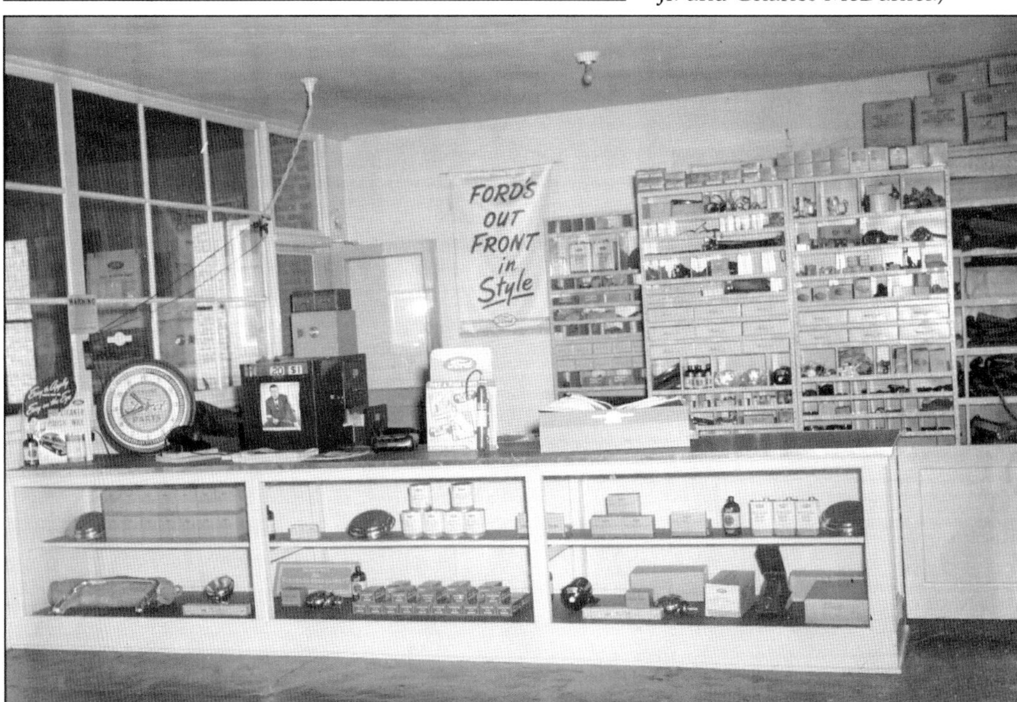

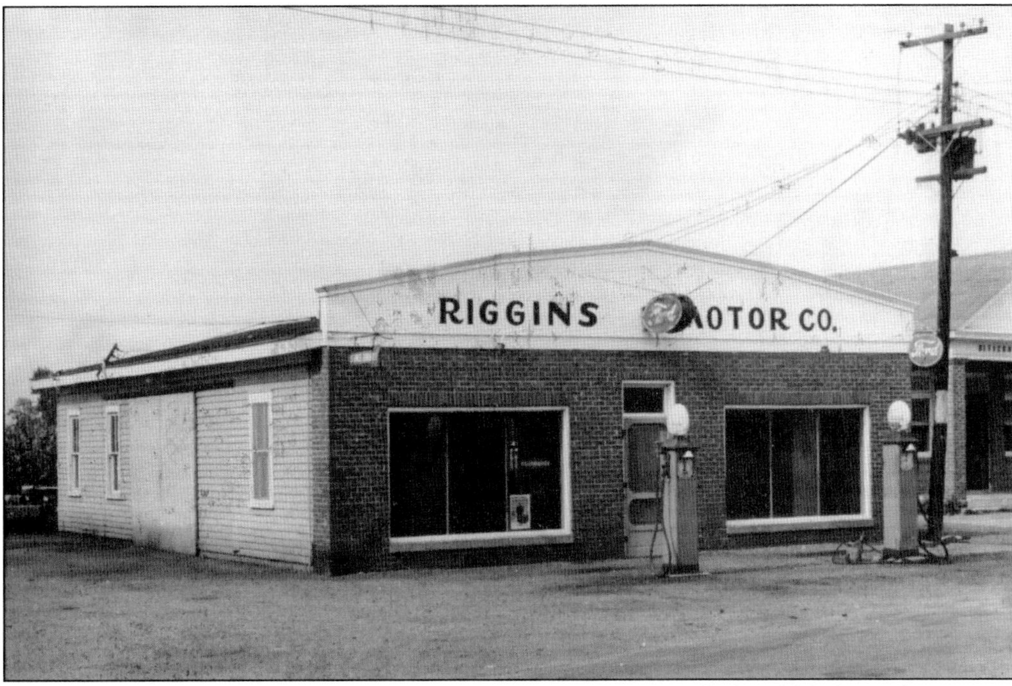


The exterior facade of the Riggins Motor Company is seen here with the old-fashioned gas pumps in front. The company later moved to a new structure, but this original building still stands and is now a photography studio. The home of Hunter Riggins Sr. and his wife, Nanny Forrest Riggins, was next to this building. Riggins Sr. died on December 28, 1978, and is buried in Peninsula Memorial Park in Newport News. (Courtesy of Hunter Riggins Jr. and Charles McDaniel.)

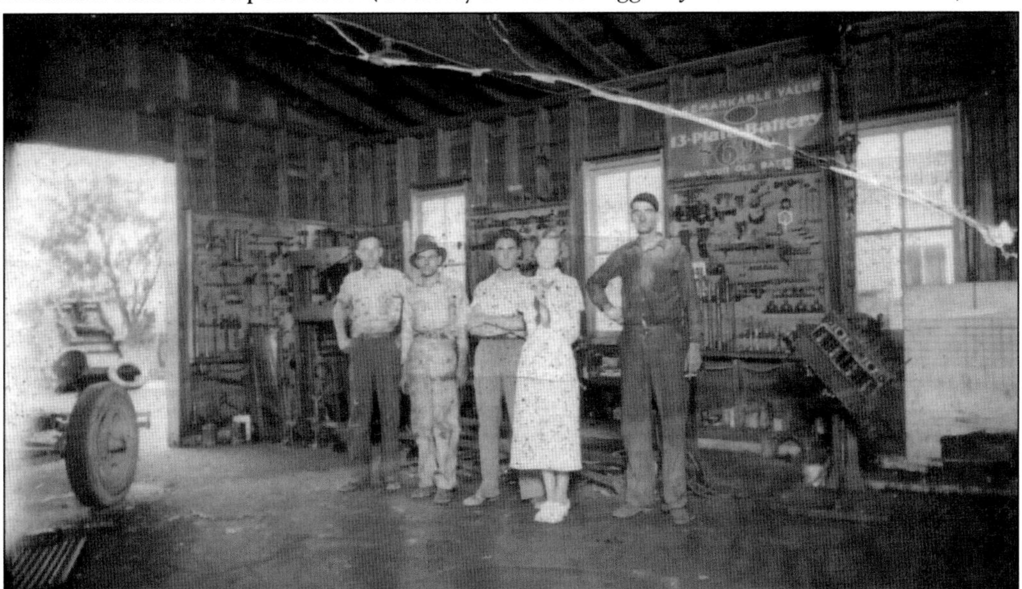

The garage at the Riggins Motor Company was a hub of activity. This photograph, taken between 1938 and 1940, shows, from left to right, Delma Freeman, unidentified, Joseph Moore, unidentified, and company owner and mechanic Hunter Riggins. (Courtesy of Charles McDaniel.)

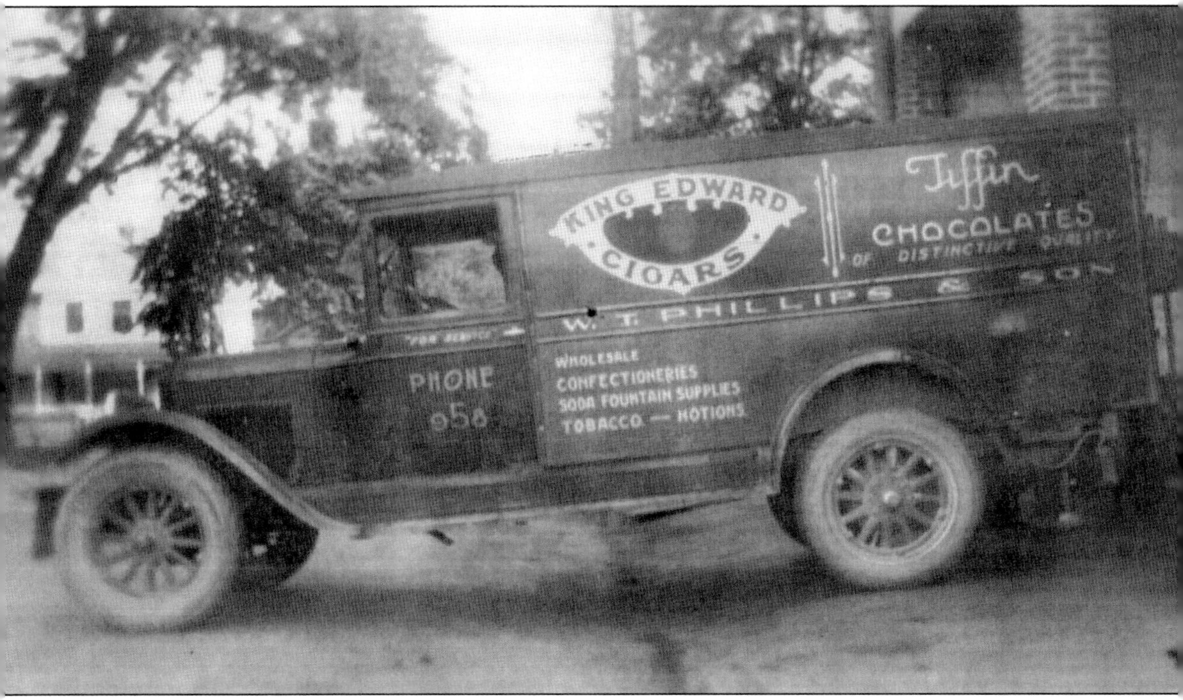


The W.T. Phillips and Son Company truck featured advertisements for their merchandise, cigars, and chocolate confections. Phillips owned the store, on the corner of Rens Road and Poquoson Avenue, in the late 1800s. The business was moved to Hampton after the store was destroyed by fire. Many Poquoson residents worked in the neighboring cities of Hampton and Newport News in the 1900s. (Courtesy of Charles McDaniel.)

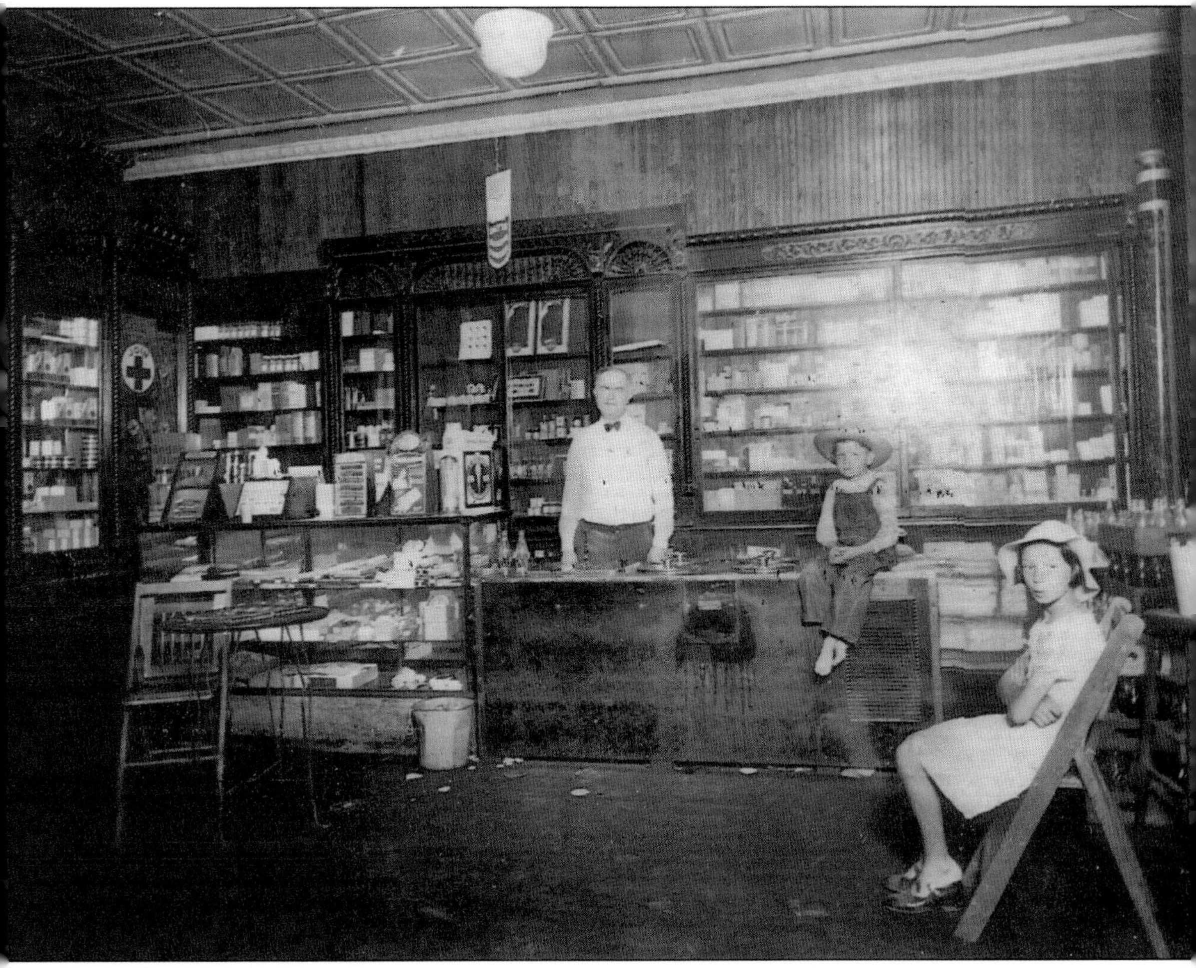

The Poquoson Drug Company was in the community of Odd. Dr. Linwood "Doc" Riggins became the postmaster for the Odd Post Office in 1933. Here, in 1937, Riggins stands behind the counter of Poquoson Drug, Leroy "Lindy" Wade sits on the counter, and Wade's sister Berlie sits in the chair on the right. The ornate cabinetry in the store was purchased by Charles McDaniel when the store was dismantled. He donated the cabinets and the Tom Hunt's store building to the Poquoson Museum in 2001. (Courtesy of Charles McDaniel and Leroy Wade.)

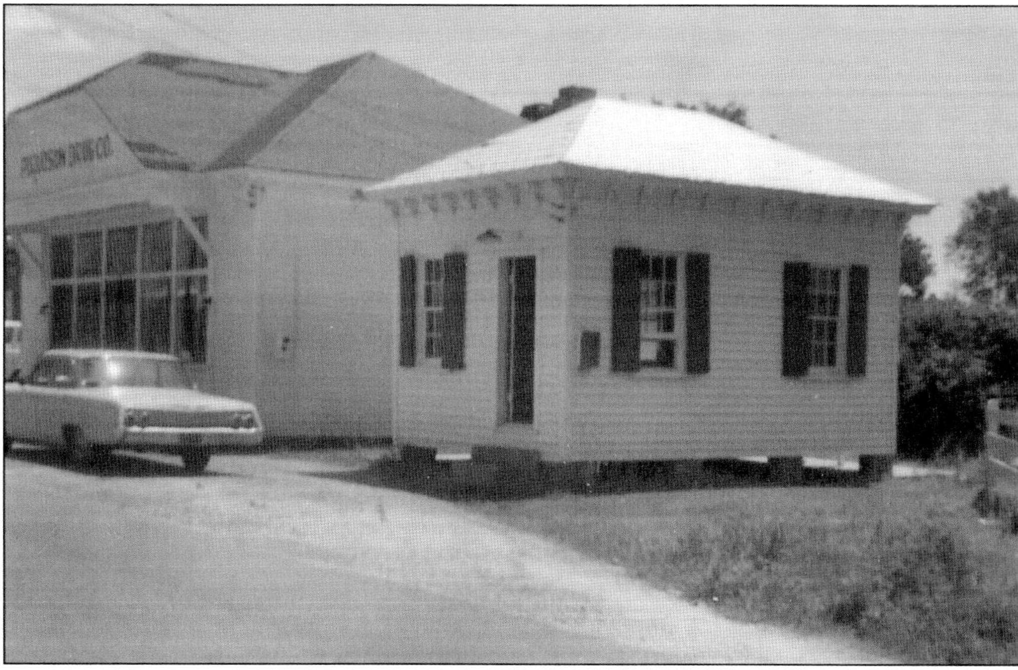

The Odd voting building was on Poquoson Avenue. The small wooden building was painted white and had shutters on the windows. It had a tin roof and was supported by brick piers. It was next to the Poquoson Drug Company, seen here on the left. The voting building was moved from its original site, where the Poquoson Police Department's parking lot is now located. (Courtesy of Charles McDaniel.)

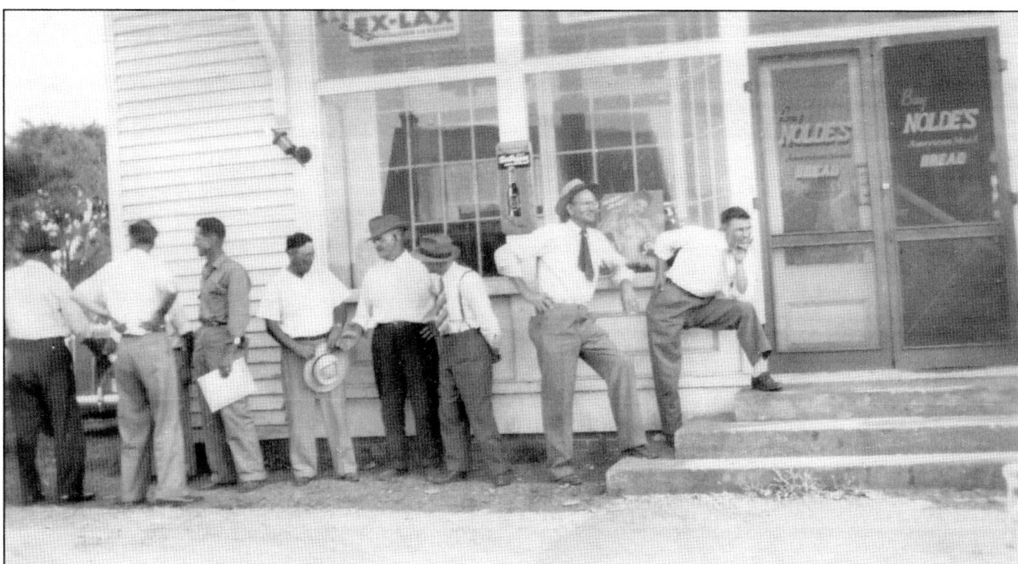


Voting was a civic duty taken seriously by the people of Poquoson. Here, locals wait to vote in front of the Poquoson Drug Company. The voting building was next to Poquoson Drug, and the line extended down Poquoson Avenue on voting day. Seen here first in line is Arthur "Jitterbug" Carmony, followed by R.E. Hunt, Linwood Burcher, Pell Phillips, Jim Elois Watkins, and Vernon Forrest. (Courtesy of Leroy Wade and Charles McDaniel.)

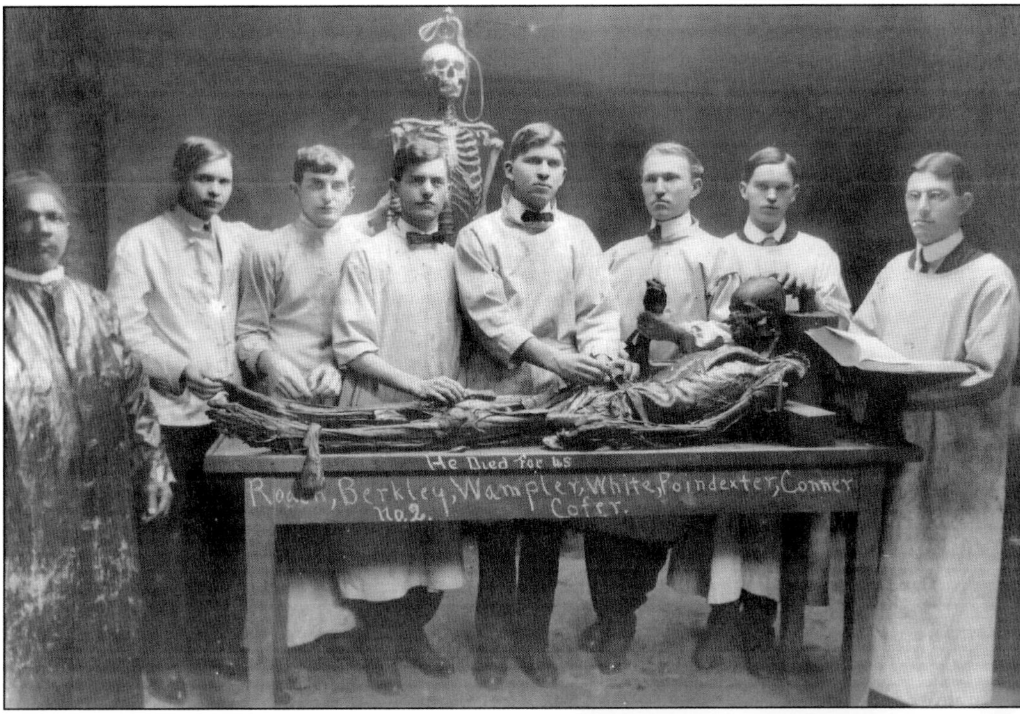


Above, a young Dr. Estridge Peterson White (third from the right) poses with other medical students while in school. The printed inscription on the photograph states, "He died for us." After he graduated from medical school, Dr. White returned to Poquoson to practice. (Courtesy of Nannie White Diggs.)

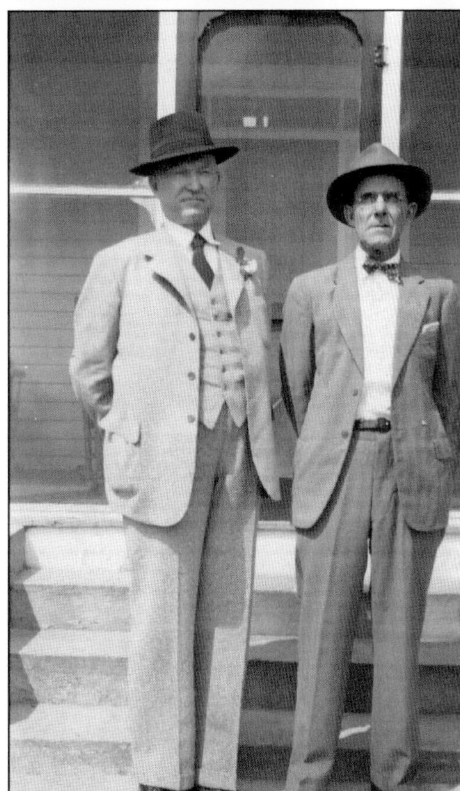

In this photograph, taken around 1940, Dr. Estridge Peterson White (left) stands outside of a house beside Joe Bush Moore, the father of Nannie Freeman, who was the business teacher at Poquoson High School for many years. Her students were well trained, often finding jobs with NASA and other government installations in the area. (Courtesy of Nannie White Diggs.)

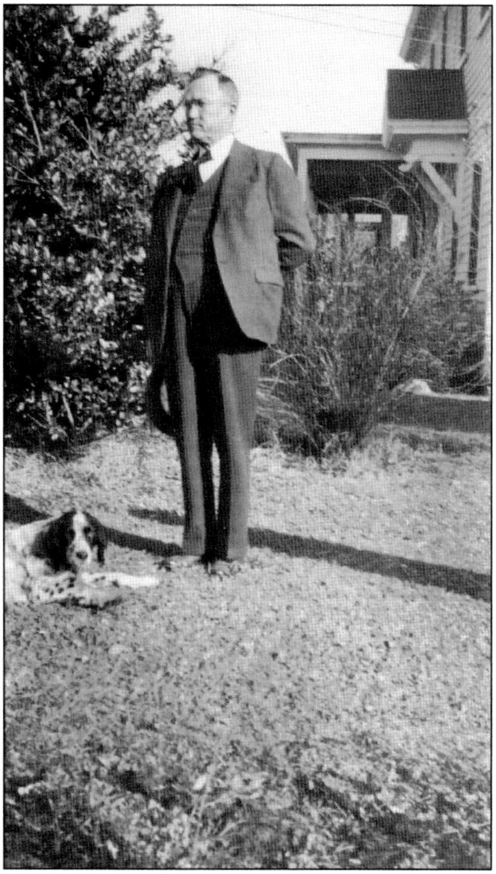

Dr. Estridge Peterson White is seen here with his dog outside his residence at 764 Poquoson Avenue. His dog was a faithful companion and a fixture around his office for many years. Dr. White was usually photographed wearing a suit. (Courtesy of Jane Smith White.)

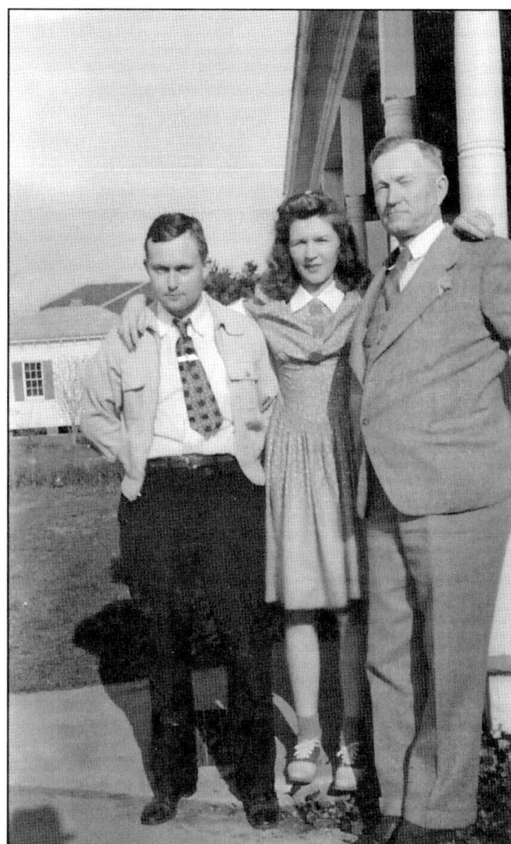

Stanley Wise White (left) and his wife, Loraine Harris White, pose for a photograph with his father, Dr. Estridge Peterson White, outside the doctor's residence in the 1940s. Stanley followed in his father's footsteps and became a doctor. He and Loraine had one daughter and two sons. Stanley was tragically killed in an automobile accident. (Courtesy of Jane Smith White.)

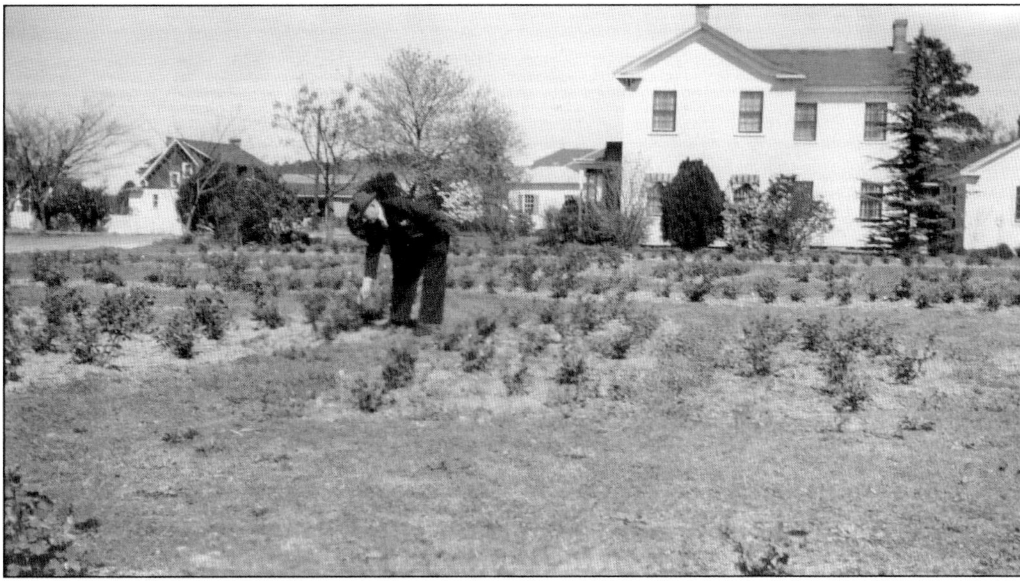

Dr. Estridge Peterson White is seen here working in his rose garden. After many long and stressful hours of work, he indulged in his hobby of cultivating beautiful roses. It was a way for him to de-stress. The rose garden was located where White's ball field once stood. (Courtesy of Jane Smith White.)

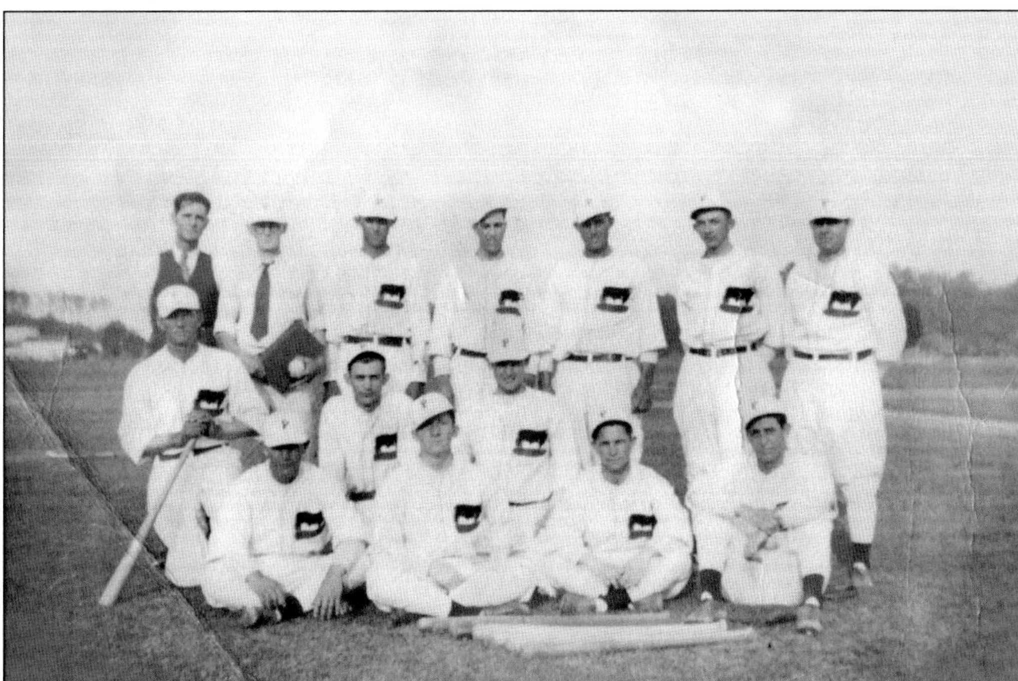

This 1920s Poquoson baseball team played at White's Field and included, from left to right, (first row) Wade Freeman, Carroll Forrest, Ned Freeman, and Duke Forrest; (second row) Vernon Forrest, Herman Forrest, and Elwood Forrest; (third row) umpire Gladwyn "Pig" Forrest, groundskeeper Luther Hunt, Ellison Holloway, "Tuffy Joe," Emerson Martin, Nelson Watkins Sr., and Beamon Forrest. (Courtesy of the family of Thomas C. Hudgins Jr.)

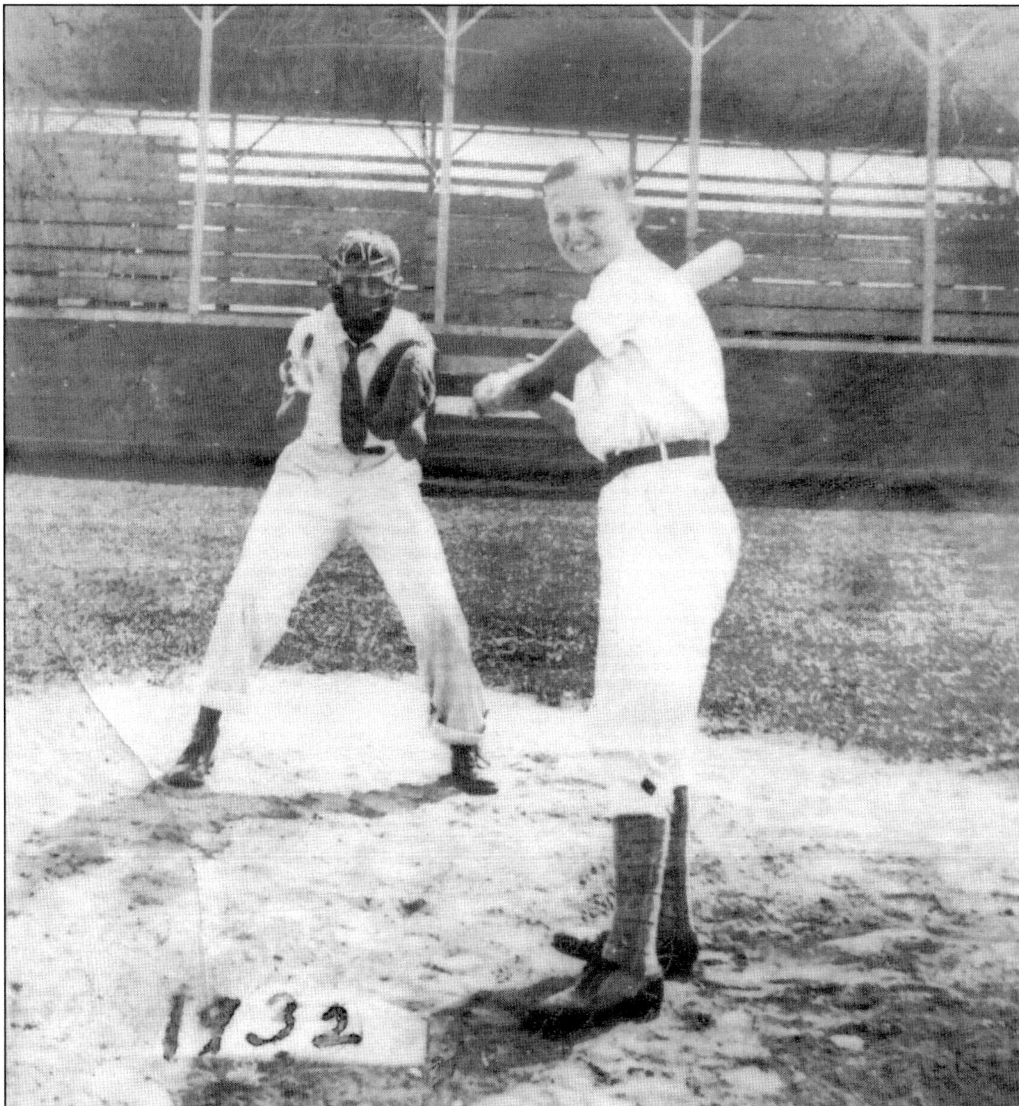


In the early 1900s, baseball was the great pastime in Poquoson. Here, a young Stanley Wise White is at bat at White's Field in 1932. The ball field had stadium-style seating and a groundskeeper, Luther Hunt, hired to maintain the field. Hunt was paid $8 on March 28, 1928, for his services. Admission to the field was 25¢, and it was considered to be better than most other baseball fields of its day. (Courtesy of Nannie White Diggs.)

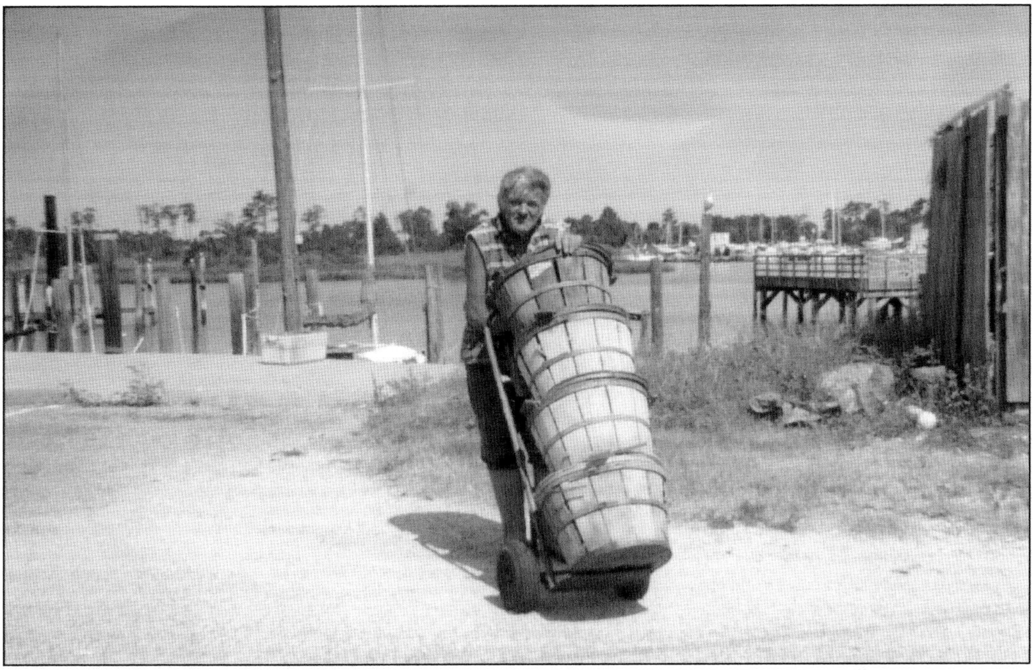

Arnie Ferguson (above) is a waterman who has worked on the water all of his life. He comes from a family of watermen and has made a good living crabbing and fishing. He is also a talented artist who carves waterfowl. (Courtesy of Georgia McDaniel.)

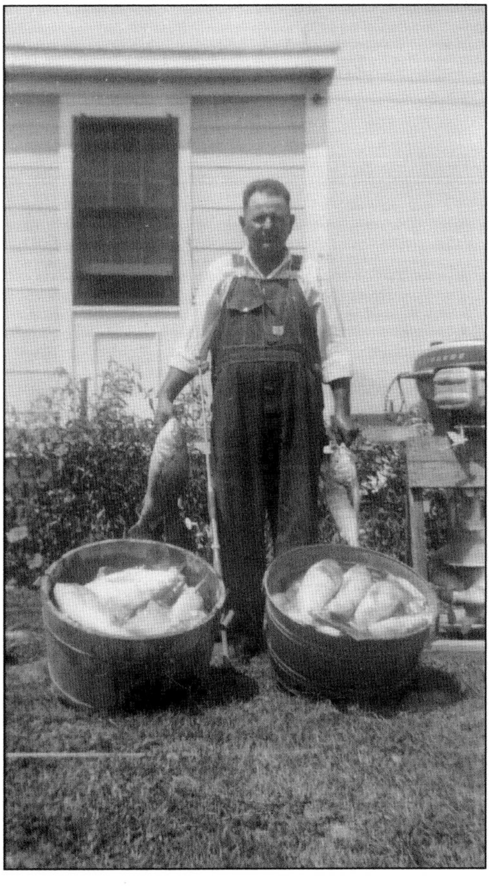

In the 1950s, Martin Luther Ketchie would come to visit his daughter Georgia McDaniel and go fishing. He is seen here after a fishing trip off Rens Road holding two bushels of croaker. (Courtesy of Charles McDaniel.)

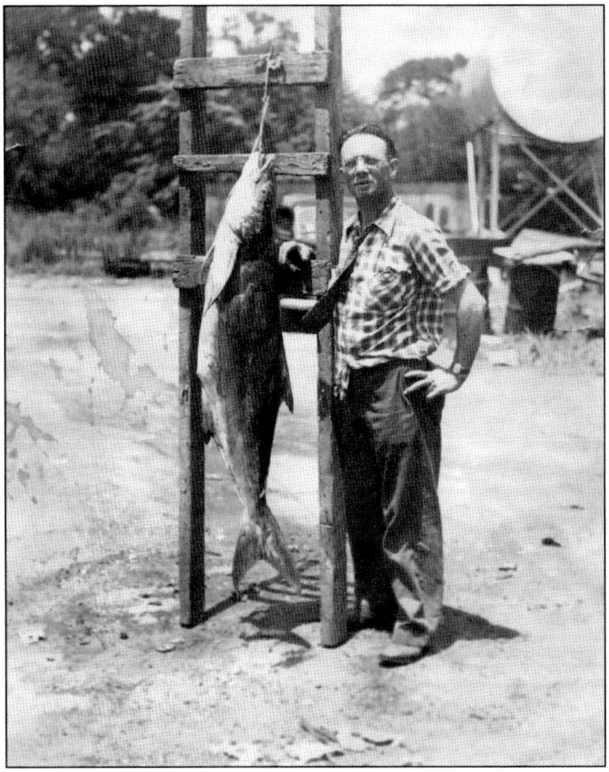

John Lemuel Firth Sr. shows off his catch of the day. Firth and his brother Alvin owned many businesses in both Hampton and Poquoson, including the Firth Brothers Trailer Park (now Wythe Creek Trailer Park) and the Firth Brothers Welding Shop and Ironworks. John Firth Sr. also helped develop the White House Cove area and many other areas of Poquoson and started the Gloucester Country Club and Golf Course. (Courtesy of Maresa Firth Spangler.)

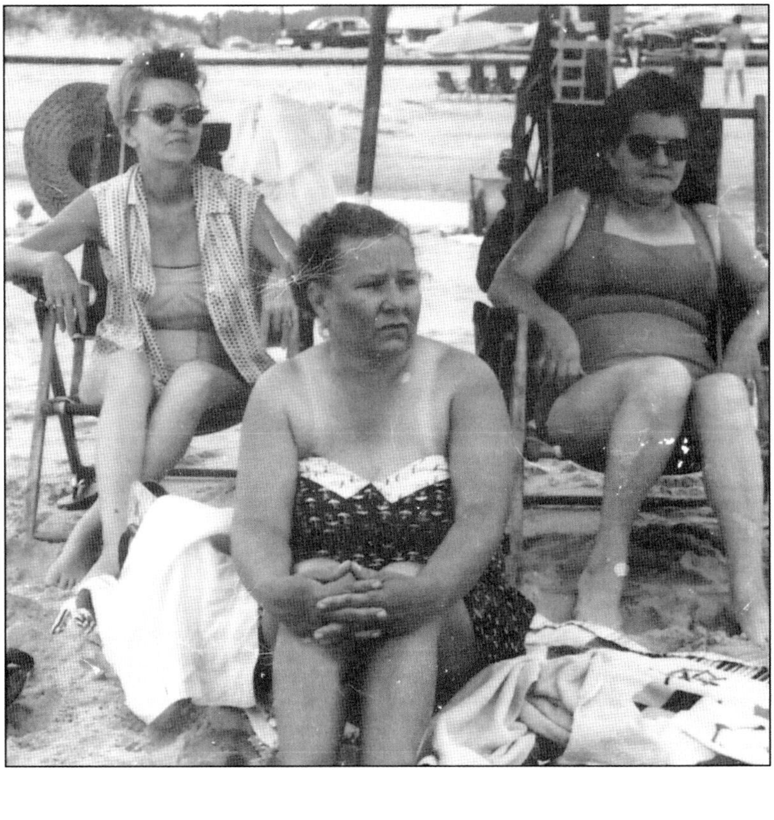

From left to right, Maude Hall, Murdie Carmines Firth, and Carrie Insley sun themselves on the beach. After World War II, going to the beach became a pastime for locals. Today, tourists from all over the country vacation on Virginia's numerous beaches. (Courtesy of Maresa Firth Spangler.)

A young Nannie White is seen here eating an apple. The Odd voting building and the Poquoson Drug Company are in the background. Nannie was the daughter of Dr. Stanley Wise White and Loraine Harris White. She married Ed Diggs Jr. Later in life, Nannie White Diggs became known for her beautiful quilts. (Courtesy of Nannie White Diggs.)

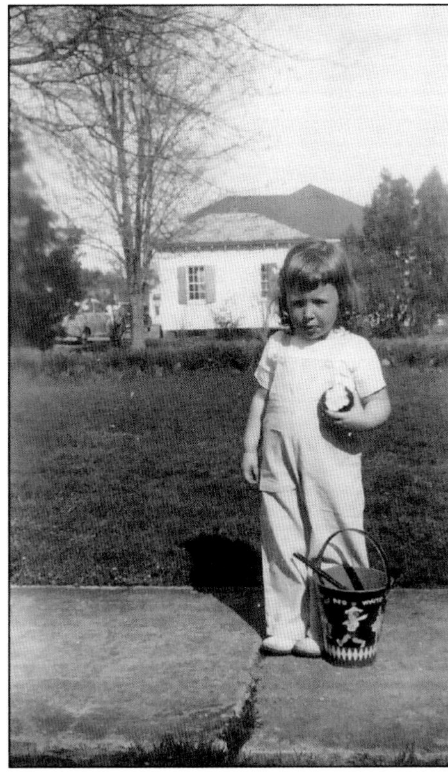

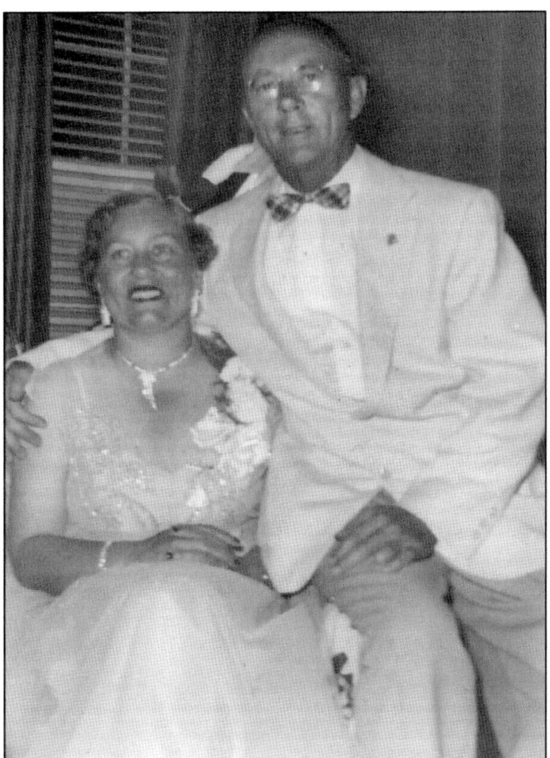

Murdie Carmines Firth and her husband, John Lemuel Firth Sr., celebrate Murdie's election to the office of Pocahontas of the State of Virginia for the Degree of Pocahontas. Murdie Carmines Firth was born to Bertha and Hope Carmines on September 14, 1914, and died on November 8, 2010. She is buried in Newport News. (Courtesy of Maresa Firth Spangler.)

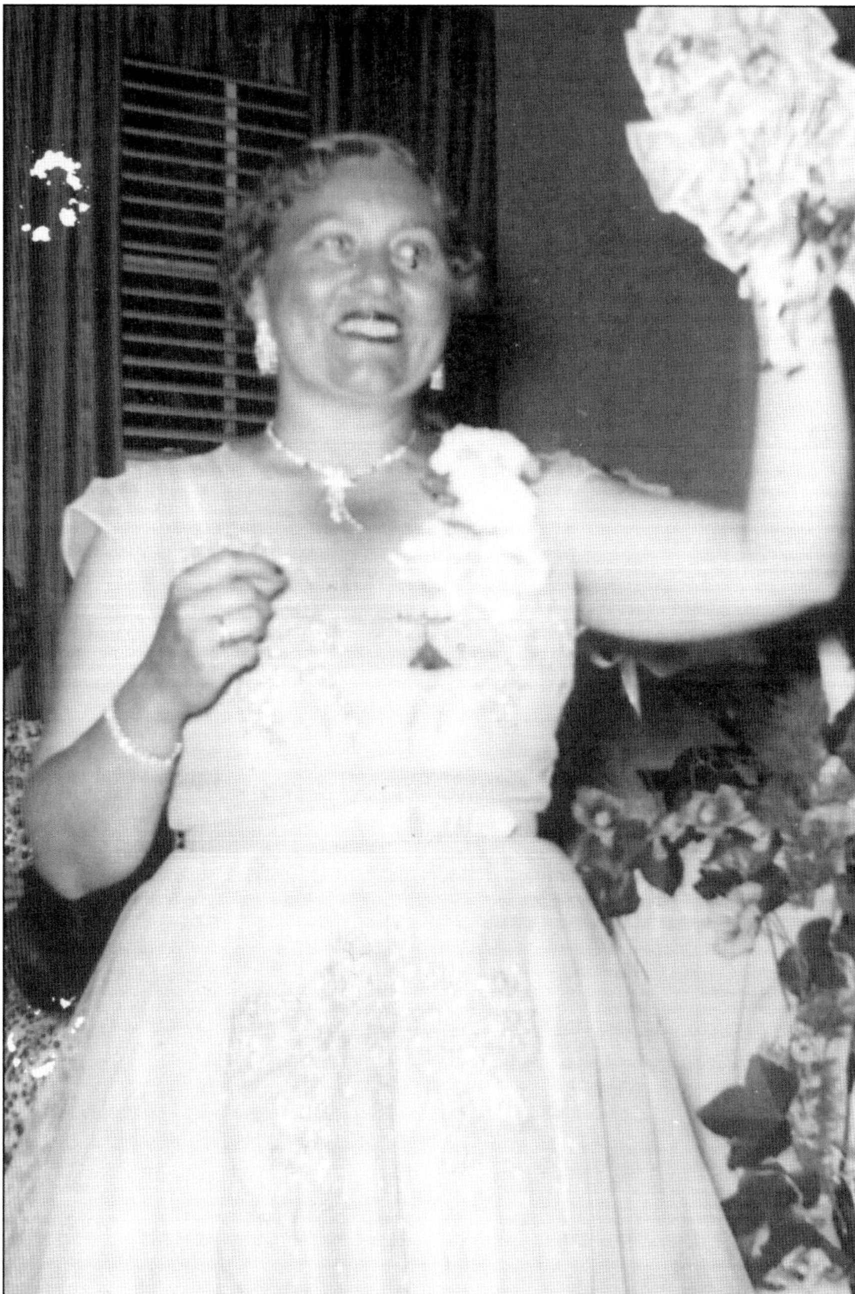

Murdie Carmines Firth raises her hand in celebration after being elected to the office of Pocohantas of the State of Virginia. The Red Men Society was a local civic club in the first half of the 1900s. The men's group was the Red Cloud Tribe No. 58, Improved Order of Red Men. The Improved Order of Red Men is the oldest fraternal society in the country with origins dating back to 1765. Its principle goals are freedom, friendship, and charity. In recent years, the Improved Order of Red Men has raised more than $1 million for the Alzheimer's Association. The women's auxiliary group, the Degree of Pocahontas, was founded in 1885. It was named after the daughter of Powhatan, a powerful Algonquin Indian chief. (Courtesy of Maresa Firth Spangler.)

# *Three*

# THE COMMUNITY OF JEFF'S

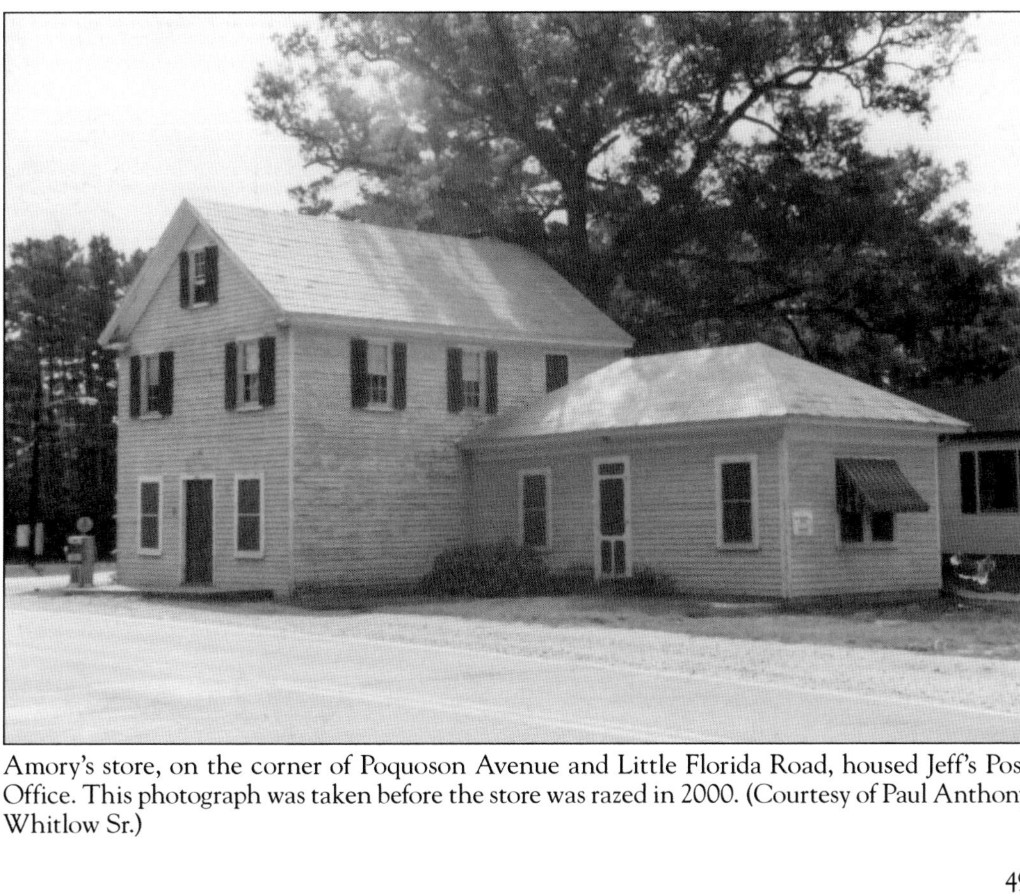

Amory's store, on the corner of Poquoson Avenue and Little Florida Road, housed Jeff's Post Office. This photograph was taken before the store was razed in 2000. (Courtesy of Paul Anthony Whitlow Sr.)

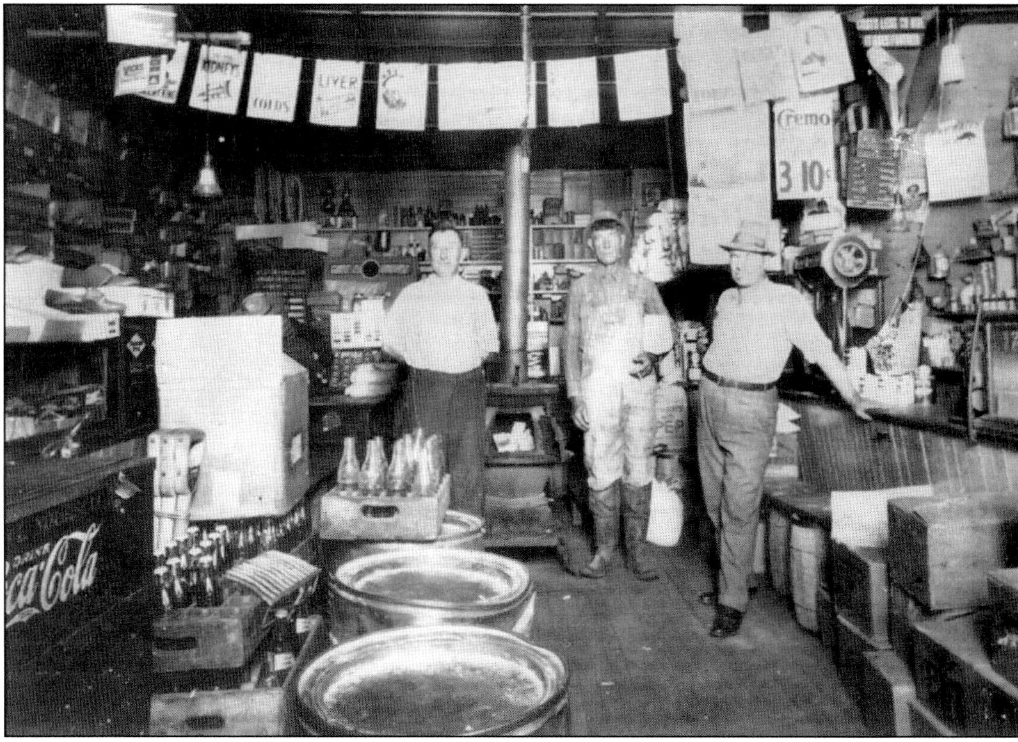


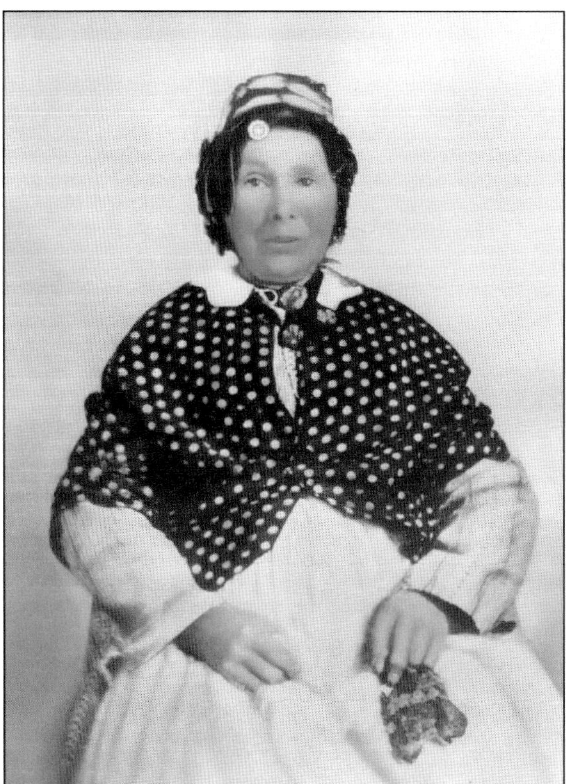

Amory's store and the Jeff's Post Office were founded by Thomas Jefferson Rowe, the first postmaster, in 1894. The store (above) changed owners and postmasters several times, but the surrounding area was called Jeff's, a nickname of the first postmaster's. John Thomas "Tom" Amory purchased the store and became the postmaster in 1914. Here, postmaster Tom Amory (left), Bill Ferguson (center), and an unidentified customer are seen in the store in the 1930s. (Courtesy of Charles McDaniel.)

Mary Rooksland Shield has been called the mother of York County. She was born around 1800 in York County, the only child of John Ferguson Shield. She was raised in Maryland but returned to the area to claim a large inheritance of land. She was married five times and bore seven children. Her children married into many of the local families, and her descendants still live in Poquoson and York County. (Courtesy of Robert V. Insley Jr.)

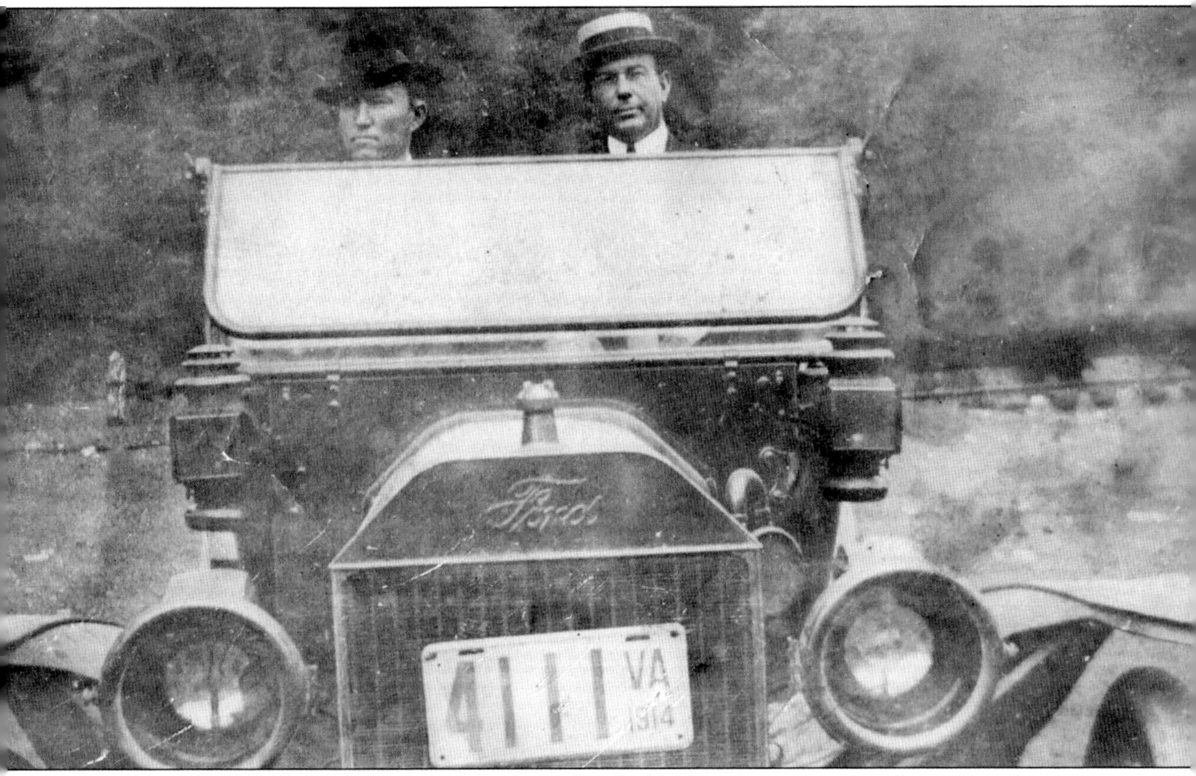


Benton Charles (right), the superintendent of schools for York County, is seen here on a drive in a Ford Model T touring car with Dr. Estridge Peterson White in 1914. The car was able to handle the dirt roads and corduroy roads in Poquoson at the time. (Courtesy of Nannie White Diggs.)

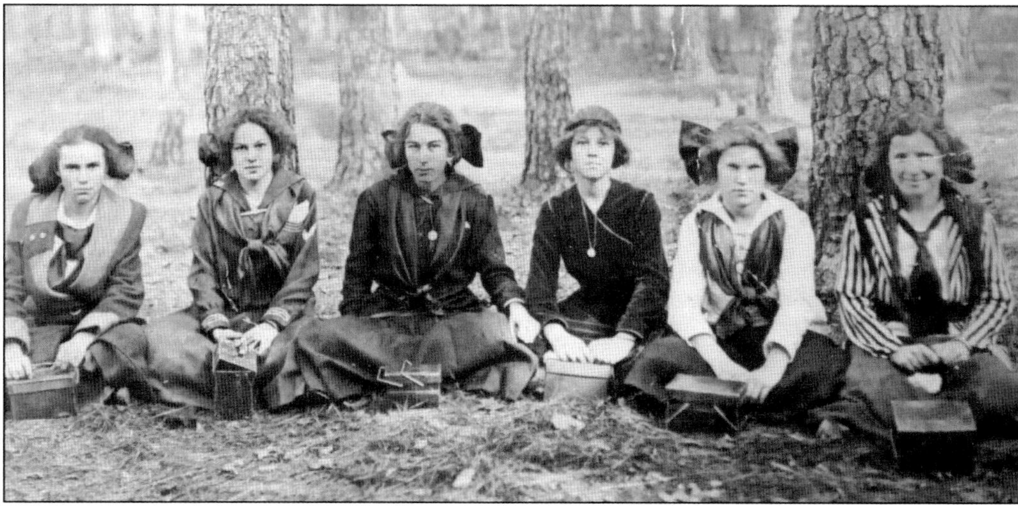

Schoolgirls from Poquoson High School have lunch under the shade of some trees. They are, from left to right, Maynie Rollins, Berta Carmines, Agnes Holloway, Marion Hawkins, and Annie and Mattie Freeman. (Courtesy of the Poquoson Historical Society.)

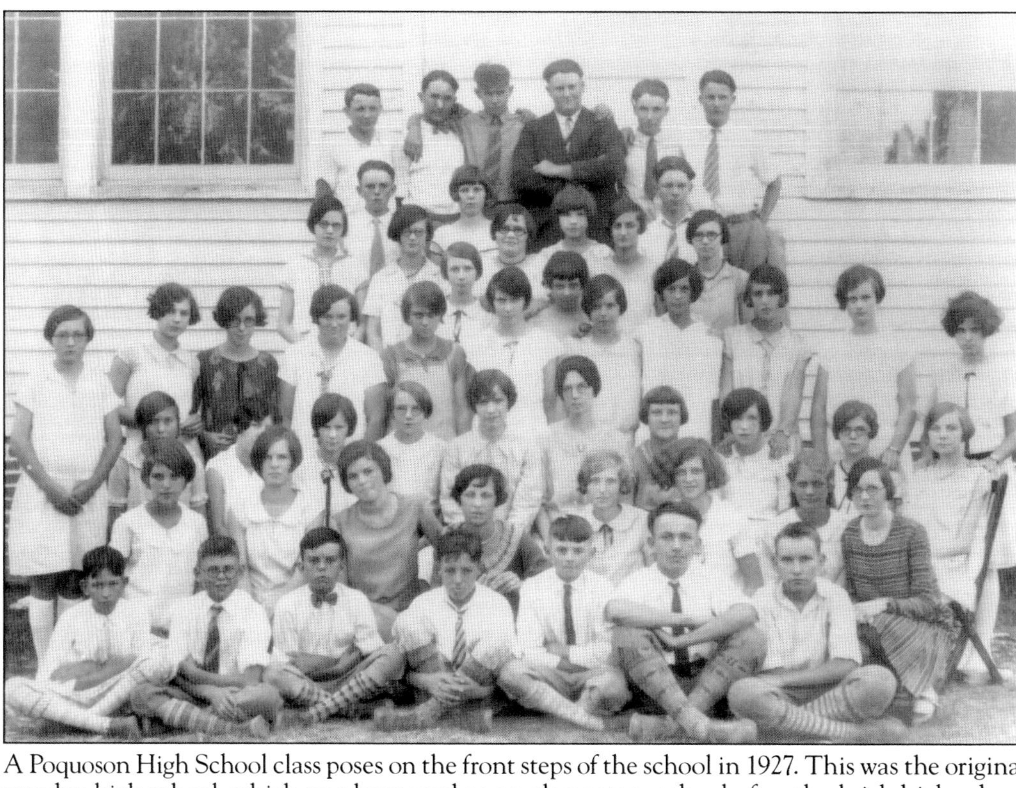

A Poquoson High School class poses on the front steps of the school in 1927. This was the original wooden high school, which was later used as an elementary school after the brick high school was built. (Courtesy of the Poquoson Historical Society.)

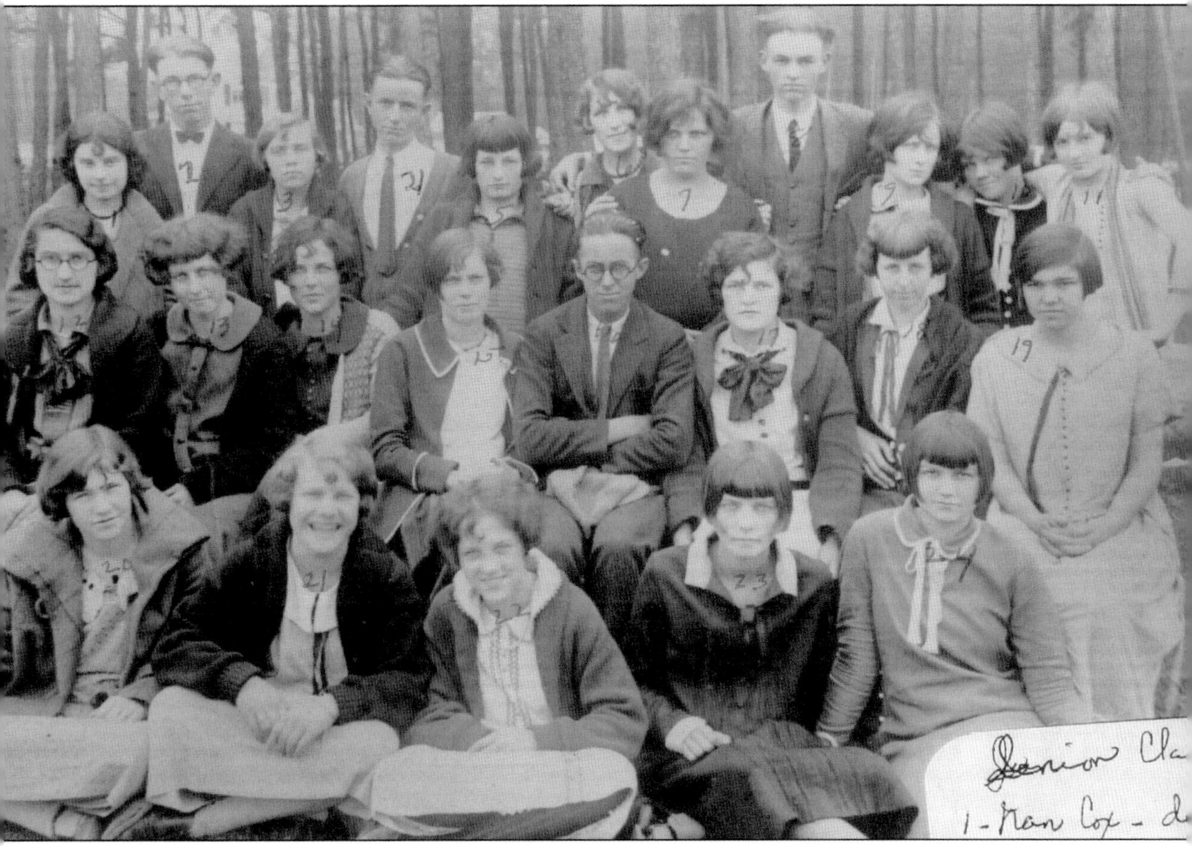


The junior class poses for a class photograph outside Poquoson High School in the early 1930s. This photograph of the 24 rising seniors was donated to the Poquoson Historical Society years ago, and the list of the students' names was lost. (Courtesy of the Poquoson Historical Society.)

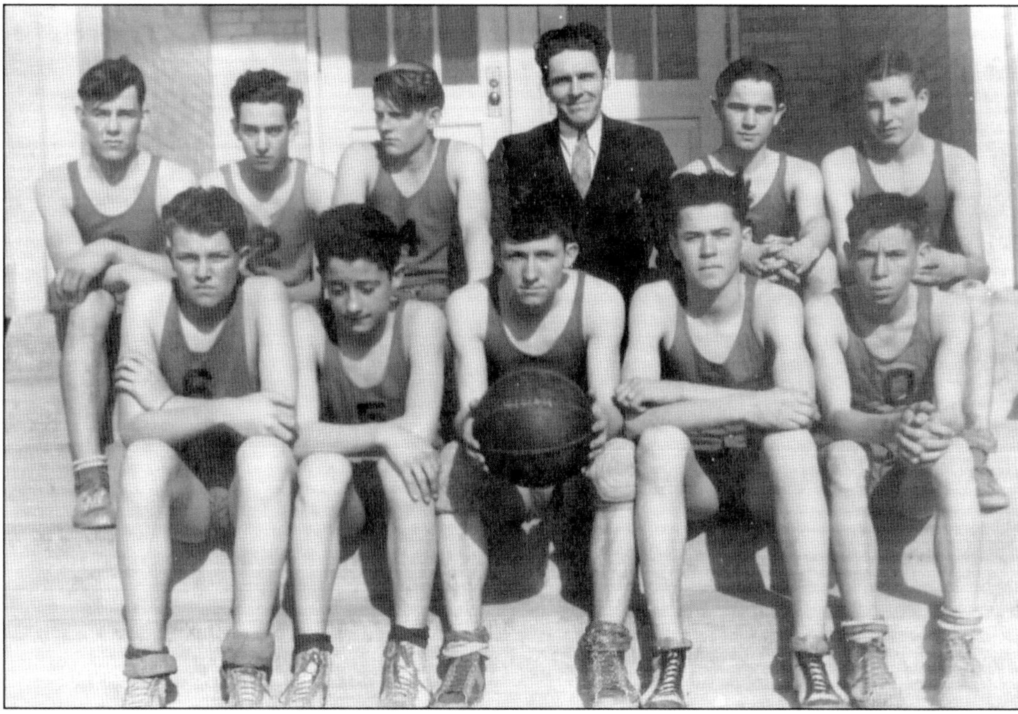

The 1932–1933 Poquoson High School basketball team included, from left to right, (first row) John H. Lawson, Robert Crutchfield, Carroll T. Forrest, Frank Carmines, and Elmer Insley; (second row) Charles Hall, Melvin Forrest, Mosco Richardson, unidentified coach, Ned Freeman, and David Hopkins. (Courtesy of the Poquoson Historical Society.)

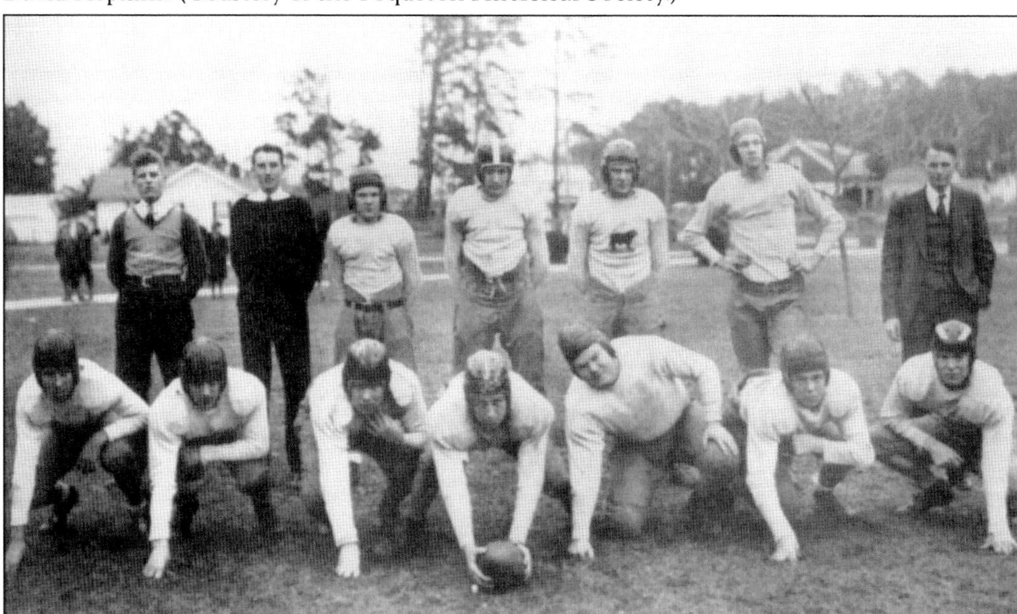

The 1939 Poquoson High School football team poses for a team photograph in their leather helmets. Coach Ed Cox was a well-known science and Latin teacher in Poquoson. (Courtesy of the Poquoson Historical Society.)

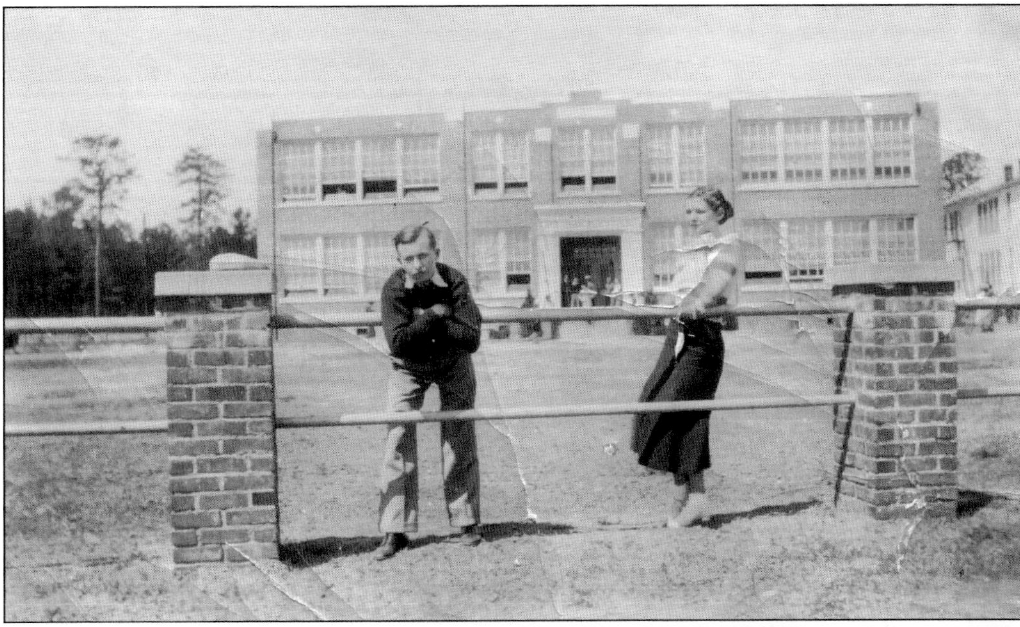

Above, Stanley Wise White and his girlfriend, Loraine Harris, lean on the fence in front of Poquoson High School in 1935. The elementary school is in the right background. (Courtesy of Nannie White Diggs.)

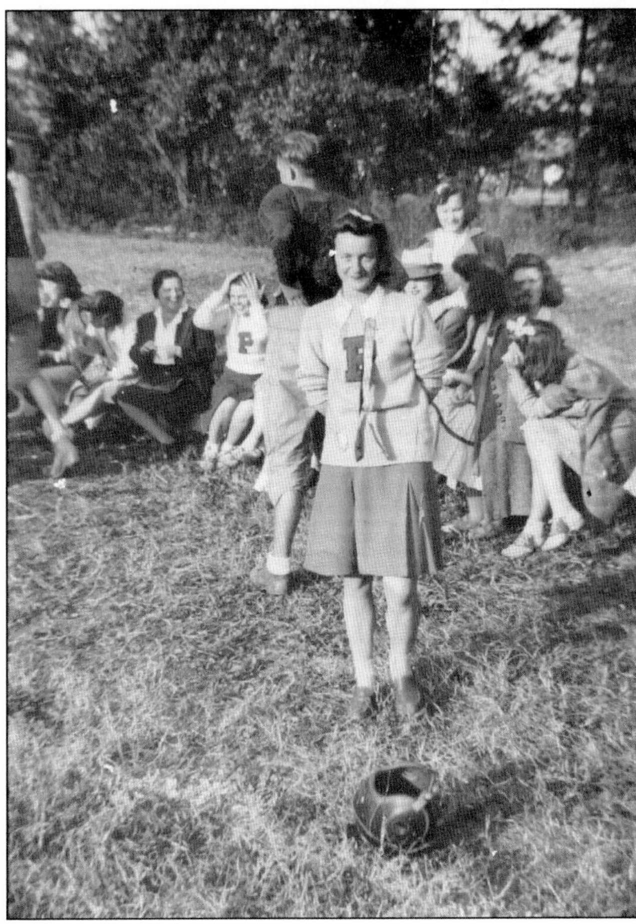

Edith Charlene Forrest was a cheerleader at Poquoson High School in 1943. She is seen here waiting for a game to begin. She was the daughter of Robert Claytor Forrest and Mary Augusta Topping and was a member of Trinity United Methodist Church. She married Wallie Gene White on December 24, 1944. The couple was always seen together. They both passed away in 2012, within weeks of each other. (Courtesy of Jane Smith White.)

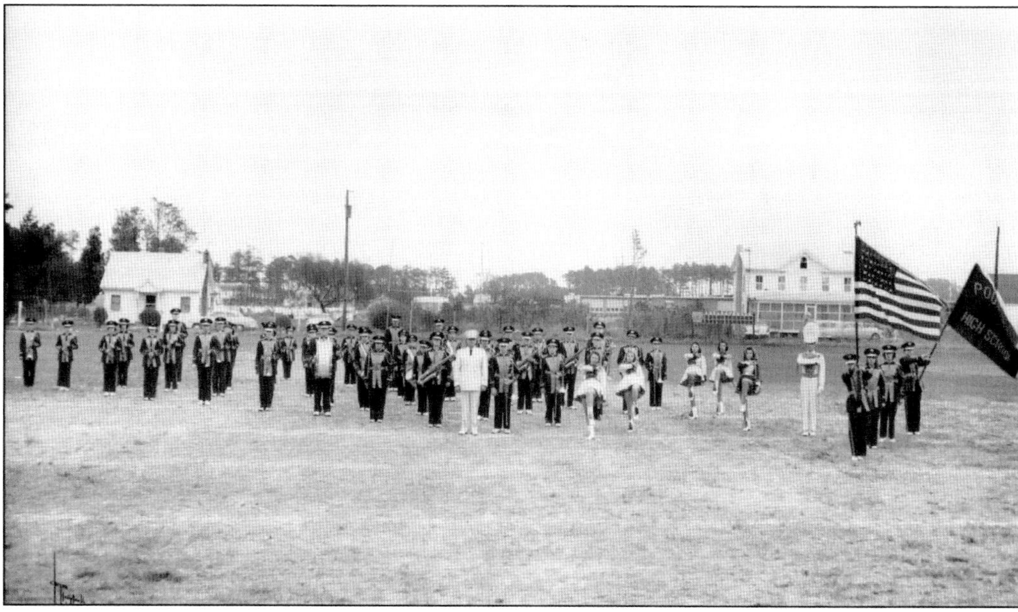

The Poquoson High School marching band poses for a photograph on the field in 1960. Note the drum major and the majorettes on the right and the band director, William T. Wiggs, in the center. (Courtesy of Carroll Ann Watkins Martin.)

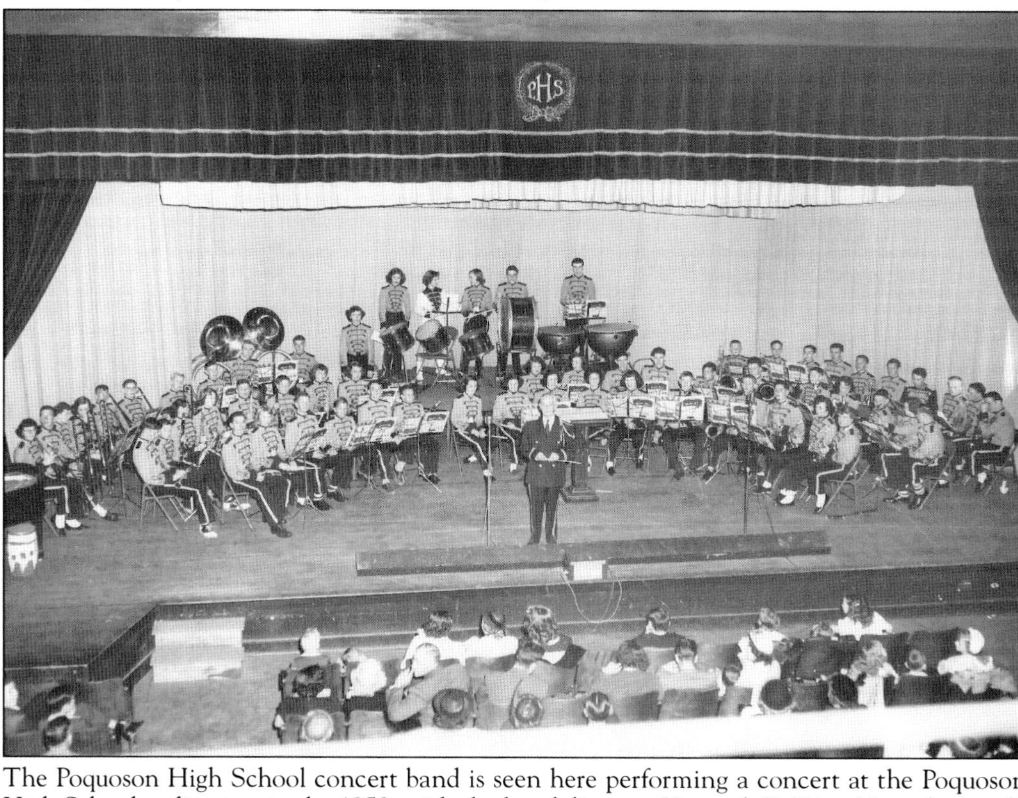

The Poquoson High School concert band is seen here performing a concert at the Poquoson High School auditorium in the 1950s with the band director, Kenneth R. Rice. Note the band's formal, military-style uniforms. (Courtesy of the Poquoson Historical Society.)

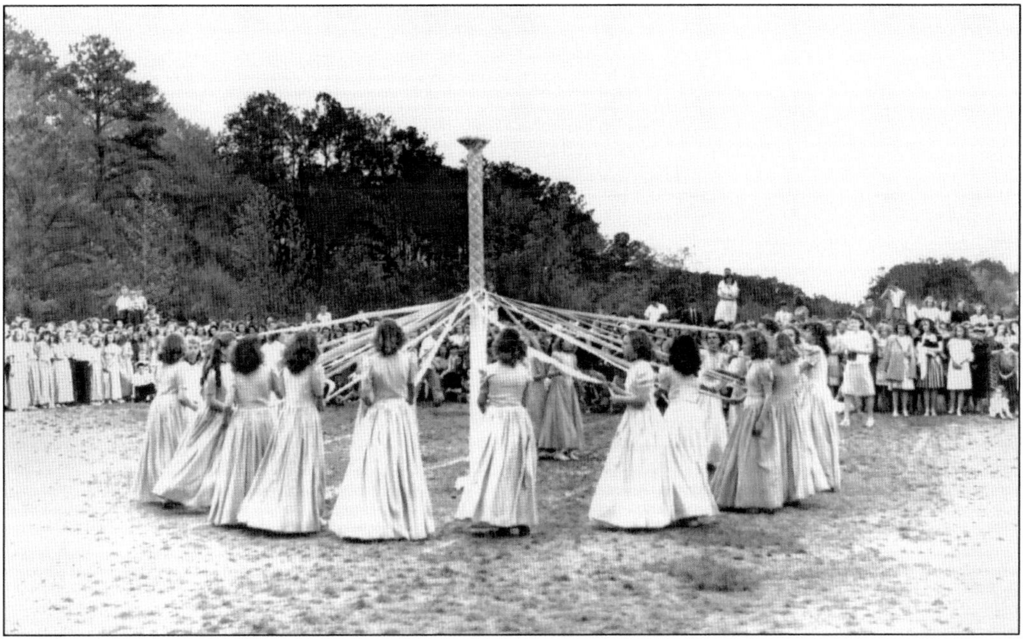

May Day celebrations were important events at Poquoson High School in the 1940s and early 1950s. Here, the May queen's court performs the maypole dance, during which the ribbons attached to the top of the pole are interwoven around the pole. (Courtesy of the Poquoson Historical Society.)

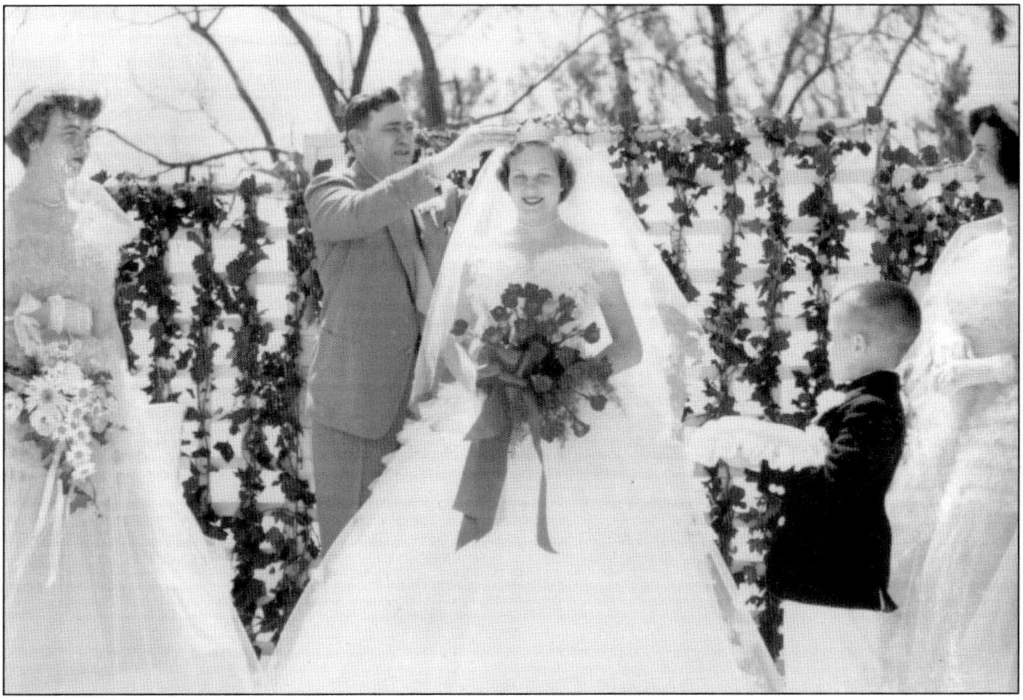

In 1954, Poquoson High School had its last May Day celebration. The May Day pageants had been an important event to local residents. The last May queen was Rose Deloris Forrest, who was crowned by the superintendent of schools. (Courtesy of Carlton Paige Forrest.)

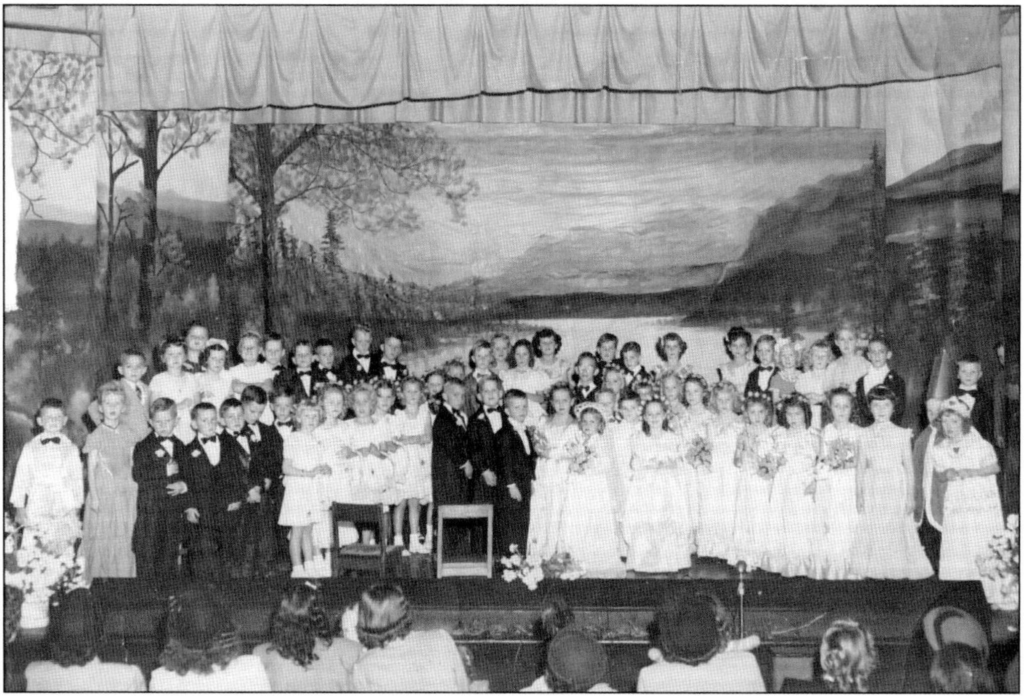

Theatrical productions were performed regularly during the school year. Here, first graders at Poquoson Elementary School perform a Jack and Jill wedding in the late 1940s. (Courtesy of Barbara Hudgins Whitlow.)

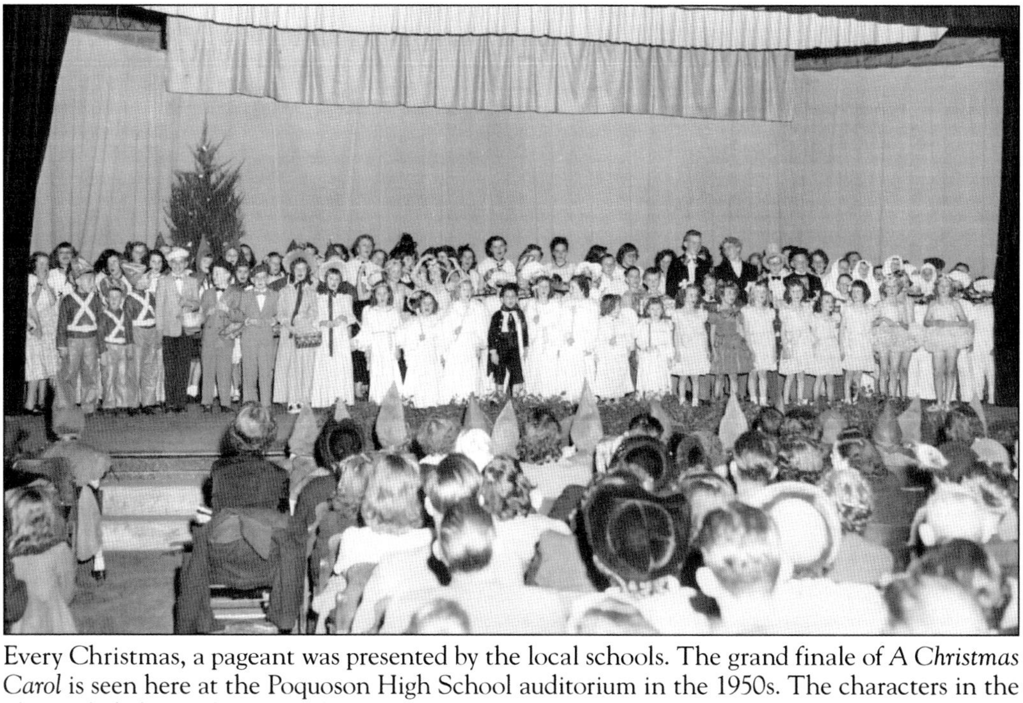

Every Christmas, a pageant was presented by the local schools. The grand finale of *A Christmas Carol* is seen here at the Poquoson High School auditorium in the 1950s. The characters in the play included French boys and girls, angels, dolls, ballerinas, and Tiny Tim, played by Bill Reed Freeman. (Courtesy of Barbara Hudgins Whitlow.)

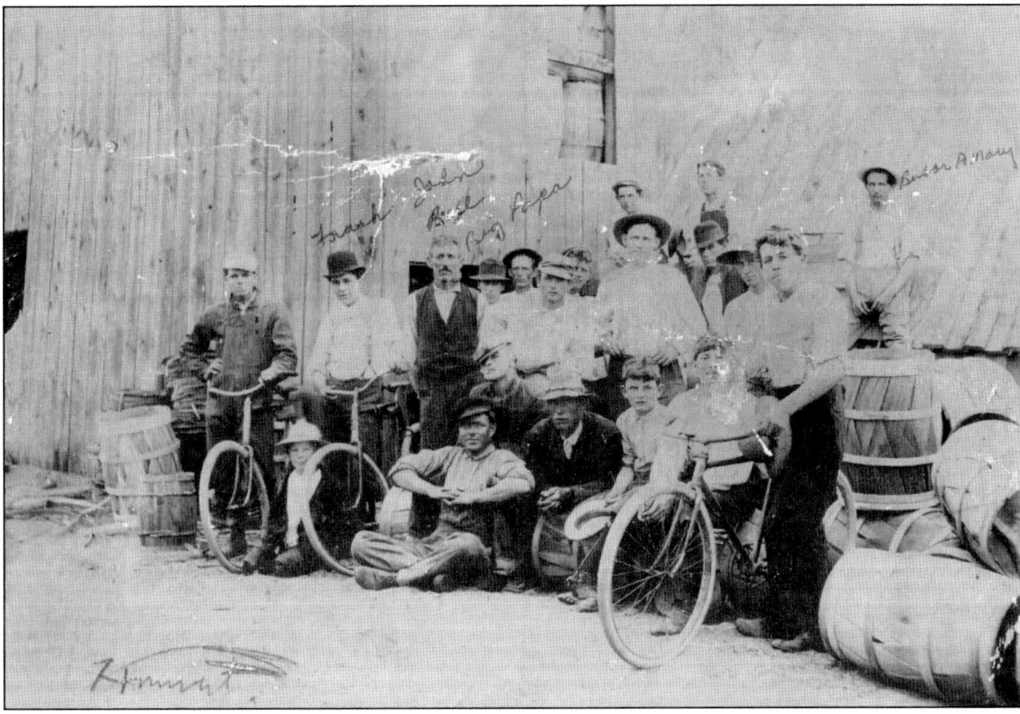

Above, workers from the Barrel Factory pose for a group photograph. The factory was on Forrest Road, also known as Barrel Factory Road, and barrels were made there for people to ship their produce and fish to market in. The business was started by Herbert Amory and his brother-in-law Henry Buchanan in 1906 and bought by George W. Amory Sr. in the early 1930s. He moved the business to the 1200 block of Poquoson Avenue, but the business closed in the late 1930s. (Courtesy of the family of Rose Ward Huggett.)

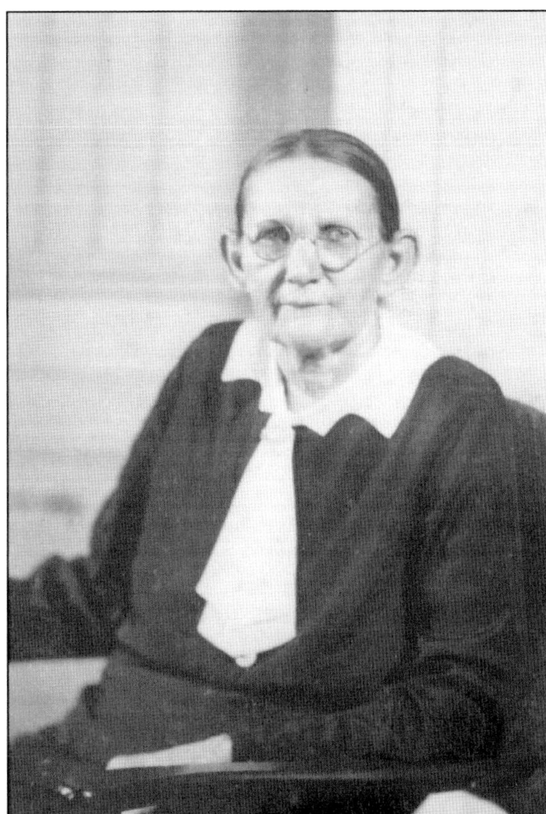

Sarah Ward Freeman was born to Rebecca Elizabeth Forrest and Wesley Ward on September 25, 1866. She and her husband, John Freeman, were the parents of Rebecca Freeman Dryden, a beloved shopkeeper in Jeff's. (Courtesy of Patricia Smith Apelt.)

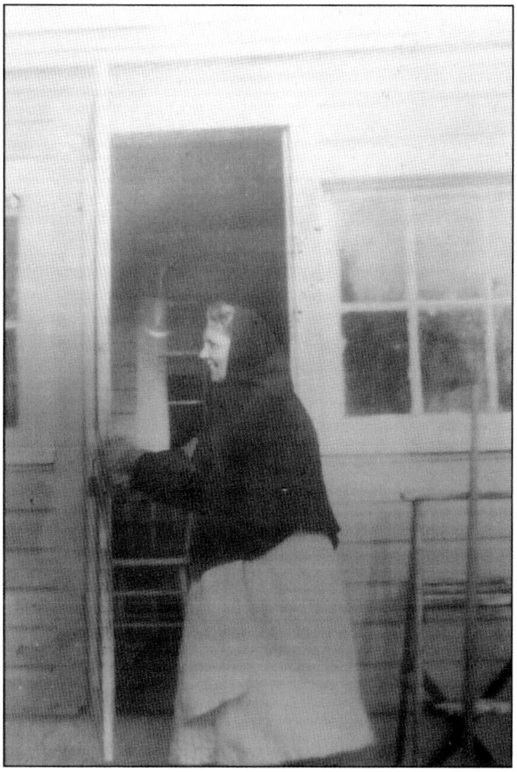

Becky Dryden is seen here entering her house at 968 Poquoson Avenue. She was known for wearing a kerchief around her head to protect her hair in cooler weather. (Courtesy of Patricia Smith Apelt.)

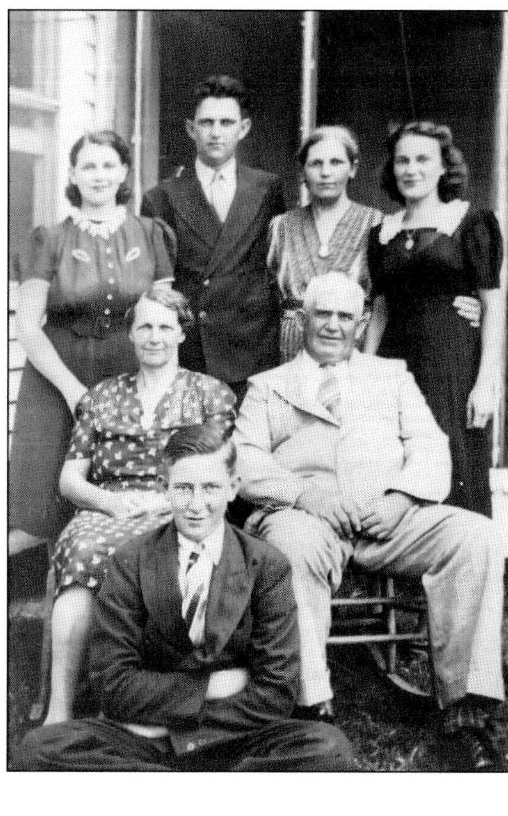

The Dryden family poses for a family photograph. They are, from left to right, (first row) Freeman Dryden; (second row) Becky Dryden and Wallie Judkins Dryden; (third row) Rebecca Dryden, Jack Dryden, Charlotte Dryden, and Mary Anne Dryden. (Courtesy of Patricia Smith Apelt.)

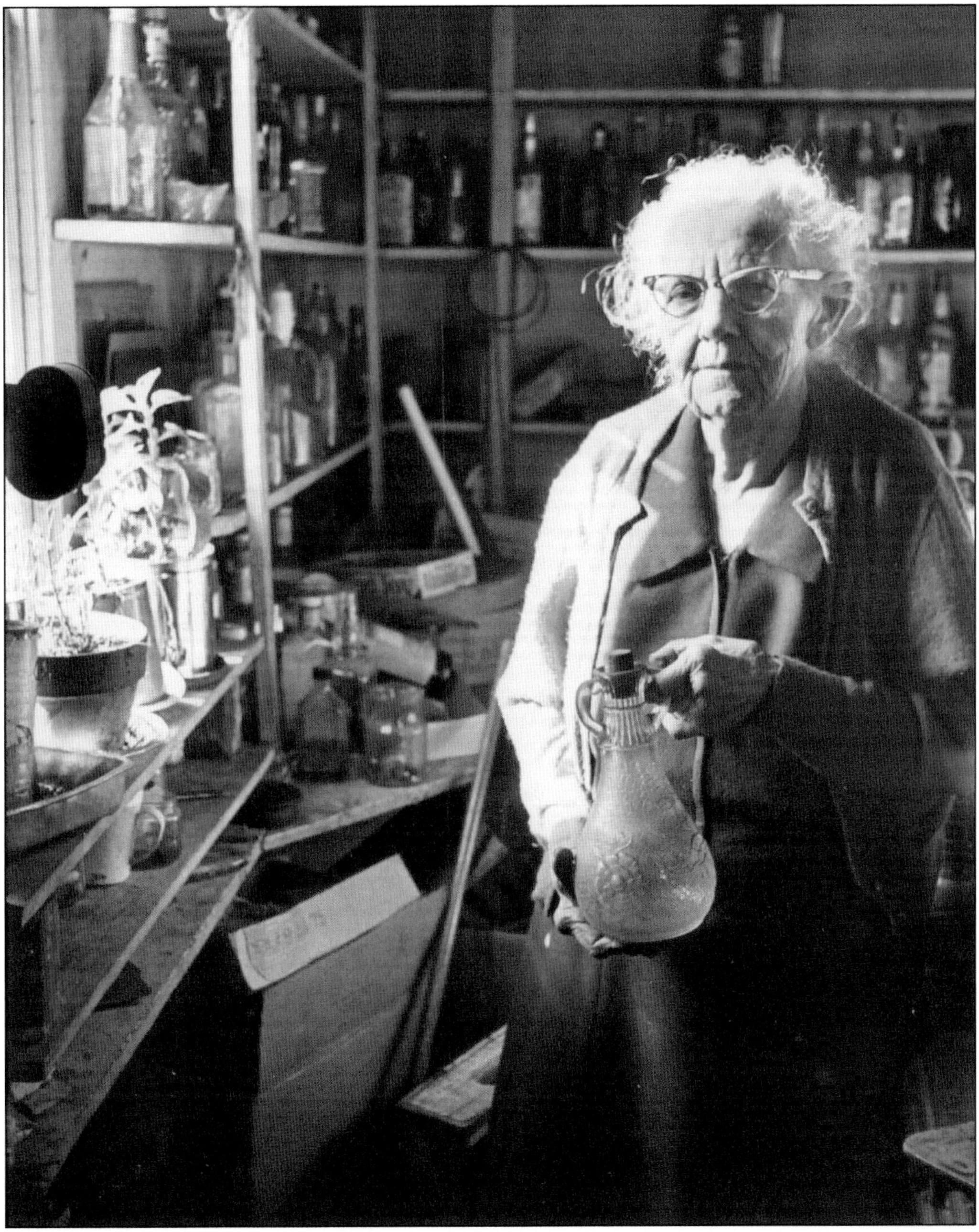

Becky Dryden, known to the locals as Miss Becky, is seen here in the mid-1970s in the small general store she ran out of a building on her property. She sold everything, including candy that local children came in to buy after school and even individual cigarettes. She ran the store well into her later years. Her grandson Henry Freeman remembered that she knew where everything was in the store without having to look. After the store was closed, her son Freeman Dryden sold produce out in front of it. Her home and store now make up the property of the Poquoson Museum and house the archives of the Poquoson Historical Society. (Courtesy of Henry Freeman.)

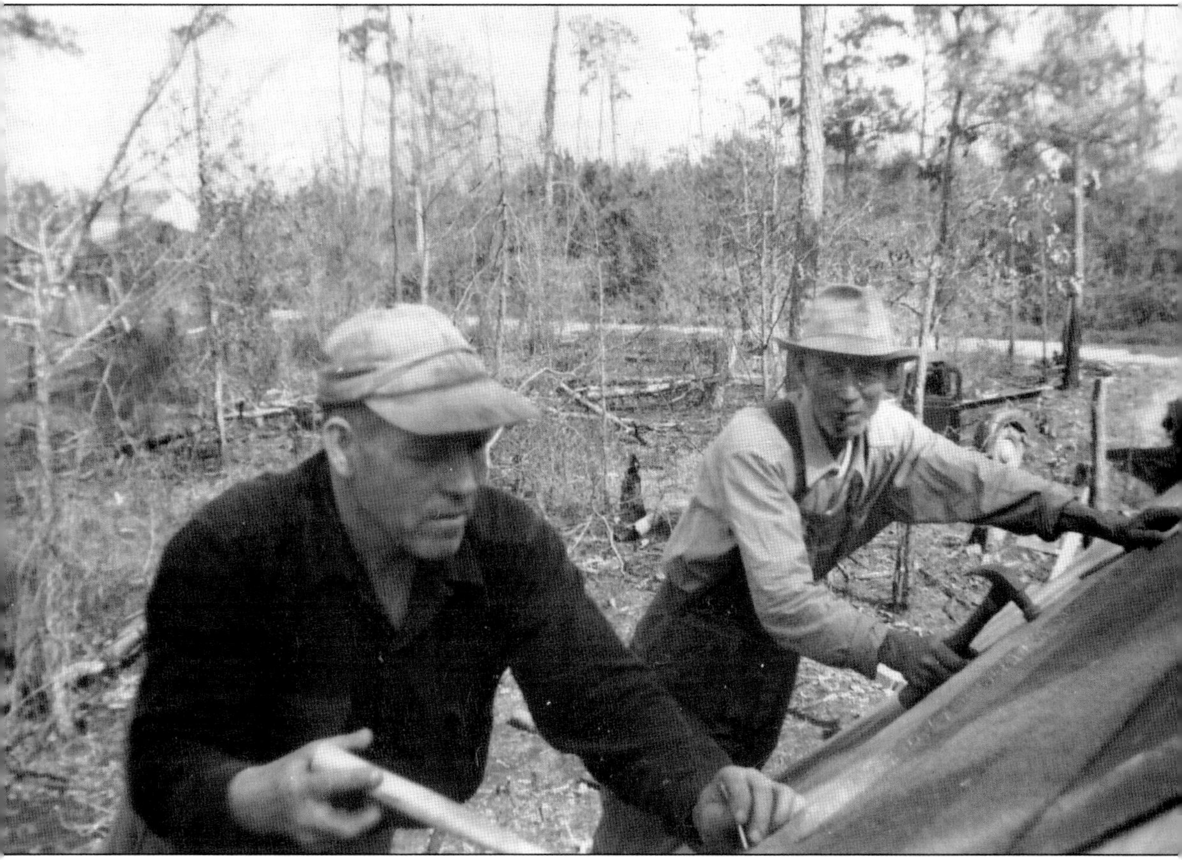

The Carmines family lived on Poplar Road, across Poquoson Avenue from the Dryden family. Ray Carmines Sr. lived at the end of Poplar Road. He is seen here working on the roof of the old Leroy Carmines house with his son Ray Carmines Jr. The house was abandoned in the late 1900s and used as a haunted house attraction for local children until 2003, when it was razed. (Courtesy of Charles McDaniel.)

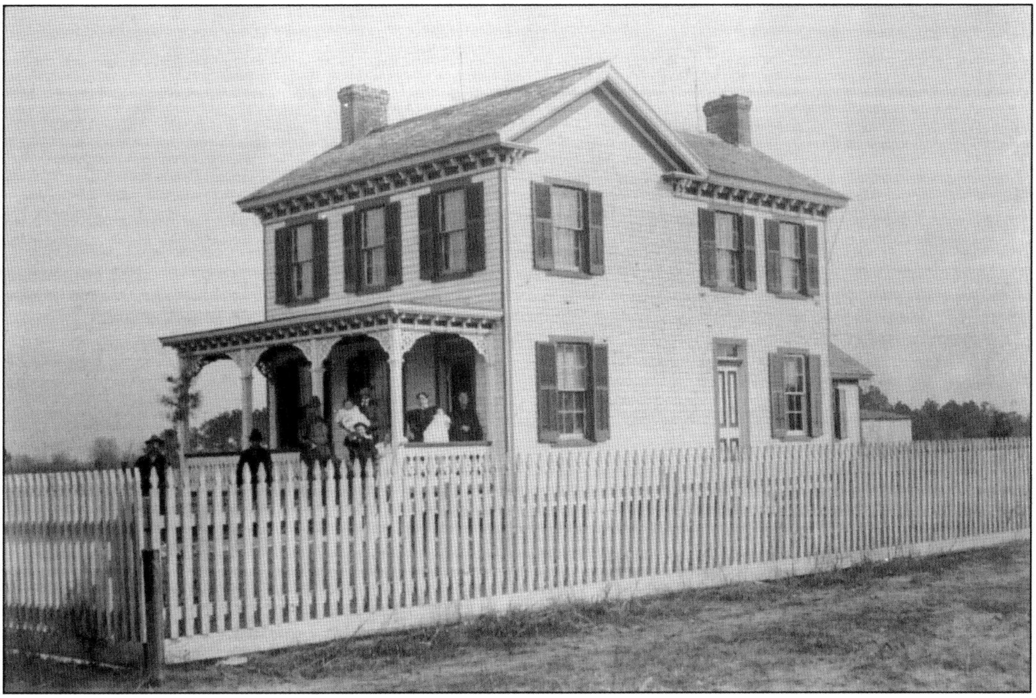

This house, at 864 Poquoson Avenue, was the home of William White and his wife, Columbia Moore, the daughter of Levi Moore. Their daughter "Matt" and her husband, Segar Watkins, also lived in this house. (Courtesy of the Poquoson Historical Society.)

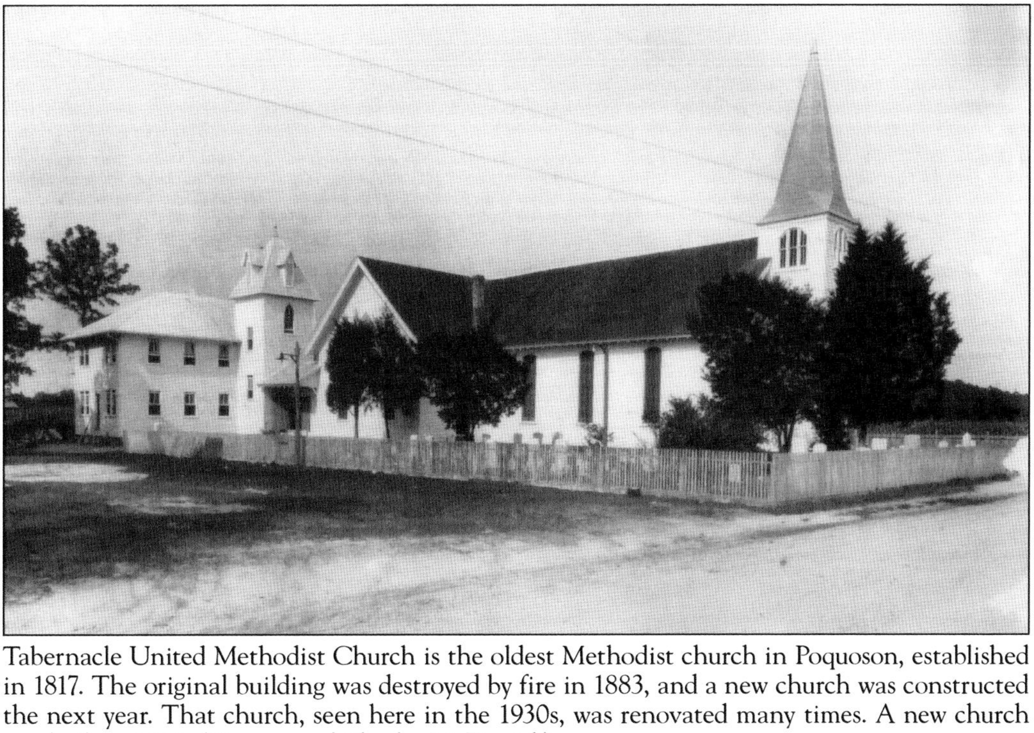

Tabernacle United Methodist Church is the oldest Methodist church in Poquoson, established in 1817. The original building was destroyed by fire in 1883, and a new church was constructed the next year. That church, seen here in the 1930s, was renovated many times. A new church was built in 1972. (Courtesy of Charles McDaniel.)

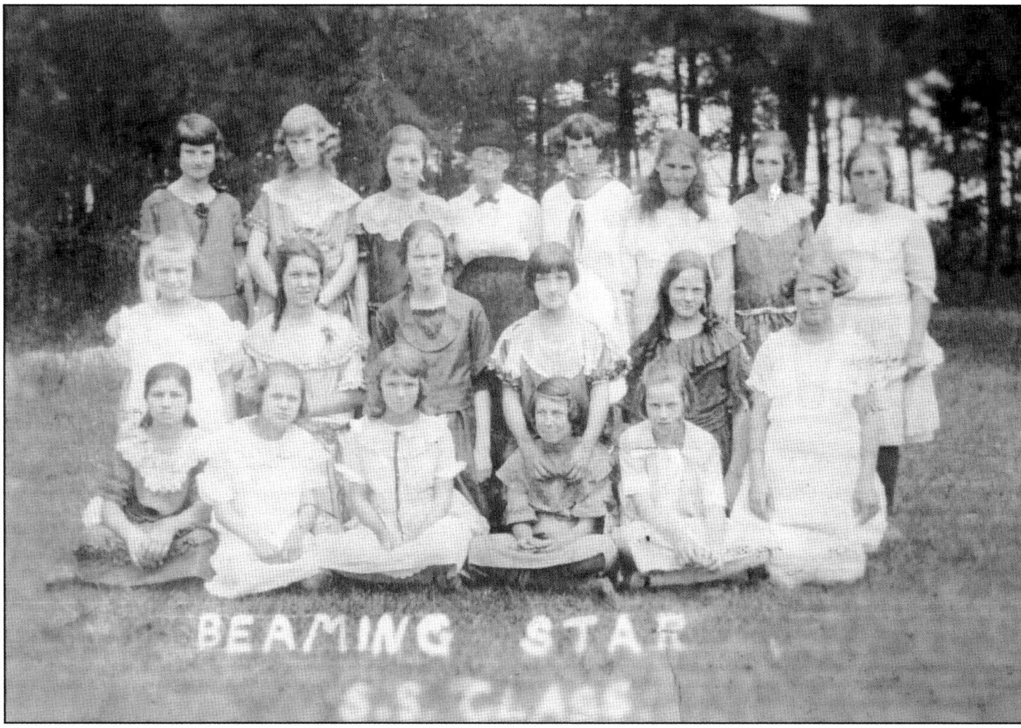


Sunday school students from Tabernacle United Methodist Church pose for a photograph in the early 1900s. This group was called the Beaming Star class. (Courtesy of Patricia Smith Apelt.)

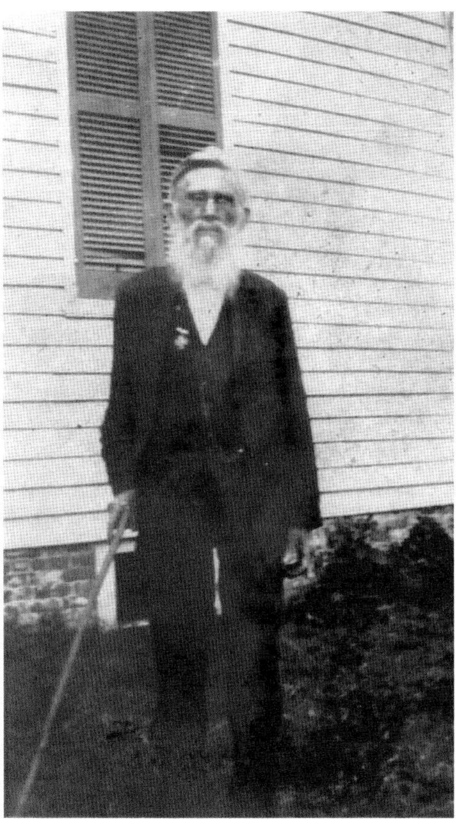

An unidentified elderly Civil War veteran stands tall in 1911. The gentleman is wearing a Southern Cross of Honor medal on his vest. The old man was a resident of the Poquoson Magisterial District of York County (Courtesy of the Poquoson Historical Society and Tim Smith.)

# *Four*

# THE MESSICK AND EARNEST COMMUNITIES

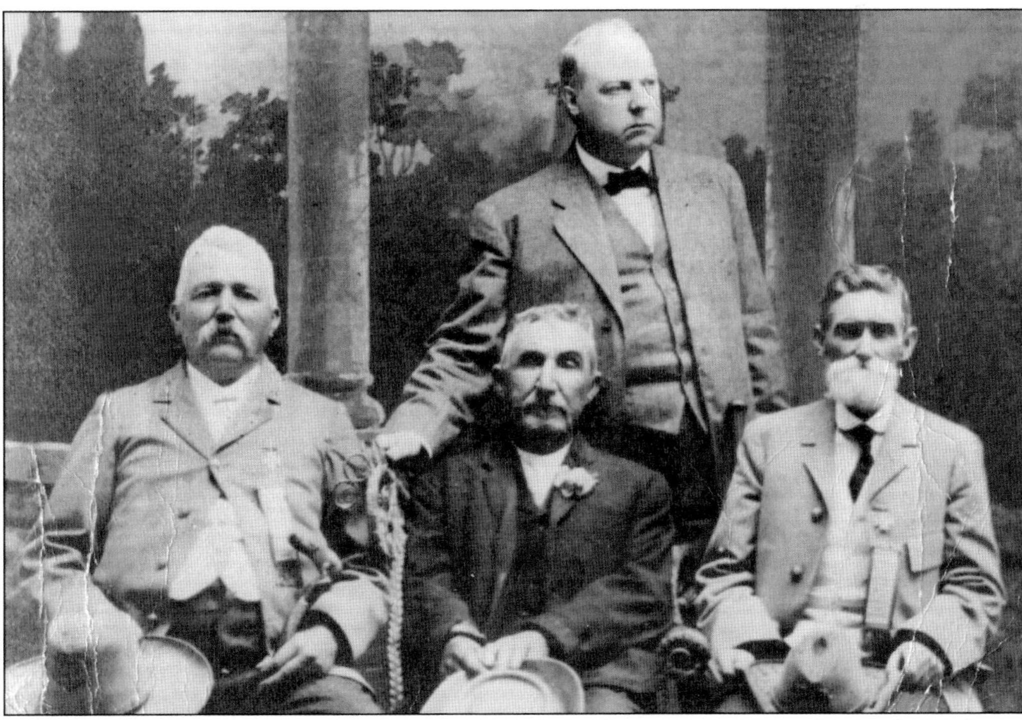

Many men from Poquoson and York County fought for the Confederacy in the Civil War, four of whom are seen here at a veterans' reunion in 1911. They are, from left to right, (seated) Robert Keith Custis, 3rd Virginia Cavalry, CSA; Wesley Messick, crew member, ironclad CSS *Virginia*, which was originally the USS *Merrimack*; and Pvt. John Montgomery, 115th Regiment, Virginia Militia, CSA; (standing) Capt. William Stores, 32nd Virginia Infantry. (Courtesy of Robert V. Insley Jr.)

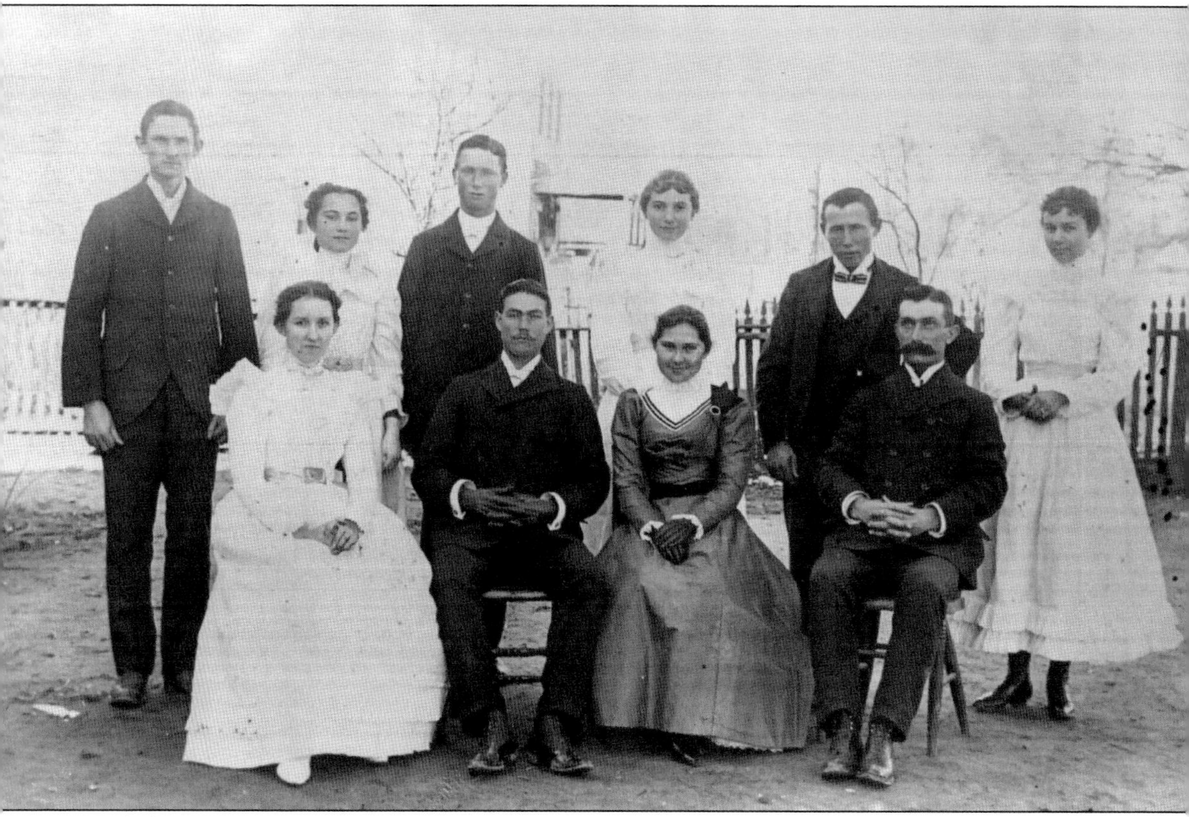

Clyde Smith and Lidia Watkins were married in the late 1800s. This wedding photograph shows the bride and groom sitting in the center of the first row, flanked by Janie Messick and Tom Amory. In the second row are, from left to right, Eddie Messick, Lizzie White, George Lawson, Sadie Huggett, Johnson Wainwright, and Sadie Holloway. The bride and groom are both wearing dark gloves. Clyde Smith was renowned for his log canoe boatbuilding; the Mariner's Museum documented the building of one of his last log canoes, from choosing the proper trees in the forest to launching the craft in Bennett's Creek on North Landing Road. His canoes were used by fishermen throughout the Chesapeake Bay. (Courtesy of Jane Smith White.)

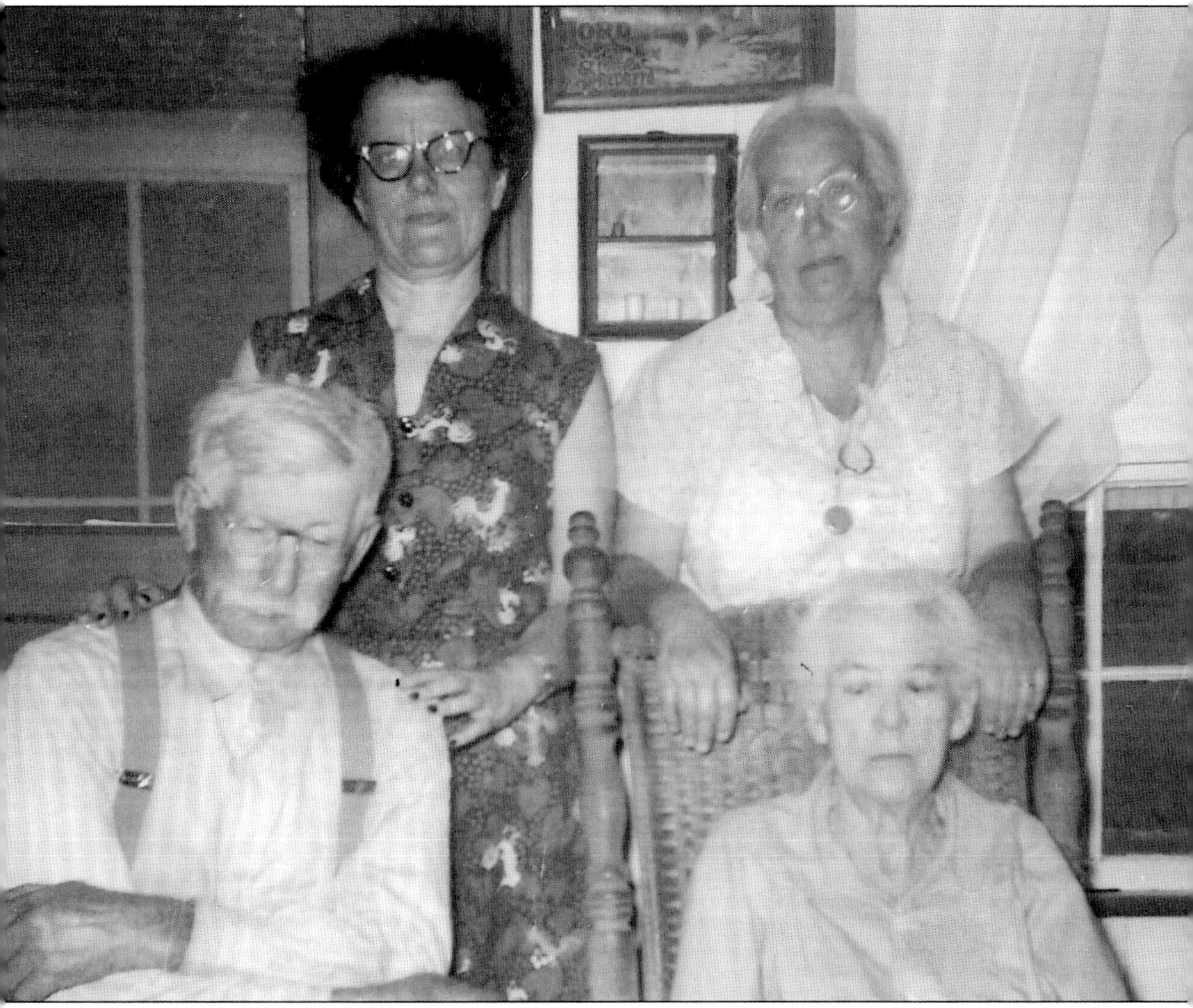

Capt. William "Billy" Newton poses for a photograph with his wife, Sarah, and their daughters, Sarah Newton Forrest (standing, left) and Mary Newton Holloway. Sarah Newton's quilting thimble, scissors, needle, and thread are displayed on the shelf behind them. Their home was built in the Eastern Shore style, and it still stands on Poquoson Avenue. It is one of a few old houses left in Poquoson, as most have either been razed to make way for modern housing or modified and added onto until they are unrecognizable. Captain Newton was known for his boatbuilding and built the small log canoes in the backyard of his house. An article was written about his boatbuilding skills in *National Geographic* magazine. He was born on July 28, 1873, and died on January 30, 1966. Sarah Newton was born on February 14, 1877, and died on June 22, 1958. (Courtesy of Joyce Butler Holloway.)

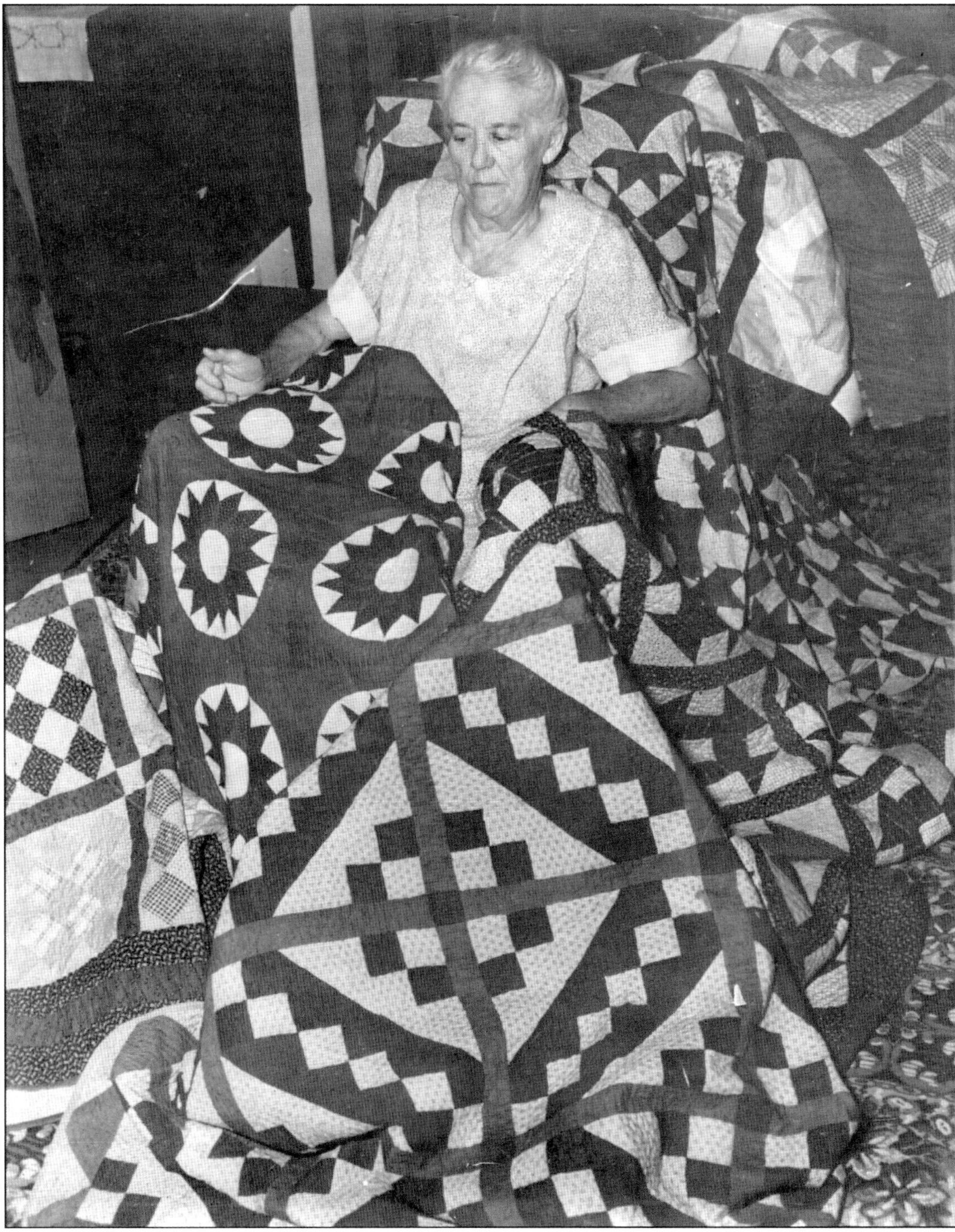

Sarah Newton, the wife of Capt. William "Billy" Newton, is seen here in the 1950s with just a few of the quilts she made through the years. Making quilts was her passion; as with many women of her generation, handwork such as quilts, knitted and crocheted throws and pillows, tatting, and embroidery was a form of relaxation. The items were either given as gifts to family and friends throughout the year or used to restock worn-out items. It is said that every quilt is a story because scrap cloth from making clothes was used to make the squares of quilts. Sarah Newton was blind in her later years, and the recipients of her quilts were fortunate to have one of her hand-sewn treasures. (Courtesy of Joyce Butler Holloway.)

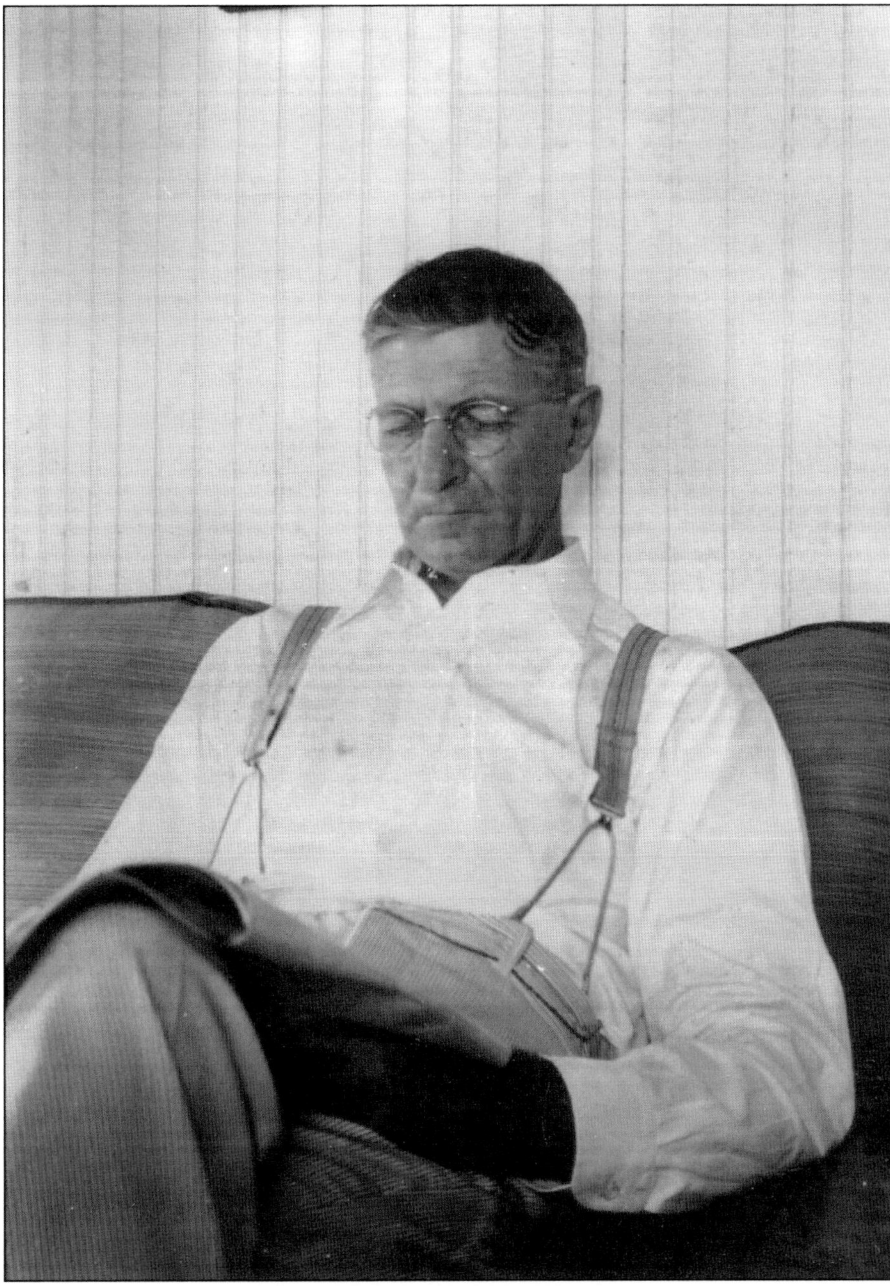

Ira B. Forrest was one of the last postmasters of Messick. He was appointed in 1918 and served until his death in 1959. During World War II, Ira Forrest personally delivered letters to families of active duty servicemen after office hours. He felt it was his duty to get the information to the local residents as quickly as possible, especially during the war. He was married to Lola Bradshaw and was the father of two local politicians and businessmen, H. Gray Forrest and Carroll Thomas Forrest, the latter of whom became the first mayor of Poquoson and married Jessie Faye Forrest. Ira was a descendant of Abraham Forrest, who was originally from Mathews and was awarded 60 acres of land in Poquoson for his service in the War of 1812. (Courtesy of the Poquoson Historical Society.)

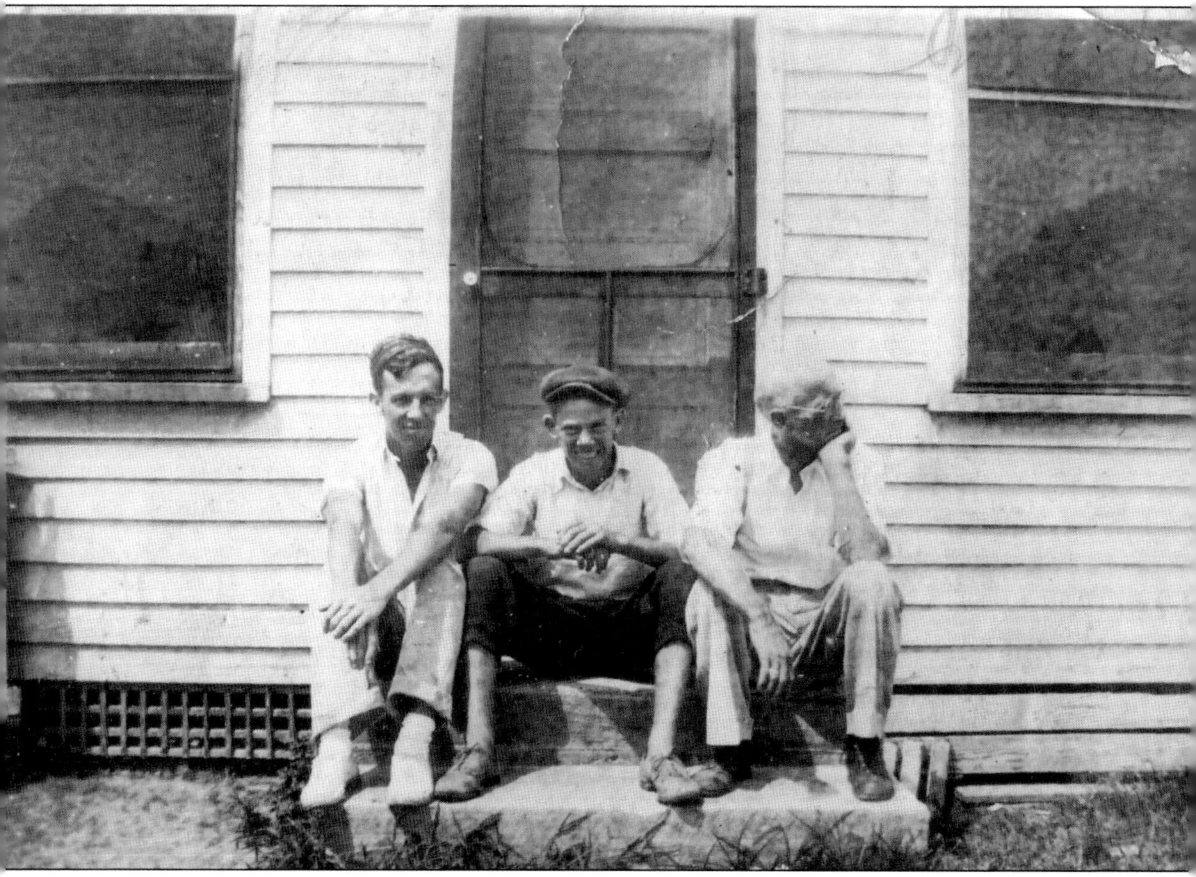

From left to right, Gray Forrest, Ivey Forrest, and Robert Lee Forrest sit on the porch of the Messick store, which was owned by Robert Lee and operated by Ira Forrest. Robert lee Forrest, a local oysterman, was born on August 27, 1865, and died on December 8, 1940. He married Melissa Virginia Holloway on January 22, 1885. His father, Robert James Forrest, was born in Mathews County on December 25, 1836. He was married to Mary Francis Weston and had seven children with her, including Robert Lee Forrest. He also had two children with his second wife, Ann Deborah Holloway. Robert James Forrest was the flag bearer for the 32nd Virginia Infantry, Company I. The flag was shot out of his hands 13 times, but he always recovered it. (Courtesy of the Poquoson Historical Society.)

Harry "Jimmy" Gray Forrest, seen here, was the son of Ira B. Forrest. His brother Carroll Thomas Forrest was the first mayor of the Town of Poquoson in 1952. Harry Gray Forrest served both in York County and in Poquoson as an elected official. (Courtesy of the Poquoson Historical Society.)

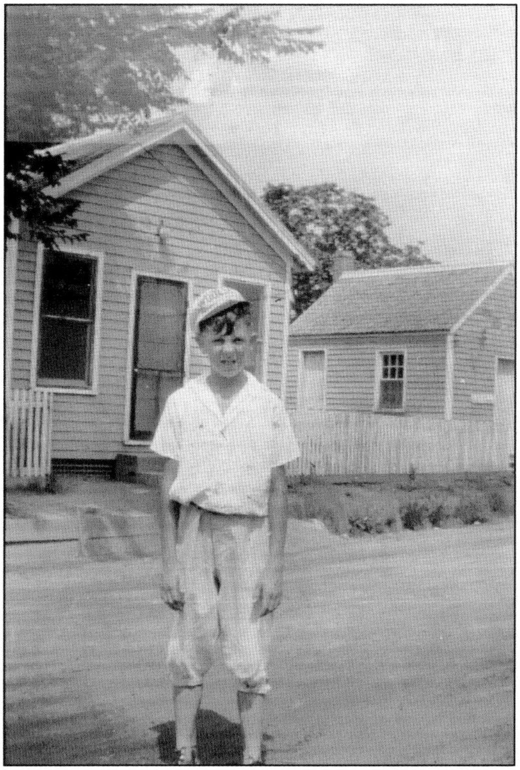

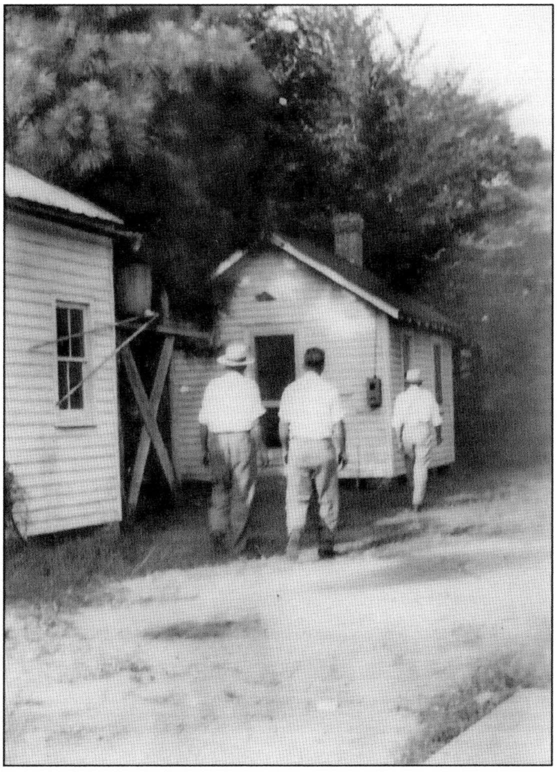

The Messick registrar's office was a small wooden building behind the Messick Post Office on Poquoson Avenue. Here, men from the community go to vote in 1940. The registrar's office was built in 1921 and owned by Ira Forrest. Charlene White worked there during voter registration and voting. Nell Forrest Hudgins and Gladys Holloway Lawson remember voting through the window of the building. It is now located on the Poquoson Museum grounds. (Courtesy of Melissa Forrest Gardy.)

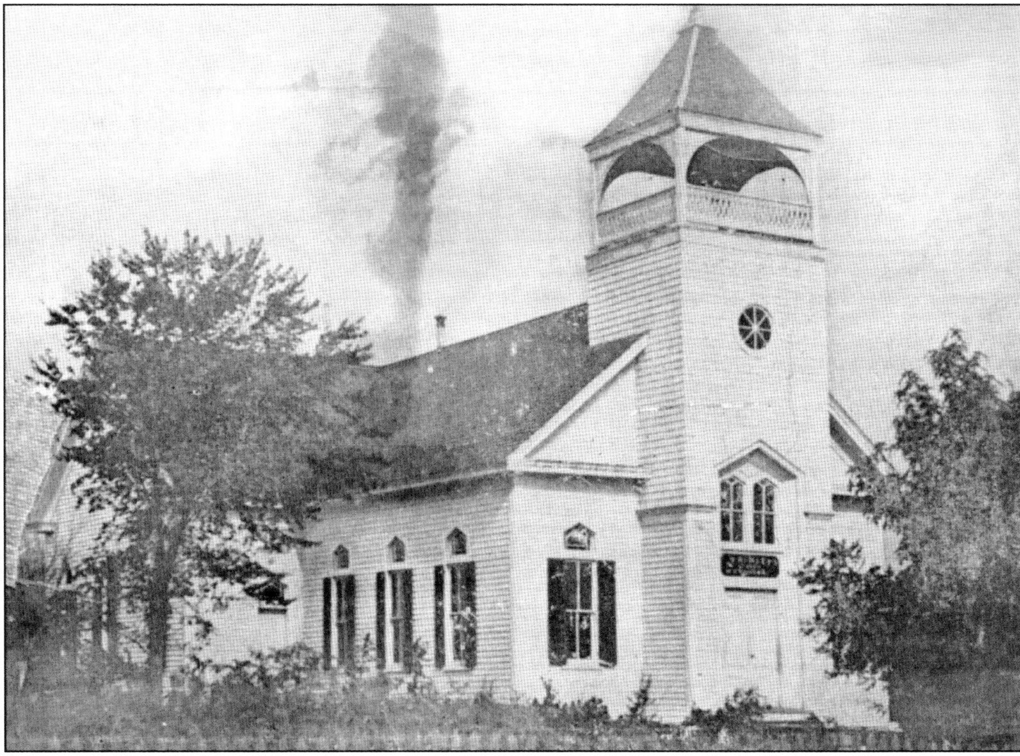

Trinity United Methodist Church is on Poquoson Avenue. This wooden structure was used from 1882 until the 1930s, when the church was expanded. Trinity was the second Methodist church in Poquoson, and for years, it shared a minister with Tabernacle United Methodist Church. (Courtesy of Trinity United Methodist Church.)

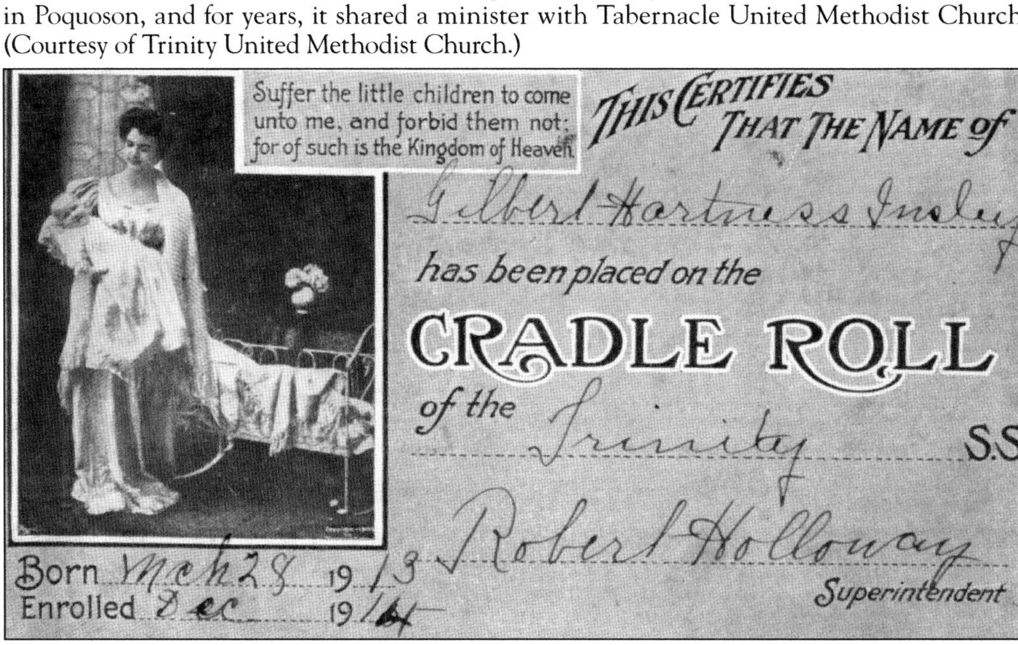


Babies born to Trinity church members could be enrolled in the Cradle Roll. Gilbert Hartness Insley was one of several children named after the minister at that time, Rev. R.N. Hartness. (Courtesy of Sonny Insley.)

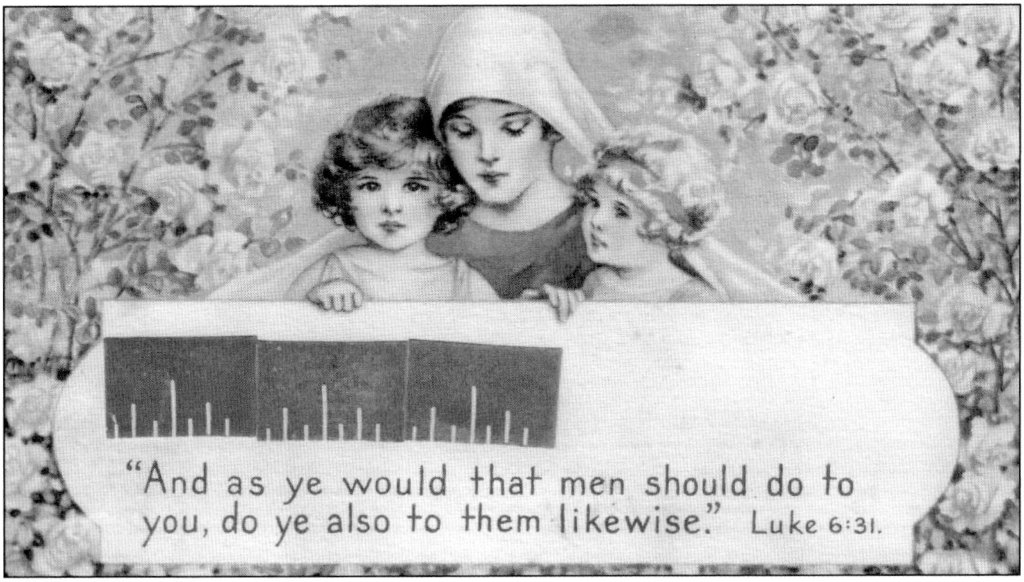


Trinity United Methodist Church Sunday school teachers used these attendance measure cards for the children. Fragments of a paper ruler were glued to the card every time the child attended Sunday school. Nell Forrest Hudgins was the owner of this attendance measure as a child. (Courtesy of Barbara Hudgins Whitlow.)

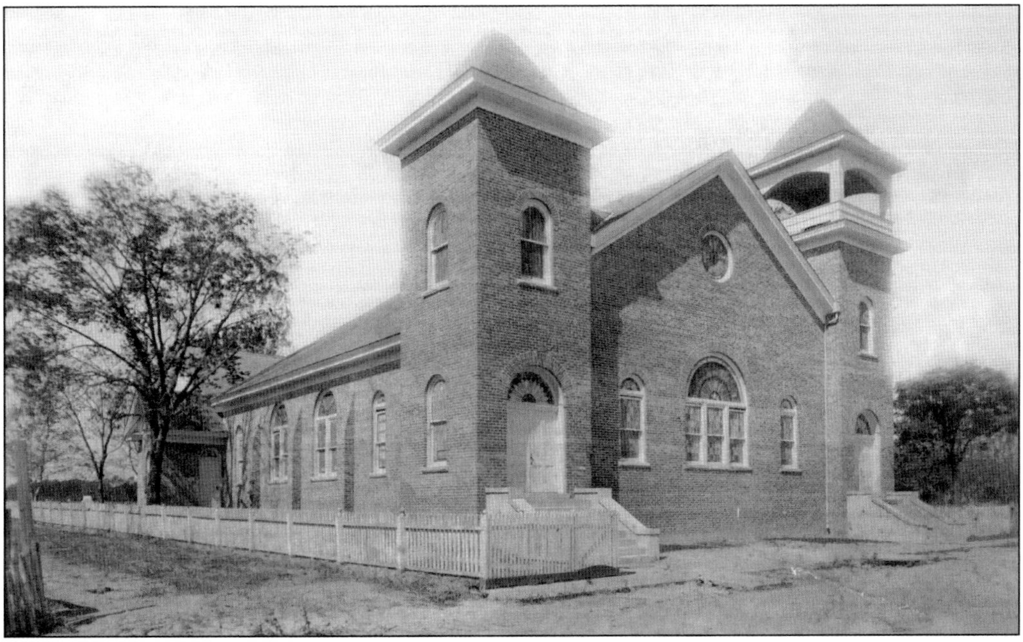

The original wooden Trinity United Methodist Church was built in 1882. Capt. John Lemuel Bradshaw brought the wood to build that first church from Suffolk in his Chesapeake Bay freight boat. The wood was then hauled by horses, owned by James Taylor Rollins, from Amory's wharf to the building site. In 1902, a second building was added, which formed a T when it was placed at the back of the original structure. The new Trinity United Methodist Church is seen here after its expansion and renovation in the 1930s. The church was renovated again in the early 1950s and in 2001. (Courtesy of Trinity United Methodist Church.)

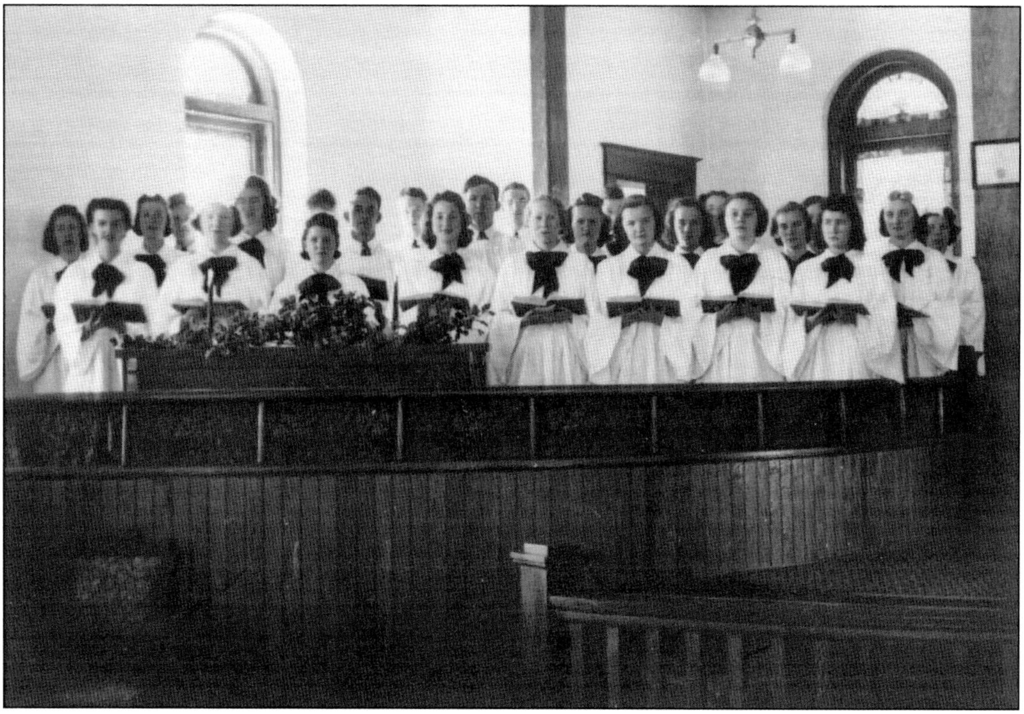

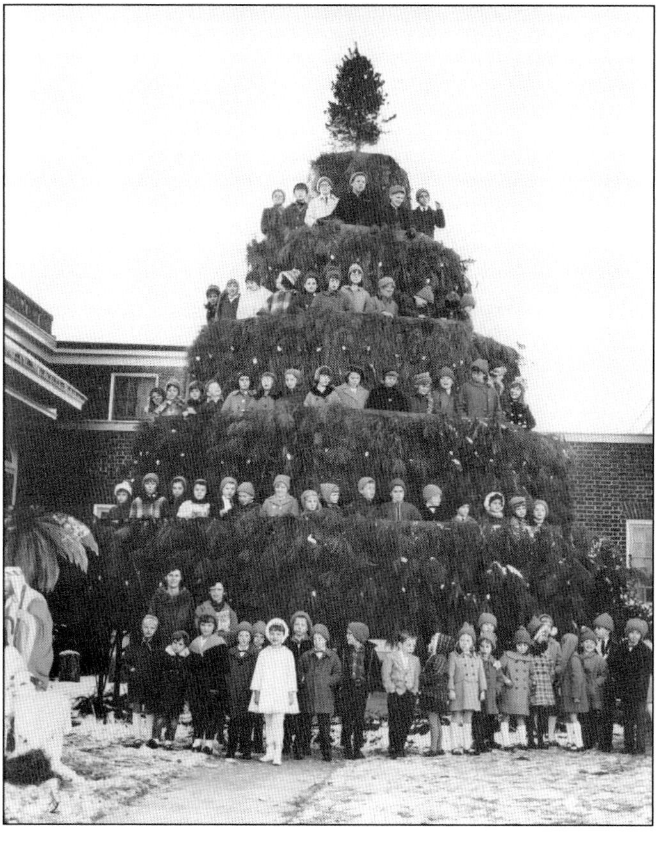

Above, the Trinity Church choir stands in the choir area, to the side of the pulpit in the 1940s. This area was moved during the renovation work in the 1950s. (Courtesy of Trinity United Methodist Church.)

This "live" Christmas tree was constructed by the men of the church and used for many Christmas seasons by the children of Trinity. It was 30 feet tall and 22 feet wide. Standing on the ground behind the children are longtime youth chorus director Harriett Page Forrest (right) and accompanist Carroll Edd Freeman Emerson (left). (Courtesy of Trinity United Methodist Church.)

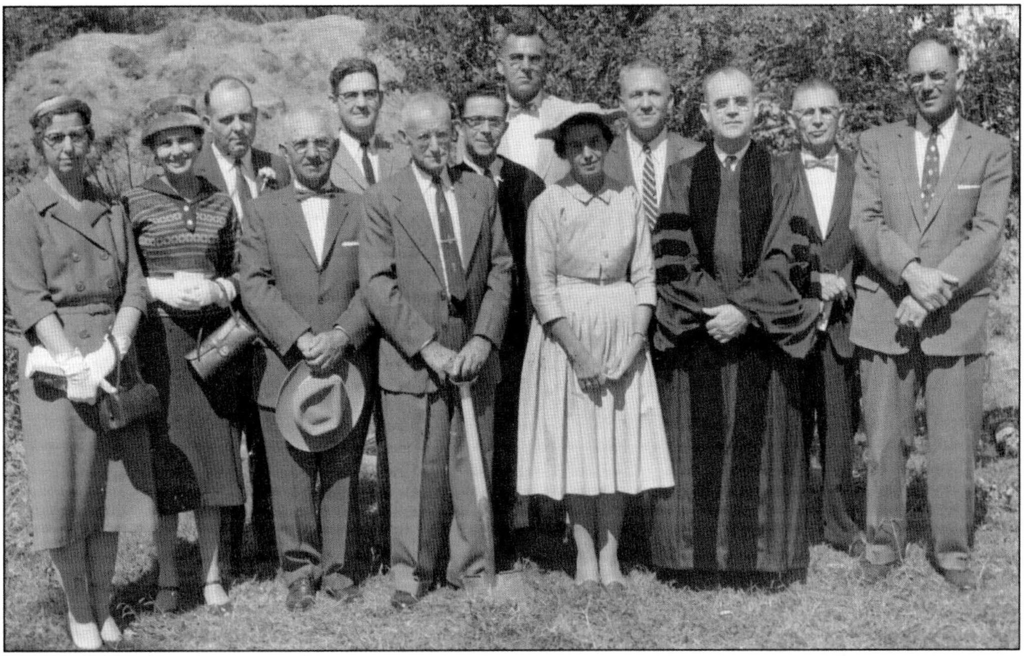

From left to right, Emily Holloway Evans, Helen Ward Forrest, Lester Carmines, Henry B. Hunt Sr., J. Elwood Forrest, Robert (Bob Manning) Holloway, Dr. Harvey Swann, Holston Evans, Mary Topping Quinn, Carroll T. Forrest, Dr. William F. Watkins, Arthur J. Page, and Charlie Powell posed for this photograph at the ground-breaking ceremony for the new multipurpose complex at Trinity United Methodist Church on September 28, 1958. (Courtesy of Trinity United Methodist Church.)

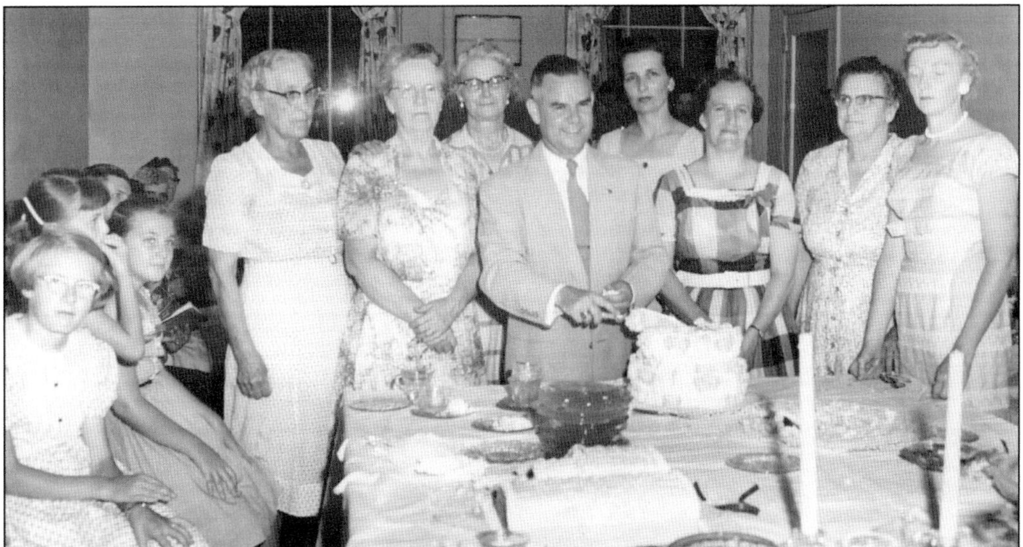

This reception was held for Rev. Douglas Williams at Trinity United Methodist Church in the early 1950s and was catered by the United Methodist Women's Society. Reverend Williams was a chaplain in the Army during World War II and was the first minister to live in the parsonage on Church Street, which was purchased after Tabernacle United Methodist Church and Trinity United Methodist Church were separated. (Courtesy of Trinity United Methodist Church.)

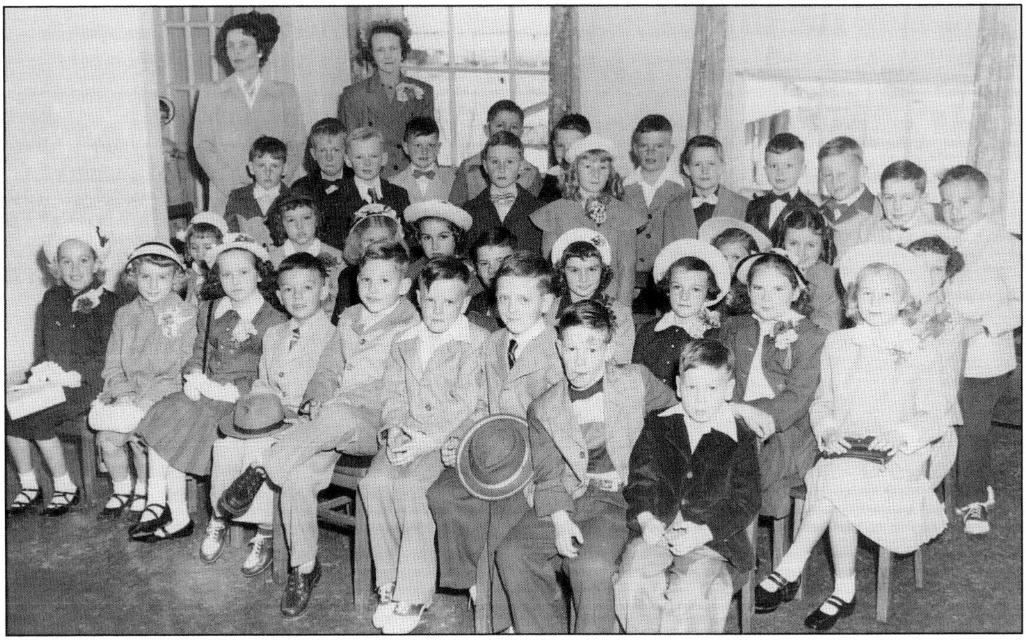

Sunday school teachers Crystal Forrest (left) and Eunice Holloway (right) are seen here with their Sunday school classes on Easter Sunday, 1951. Note the hats and gloves worn by all the girls and teachers. This was the first Easter Sunday since the church was renovated, and a professional photographer was there to document the day. Six Sunday school classes were set up around a central meeting room, which had a piano in it. Each teacher held a class in the morning before everyone met in the sanctuary for the sermon. (Courtesy of Trinity United Methodist Church.)

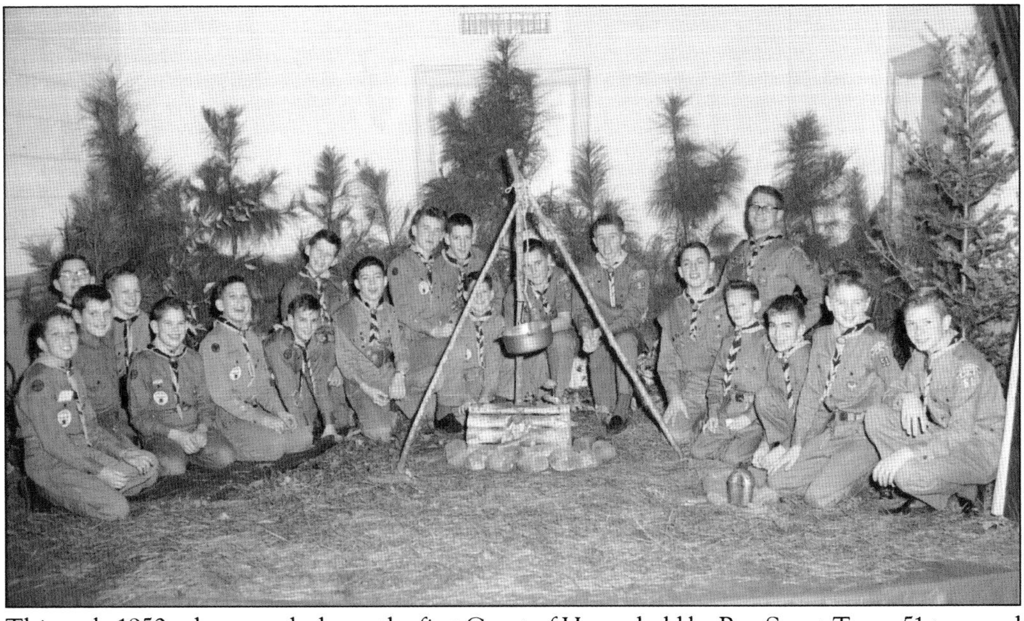

This early-1950s photograph shows the first Court of Honor held by Boy Scout Troop 51 to award the first rank of Eagle Scout. Trinity United Methodist Church sponsored the troop, and Clarence Evans was the Scoutmaster at the time. Civic duty and community pride are a large part of what Poquoson is today. (Courtesy of Trinity United Methodist Church.)

As a child, Eleanor Elizabeth Firth Chesser walked to Williamsburg behind an oxcart to visit her father, Charles Thomas Firth, who was stationed in Williamsburg with the 32nd Virginia Infantry. (Courtesy of Barbara Hudgins Whitlow.)

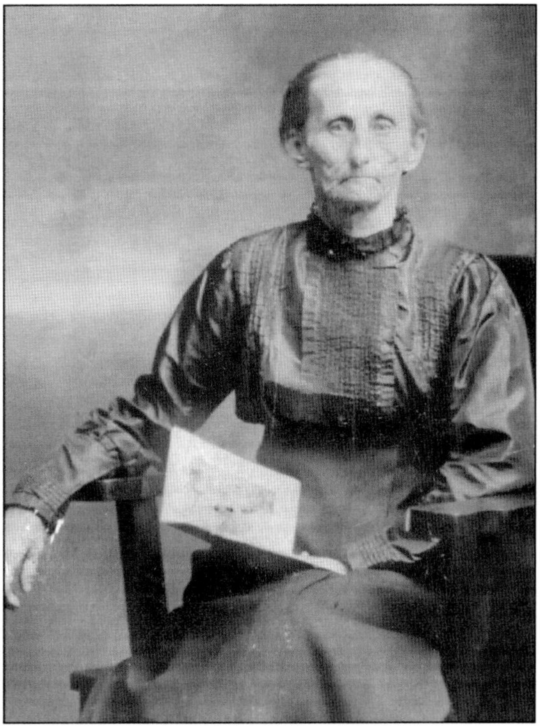

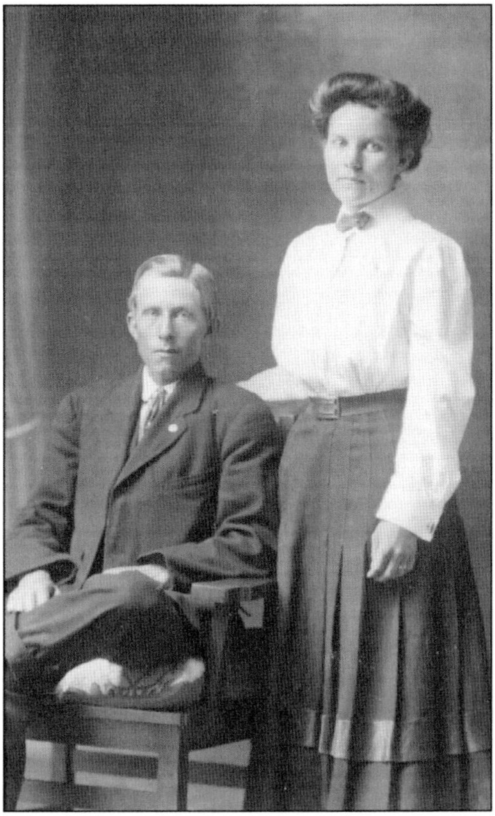

Wilton Hope Carmines and his wife, Bertha Maud Ward Carmines, were the parents of Mary Jane Carmines Mason, Murdie Viola Carmines Firth, and Roberta Sue Carmines Faulkner. They lived three doors down from Trinity United Methodist Church. The church eventually bought their property and razed the house. It is now a vacant lot where Trinity holds outdoor activities. Bertha Carmines was called Big Mama by her grandchildren. (Courtesy of Maresa Firth Spangler.)

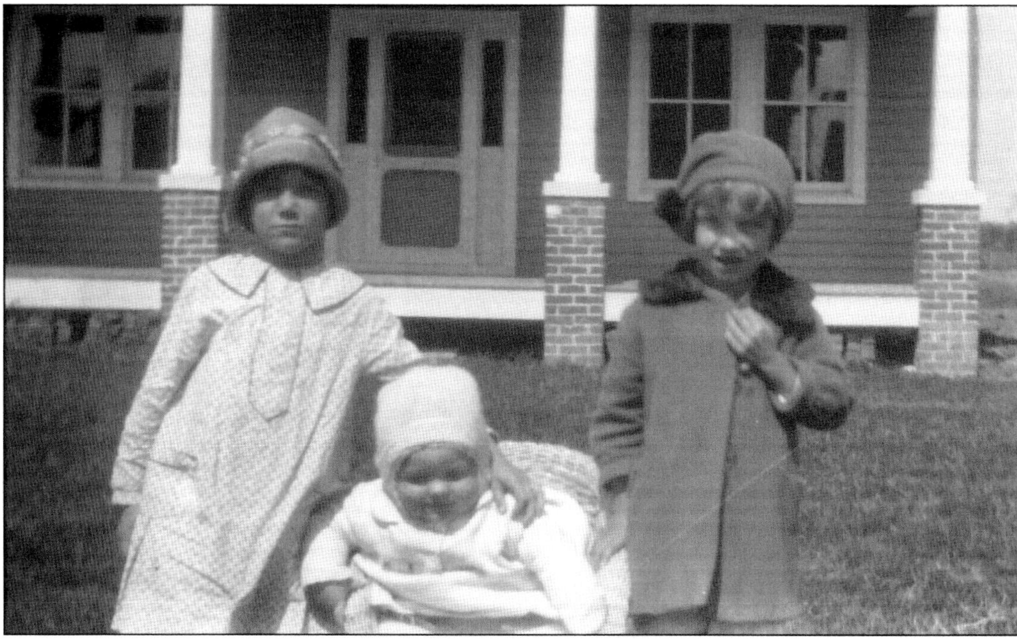

Seen here in front of Ray Carmines Sr.'s home are, from left to right, Mary Louise "Peachie" Hopkins Downs, Ray Carmines Jr., and Amelia Forrest Hunt. Ray Carmines Sr. and his wife, Eva Freeman Carmines, had a pony and a little surrey, which they rode in the annual Poquoson Fire Department Fire Carnival parade, put on by the Poquoson Fire Department Ladies Auxiliary. Ray Carmines Sr. was known for his outgoing personality and his support of Poquoson High School sports. He was the son of Leroy Carmines and Missouri Frances Rollins and one of the heirs to James Taylor Rollins. Ray Carmines Jr. ice-skated well into his late 70s. Mary Louise "Peachie" Hopkins Downs owned the Lou-Paige Beauty Shoppe in Messick. Amelia Forrest was the daughter of Frank Lee Forrest and Emma Hopkins. She married William T. Hunt. (Courtesy of Susan Downs Herring.)

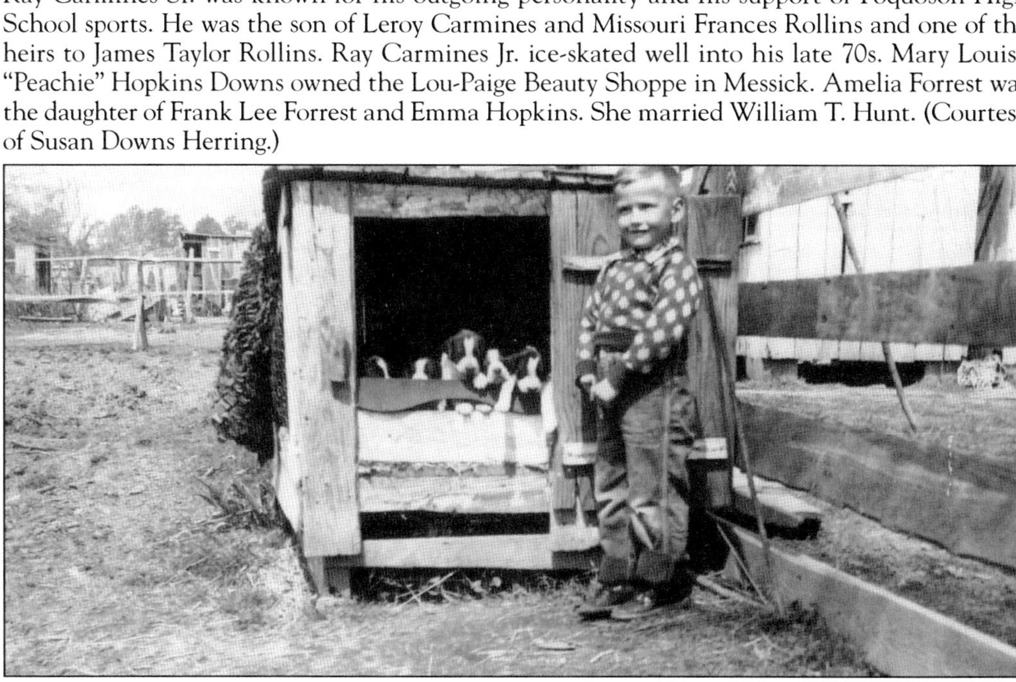

Five-year-old Sonny Insley takes care of the English Pointer puppies that his father was raising on Bay Street in the 1950s. Insley is now the owner of Marshland Expedition, which gives tours of the outer ridges of Poquoson. He also still hunts. (Courtesy of Sonny Insley.)

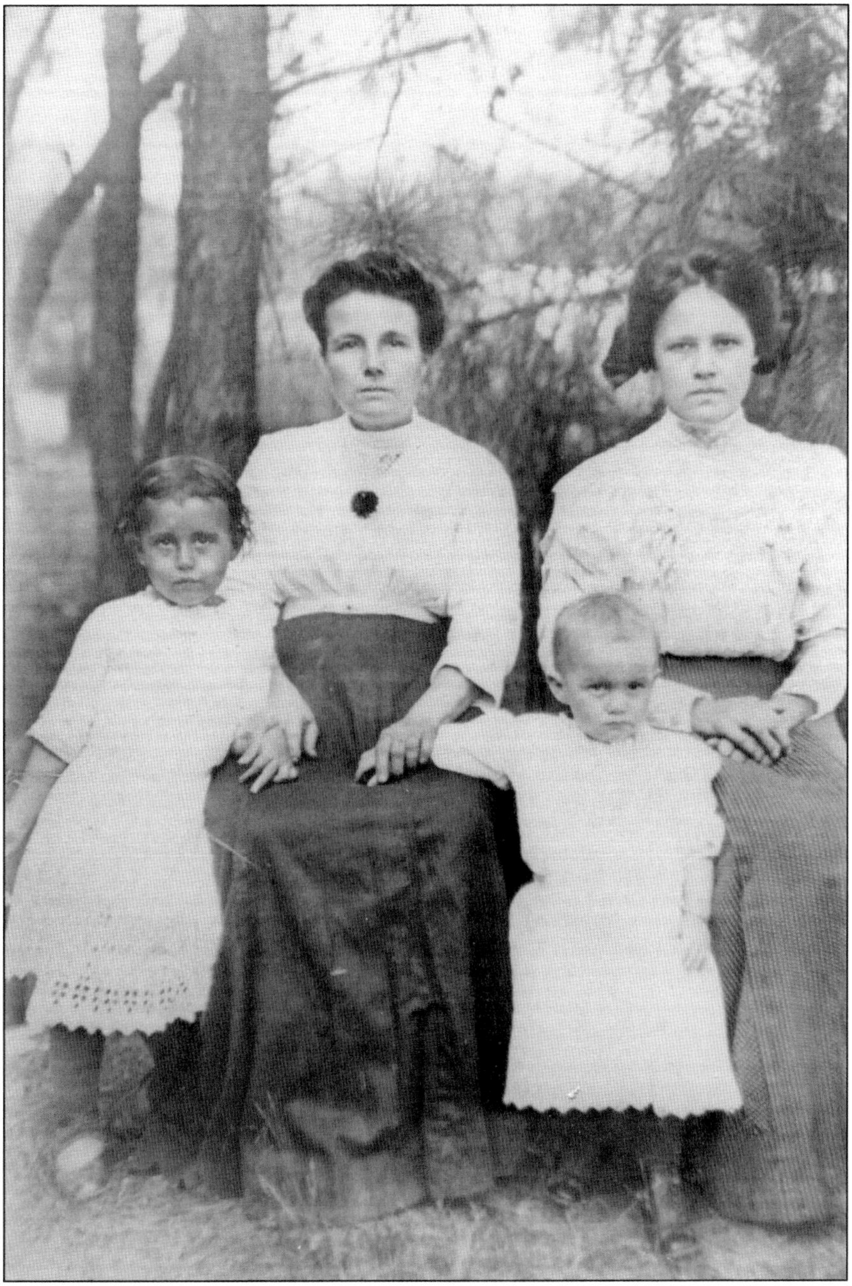

Rosanna Martin Bell is seated on the left and her daughter Carrie Bell Ward is seated next to her. Her youngest daughter, Bessie Bell, is leaning on her mother's leg, and her grandchild holds her hand. Rosanna Bell was the mother of five children. Her husband, John P. Bell, was 15 years older and died in 1923. Her eldest child, William Frank Bell, took care of "Miss Rosie" until his death in 1945, when her daughters took over her care until her death in 1956 at the age of 84. Rosanna was the daughter of Delianna Rollins and Moses Martin. Carrie Bell, Rosanna's oldest daughter, married Clinton Ward and had two children, Rose and Helen Ward. Bessie Bell was born in 1909. She would later marry Claddie Bunting and move away from Poquoson. She had two daughters, Nona and Nola Bunting. (Courtesy of the family of Rose Ward Huggett.)

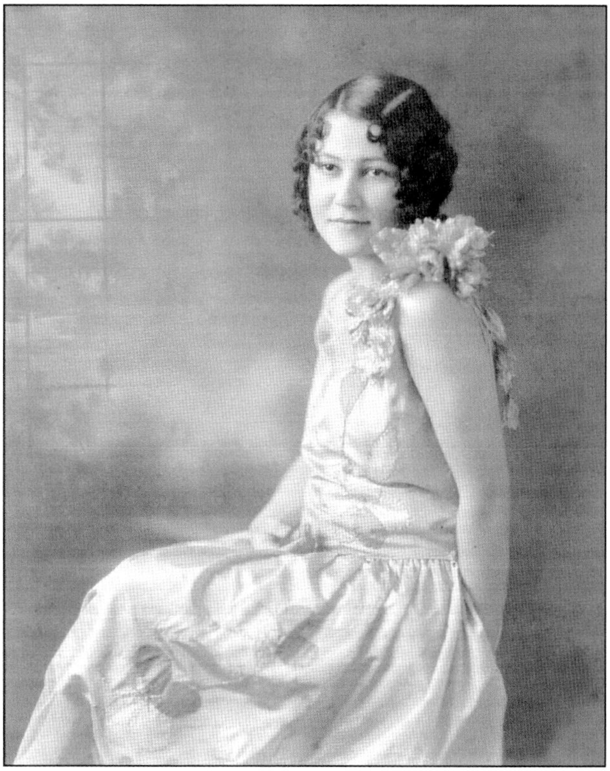

Louise Guy poses for her engagement photograph. Guy, who was from Hampton, married Marvin Forrest of Poquoson. Note the style of her hair and her dress. (Courtesy of Joyce Butler Holloway.)

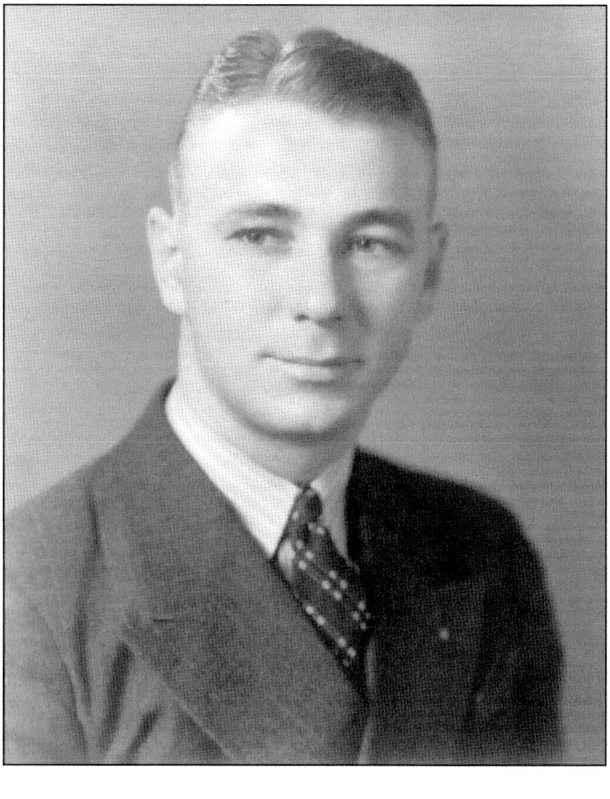

Marvin Forrest was the grandson of Lemuel Mansfield Duncan Forrest and Missouri "Lou" Hall Forrest. After graduating school, he went to business school and later married Louise Guy. (Courtesy of Joyce Butler Holloway.)

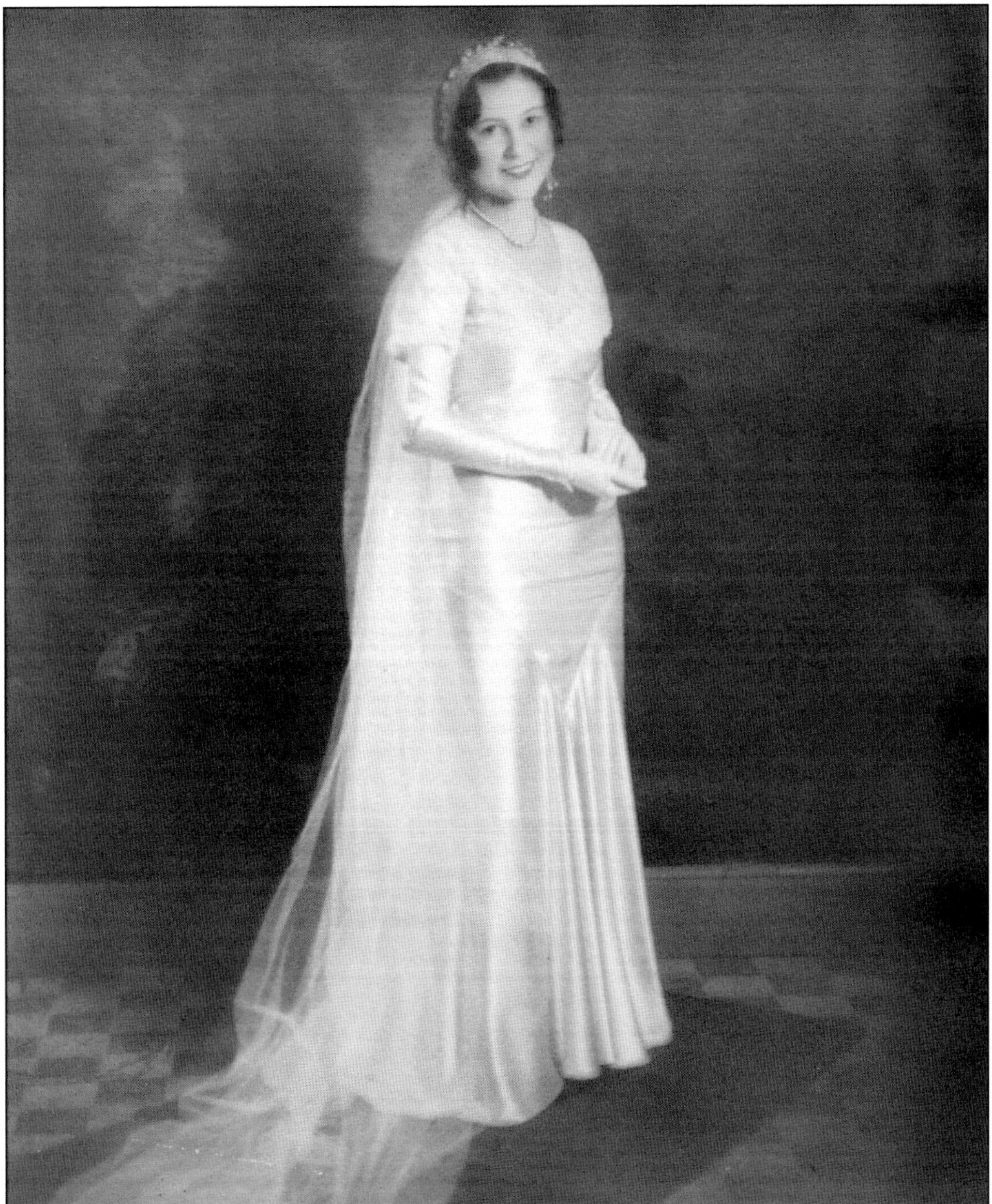

This wedding portrait shows Louise Guy Forrest posed in her long gown and veil. She was from a wealthy Hampton family and married Marvin Forrest on November 25, 1939, at Central Methodist Church in Hampton. Marvin Forrest was born in 1906 to Robert H. Forrest and Bernice L. Evans of Poquoson. (Courtesy of Joyce Butler Holloway.)

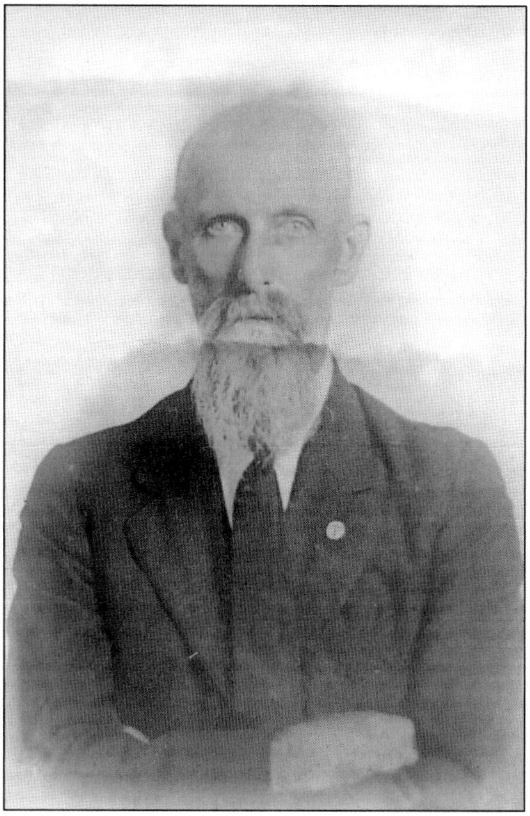

Lemuel Mansfield Duncan Forrest, seen here, preferred to be called "L.M.D." He was born on December 9, 1858, in Messick and married Missouri "Lou" Hall Watkins on January 22, 1880. She was the daughter of Henry Watkins and Sarah Anne Linton. They had nine children. (Courtesy of Joyce Butler Holloway.)

The Forrest family of Messick posed for the family portrait below. They included, from left to right, (first row) Melvin Forrest, unidentified, Marvin Forrest, and Osborne Forrest; (second row) Hatie Carmines (holding Florence), Fred Forrest, Bernie Evans Forrest, Ira Forrest, Edna Earl Forrest, Lem Forrest Jr., John "D" Forrest, Ola Forrest, Maggie Forrest, Inez Forrest, Bobby Forrest, Lilly Forrest, Missouri "Lou" Forrest, Lem Forrest Sr., and Elijah Forrest. (Courtesy of Joyce Butler Holloway.)

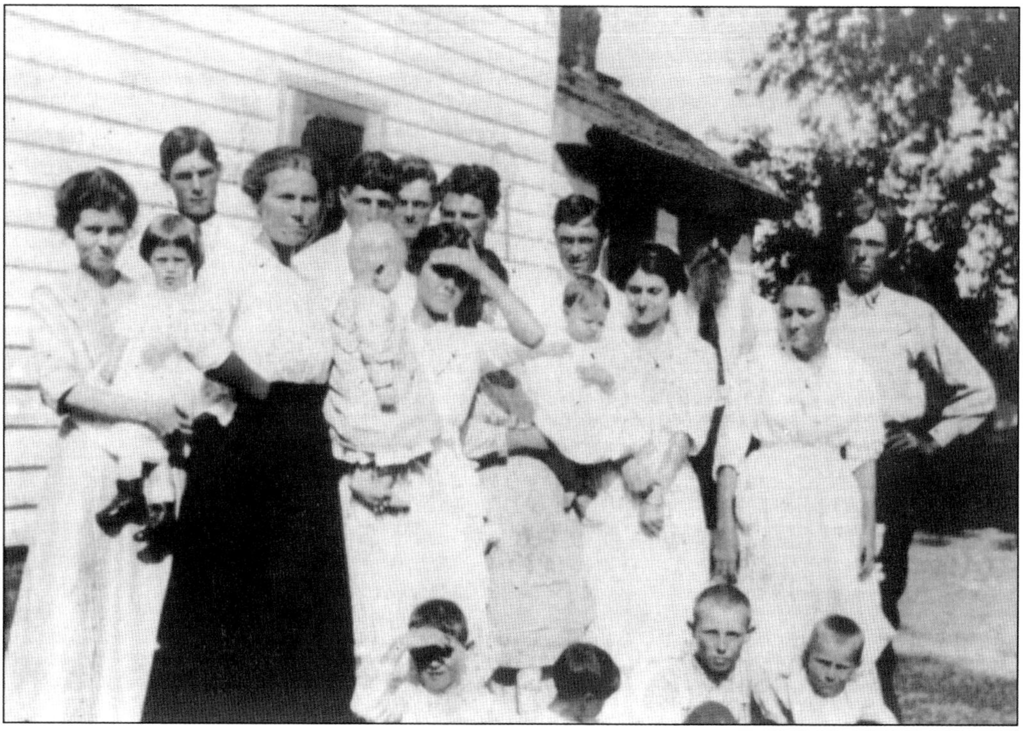

The *Kaynoo*, a five-log canoe built in Poquoson in 1879, is seen here being sailed down the river by its owners Milford Rollins, Jon B. Rollins II, and Garland Rollins. It was donated to the Poquoson Museum and is now housed at the museum property awaiting restoration. (Courtesy of Roman Rollins.)

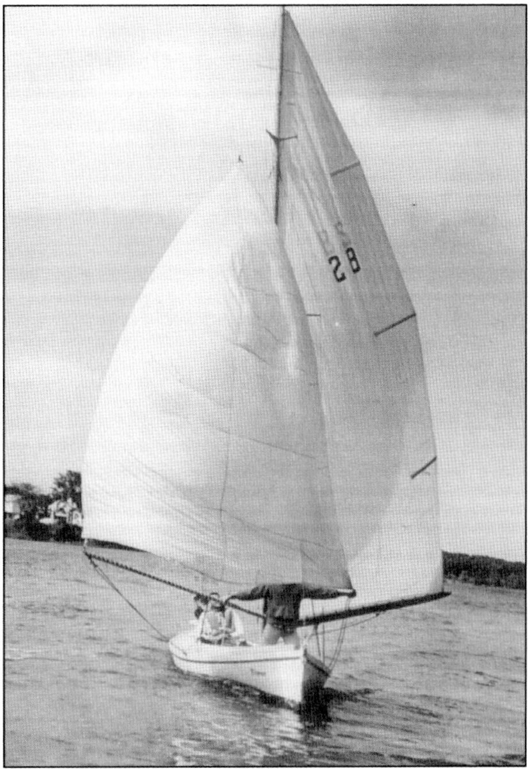

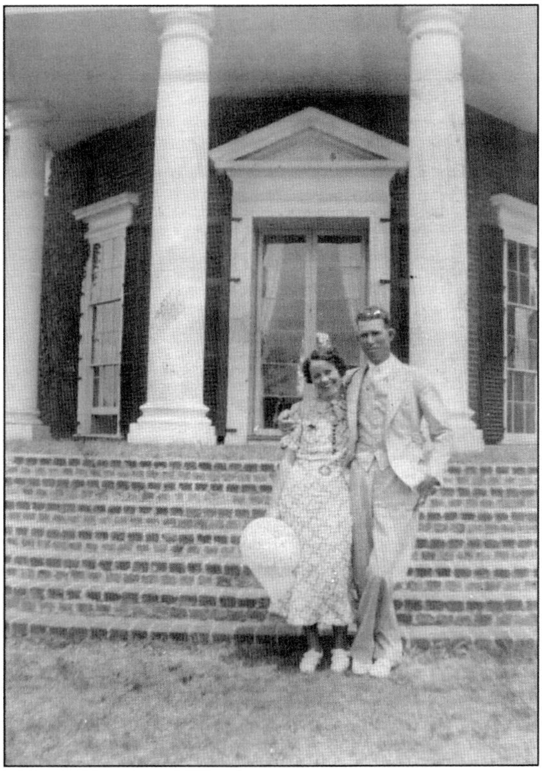

Sarah Newton Forrest and Maywood Forrest posed for this photograph on their honeymoon trip to Thomas Jefferson's Monticello in Charlottesville. Sarah Newton Forrest was born on January 13, 1909, to William B. Newton and Sarah E. Watkins. She died on January 3, 2001. Maywood Forrest was born on October 12, 1905, to Henry Stephen Forrest and Martha Jane Evans. He died at the age of 83 on May 15, 1989. They did not have any children. (Courtesy of Joyce Butler Holloway.)

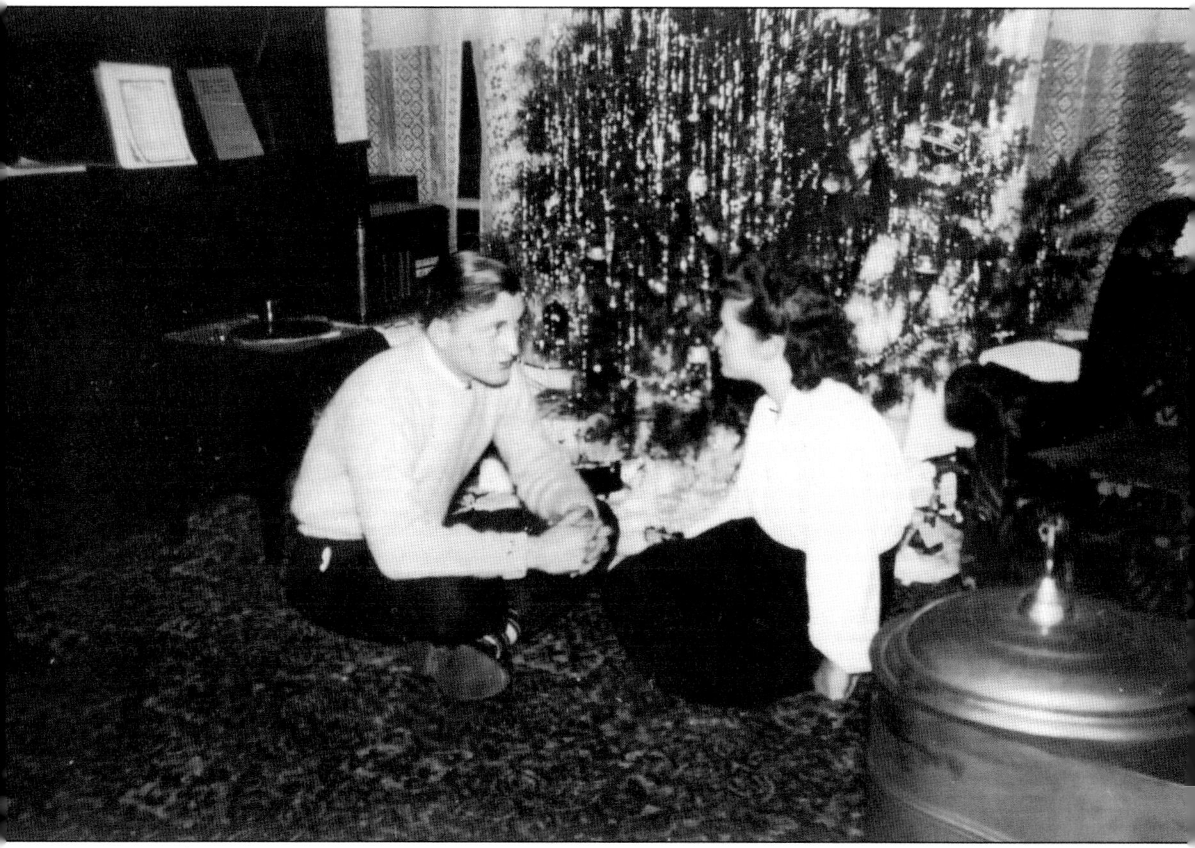

Sitting beneath the Christmas tree in 1946 are Mary Louise "Peachie" Hopkins and her husband, Wiley Downs. The couple married in 1942. This photograph was taken at their house on Lodge Road after he was discharged from the Army after World War II. Note that the tinsel on the Christmas tree was meticulously hung to give the illusion of icicles. Everything about the Christmas celebration, down to the dishes used, reflected Peachie's love for the holiday. She was born to Ira Edward Hopkins and Rebecca Rollins on September 13, 1920. Her daughter Susan Gail Downs Herring now operates Claytor Rollins Funeral Home, which has been in the family for generations. (Courtesy of Susan Downs Herring.)

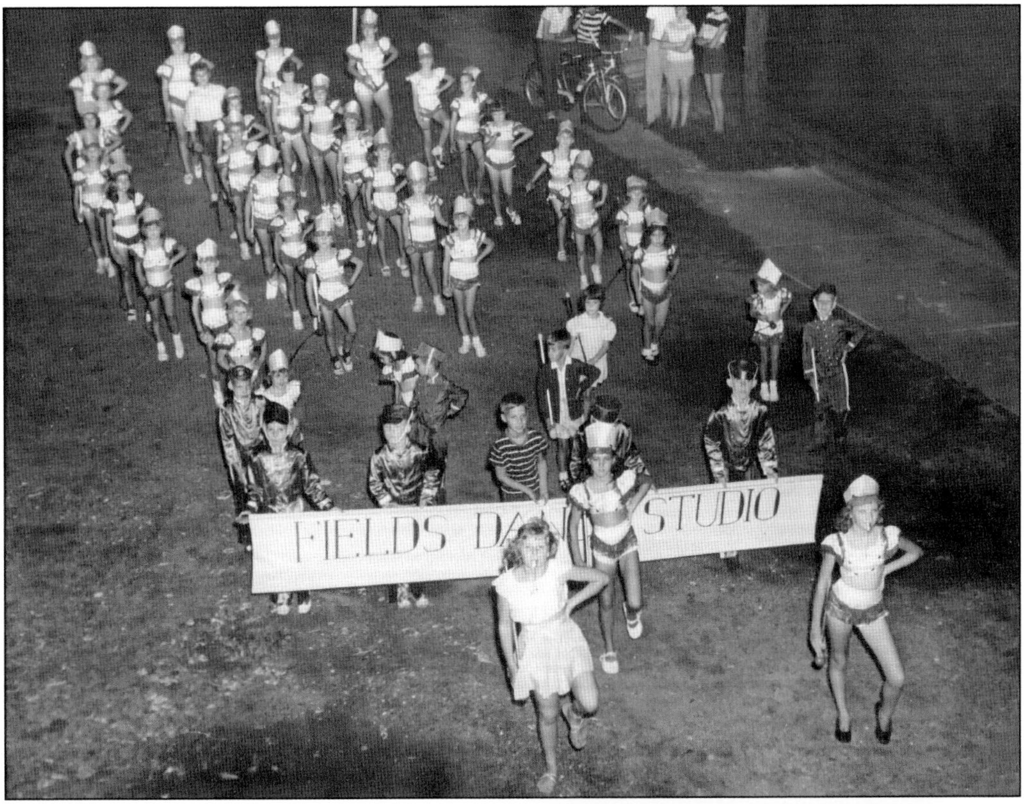


Fields Dance Studio came to Poquoson in the late 1940s. It was on the second floor of the Juniors' Lodge on Lodge Road. The studio offered dance lessons to local residents through the 1950s. Many local children were trained in dance and marching at this facility. These students are lined up for a parade. (Courtesy of Barbara Hudgins Whitlow.)

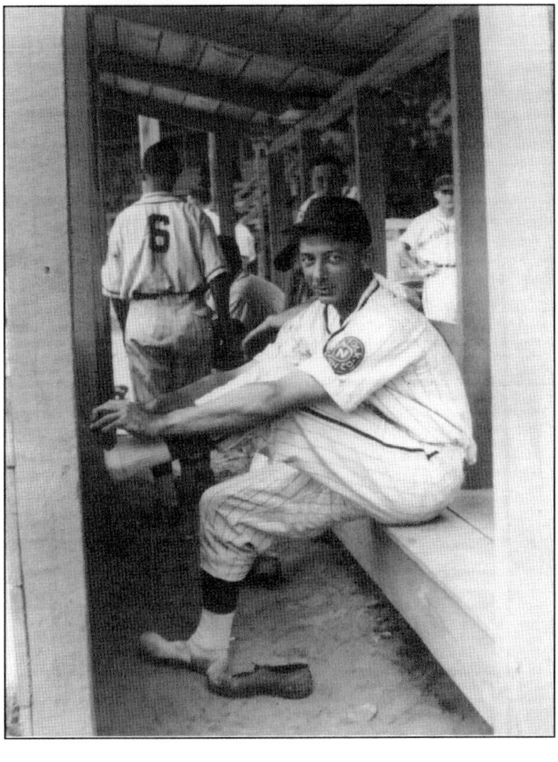

Nelson Cornell Watkins Sr. shoes up for a game at Chigger Park in Messick. Baseball was the most popular sport in the first half of the 1900s. There were two well-marked fields in Messick, Chigger Park and Messick Park, but there were also good areas for pickup games, such as Tom Epps Field. (Courtesy of the family of Nelson C. Watkins Jr.)

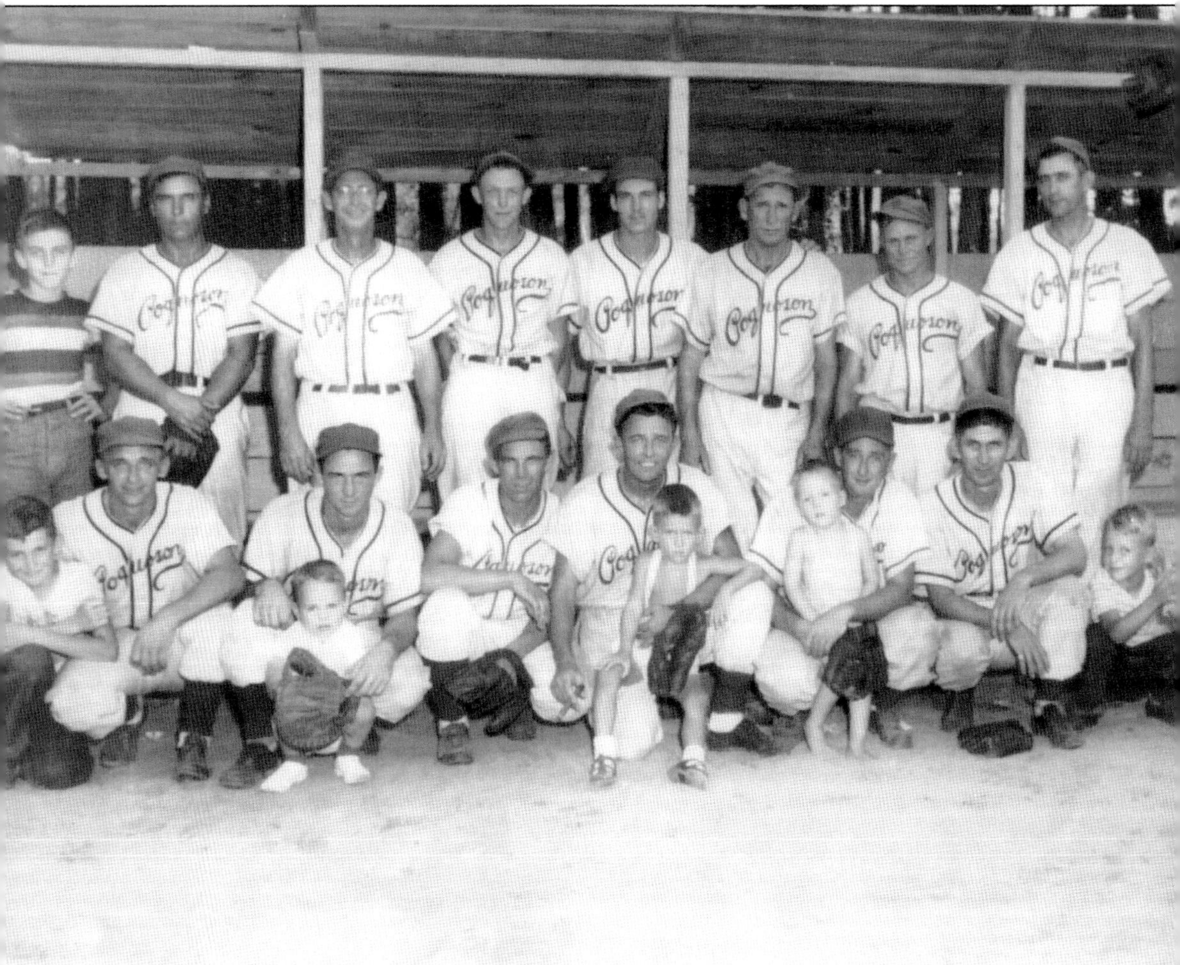

The Poquoson baseball team is seen here posing for a photograph in front of the dugout at Chigger Park, which was down a dirt lane off Poquoson Avenue between Messick Road and Amory's wharf. The seating consisted of two facing bleachers for the opposing teams. Many of the players from the team that had played at White's Field became part of the Poquoson team at Chigger Park. As the men grew older, they became managers so that they could continue their affiliation with the team. Seen here are, from left to right, (first row) an unidentified child, Henry Pancoke, Durwood Watkins (with his son Bobby), Arthur "Jitterbug" Carmony, Bill Watkins (with Benny Griebel), Preston Watkins (with his son Terry), Henry Griebel, and Sidney Patrick; (second row) Tommy Hudgins, Alvoid Shackleford, Duke Forrest, two unidentified players, Johnny Crow Bradshaw, Nelson Firth, and manager Herman Forrest. (Courtesy of Durwood Watkins.)

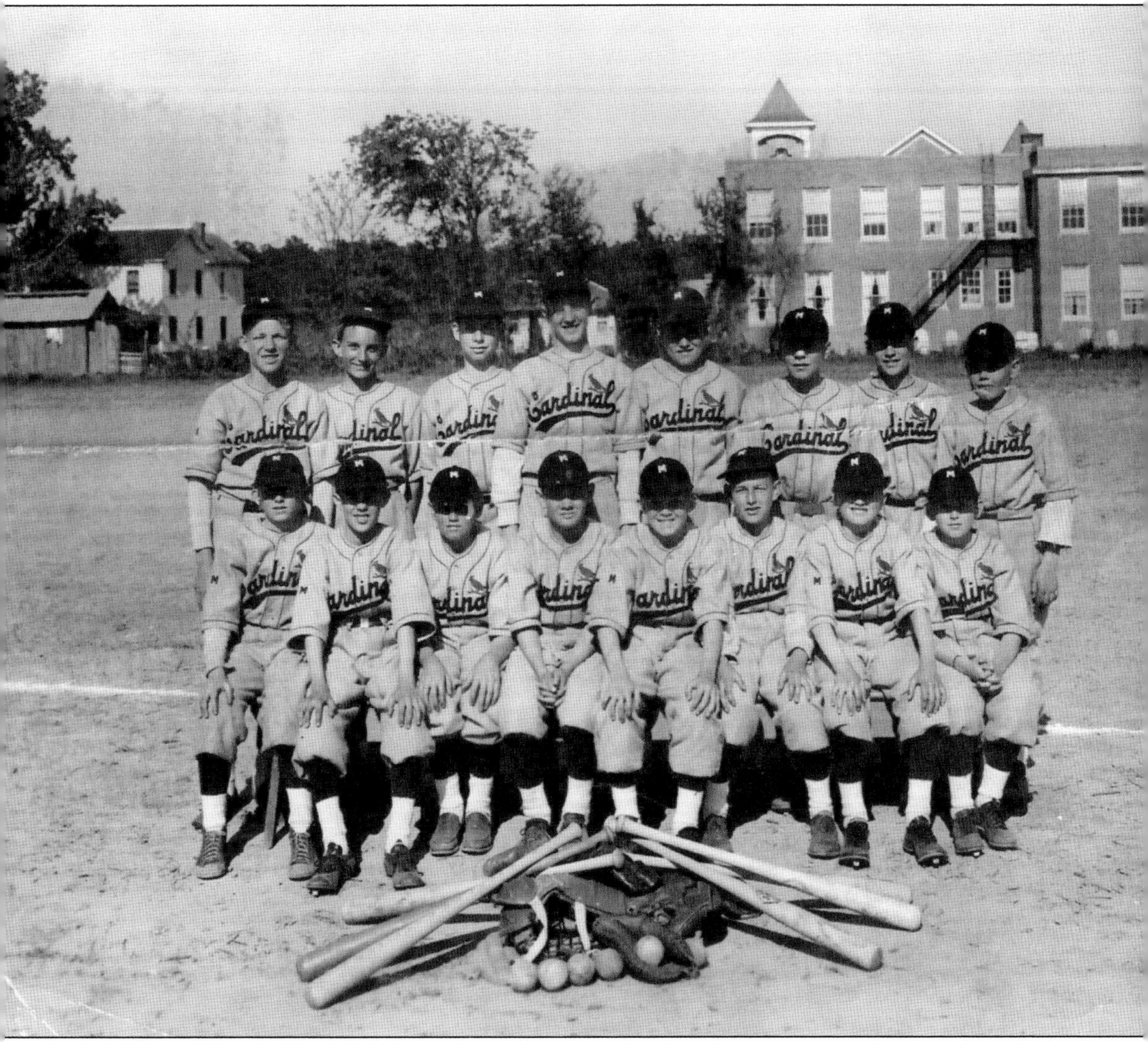

The 1944 Messick Cardinals strike a team pose on a lot behind Trinity Church with the church's bell tower in the background. The team included, from left to right, (first row) James "Cut" Firth, Martin Graham, Ernest F. Pauls, John Graham, Warren Holloway, Kenneth Forrest, Bobby Abdell, and Nelson Watkins Jr.; (second row) Marshell Topping, Percy Ward, B.T. Forrest, Randy Rollins, Buster Martin, John L. Firth, Olen Evans, and Norris Hogge. This team's coaches were Lem Firth, Nelson Watkins, and Randolph Rollins, and the bat boy was Addie Hope Firth. Many of these young men went on to play for Poquoson High School's winning baseball teams. Olen Evans eventually became the high school's baseball coach. Many of these boys continued to play baseball as grown men at Chigger Park. (Courtesy of the family of Nelson Watkins Jr.)

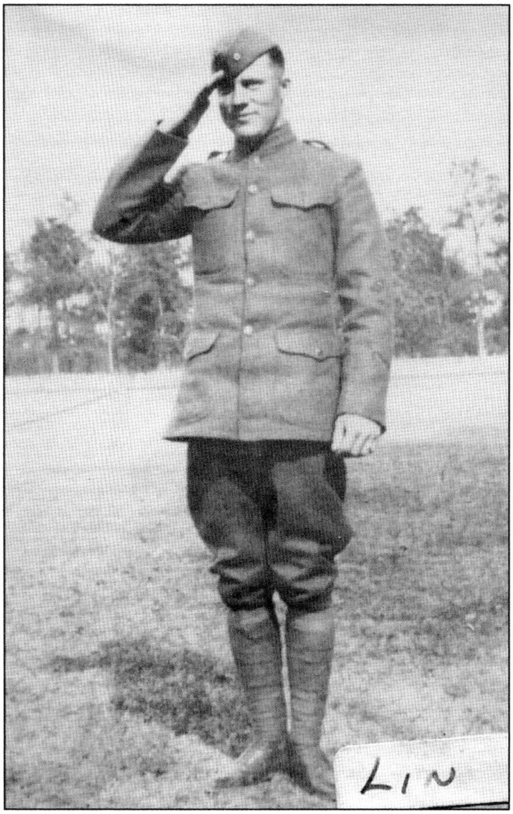


In 1917, the United States entered World War I, and many local residents went to war. Linwood Bradshaw, seen here saluting the camera, was one of them. (Courtesy of the Poquoson Historical Society.)

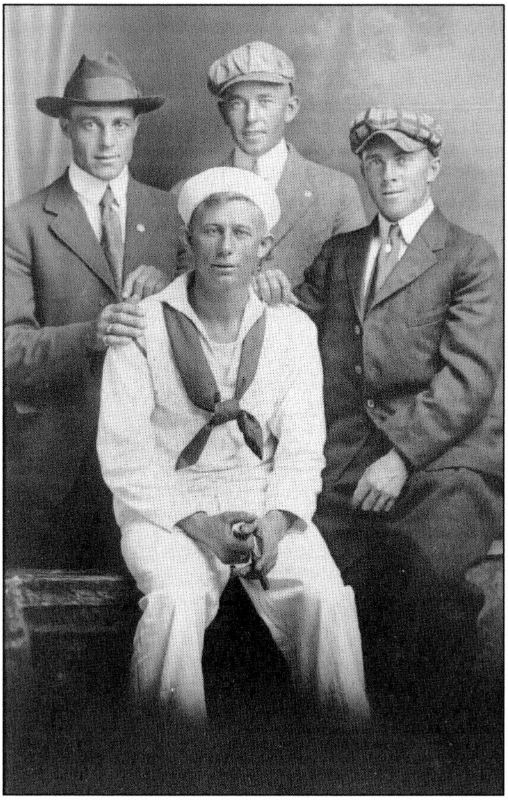

Other men from the Messick community signed up for World War I, including Charles Chesser, who joined the Navy and is seen here in the front along with other local servicemen, from left to right, Frank Bell, who was stationed in Europe; George Bradshaw; and Stanley Holloway. (Courtesy of the Poquoson Historical Society.)

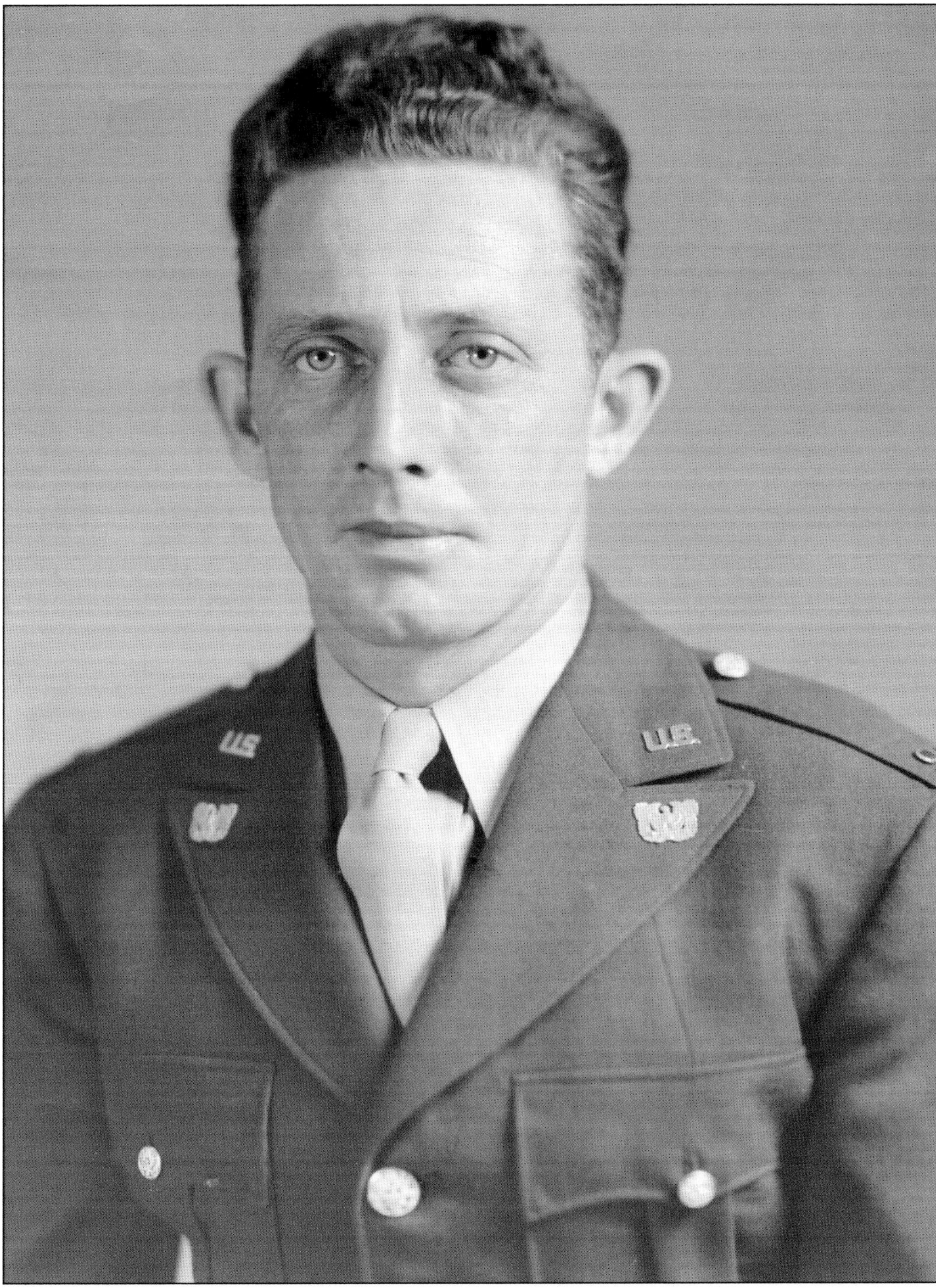

John William Paul was in the Army Air Force during World War II. He changed his last name from Pauls to Paul after he was mistaken for another John Pauls. The Army Air Force remained a branch of the Army until 1947, when the United States Air Force was founded. The Air Force became a strong organized force during the war, making strides in tactical bombing strategies and air combat tactics. (Courtesy of Sid Pauls Jr.)

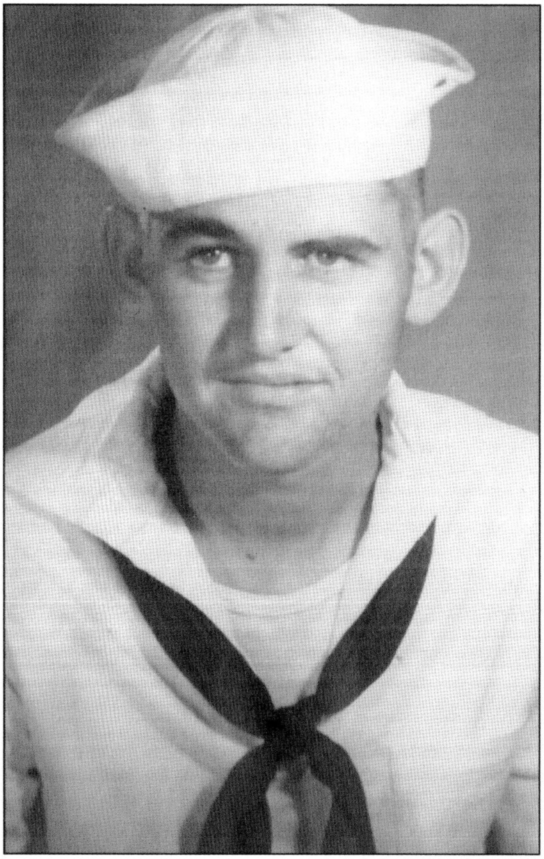

Another Messick resident to enlist was M.J. "Moody" Firman, who served in the Navy during World War II. He is a member of Trinity United Methodist Church and is known for his baked goods, which he contributes to many organizations in Poquoson. (Courtesy of the family of Rose Ward Huggett.)

Below, Clyde Russell Smith stands in the middle of Poquoson Avenue during World War II. He was stationed in Washington, DC, during the war, as a Navy clerk at the Pentagon. (Courtesy of Jane Smith White.)

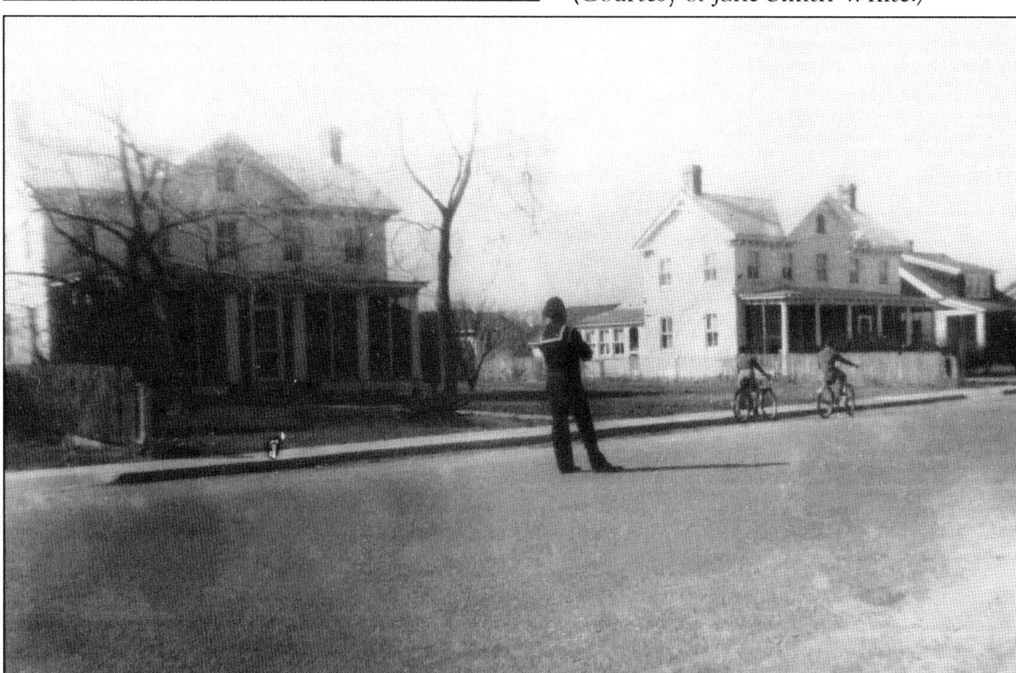

This trio of young Forrest cousins from Messick shows off their Christmas guns in the yard of their grandmother Martha Chesser Forrest. They are, from left to right, Henry Gordon Page, William Warren Forrest, and Robert Samuel Forrest. (Courtesy of the family of Robert Samuel Forrest.)

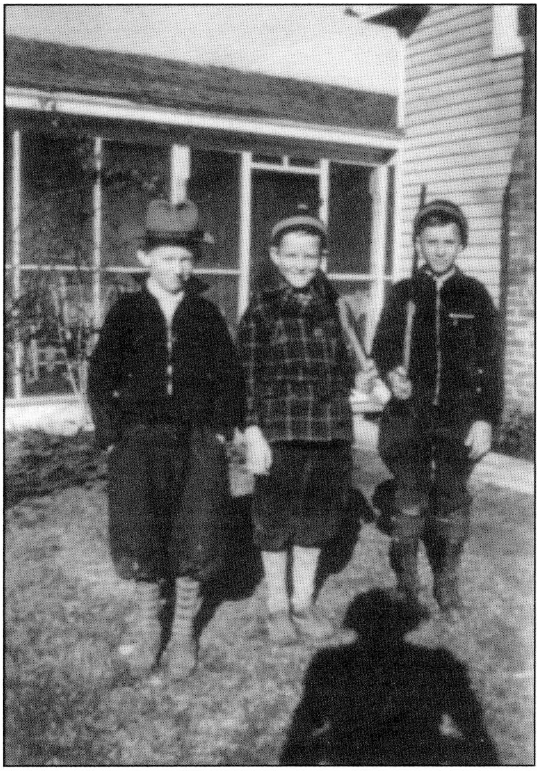

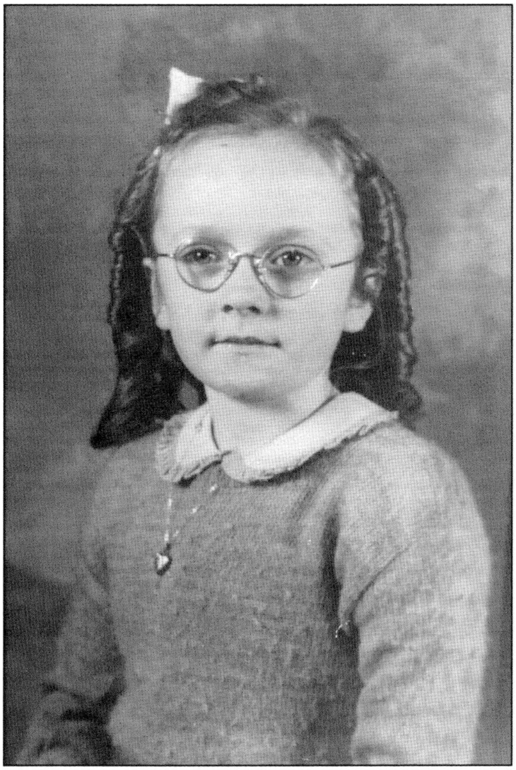

A young Frances Powell Evans Potts poses for her portrait. Potts was a longtime physical education teacher at Poquoson High School and the coach of both girls' basketball and cheerleading. The daughter of Joseph Allen Evans, she married William Potts, with whom she has three children. (Courtesy of Frances Evans Potts.)

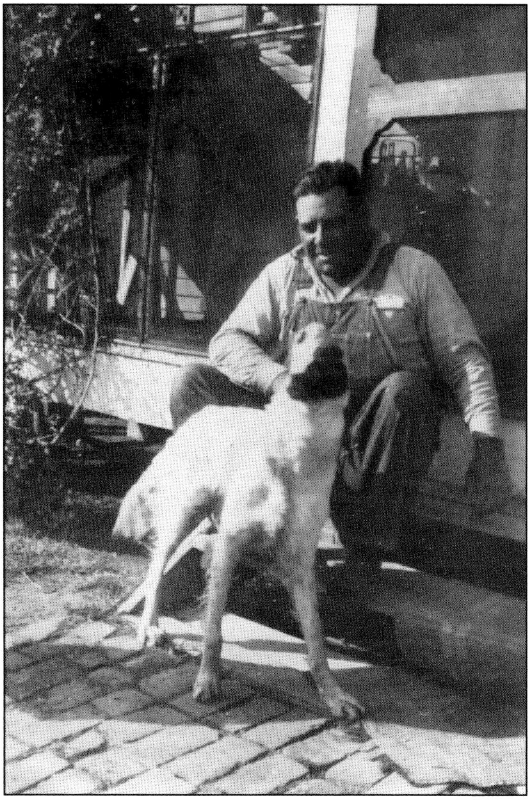

Joseph Allen Evans pets his dog on the steps to his front porch. The porch is screened in, like many porches in the area, due to the large number of mosquitoes near the coastal marshes. (Courtesy of Frances Evans Potts.)

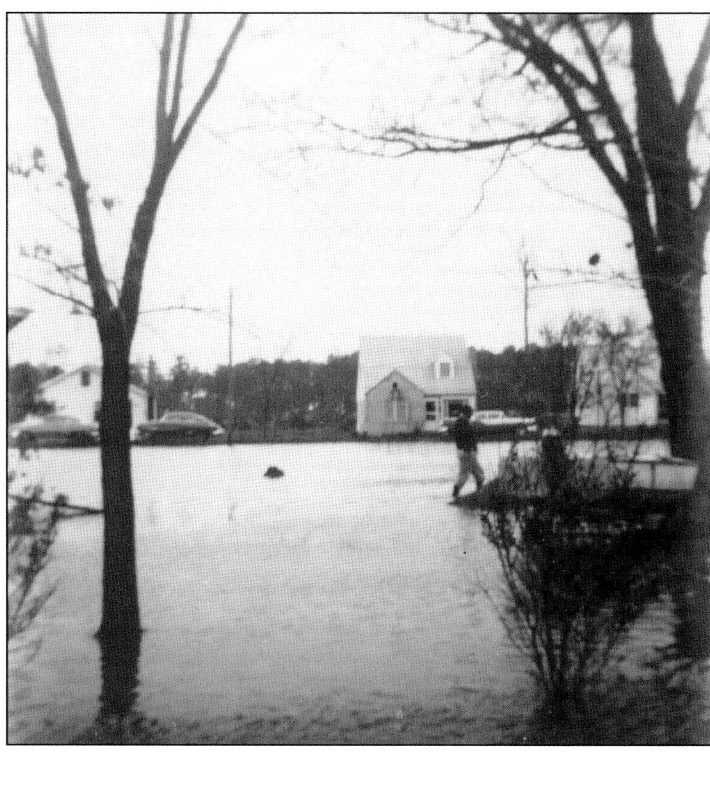

Tidal flooding caused by storms in the 1950s flooded the corner of Bay Street and Ridge Road. Note that the cars have been moved to the higher part of the roadway. (Courtesy of Sonny Insley.)

Selena Jane Rollins stands in the flooded yard of Claytor and Winnie Rollins after the Ash Wednesday storm in 1962. She was the daughter of Selena Jane Watkins Rollins and Wesley Thomas "Bink" Rollins. The house was next to the former location of Claytor Rollins Funeral Home on Poquoson Avenue. Claytor and Winnie Rollins raised Selena after her mother's death in childbirth. Selena worked at the funeral home as a bookkeeper until her death. (Courtesy of Susan Downs Herring.)

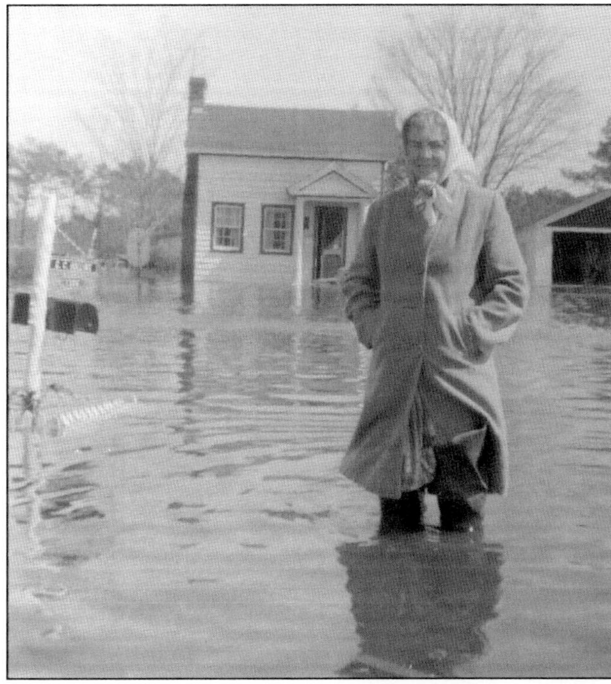

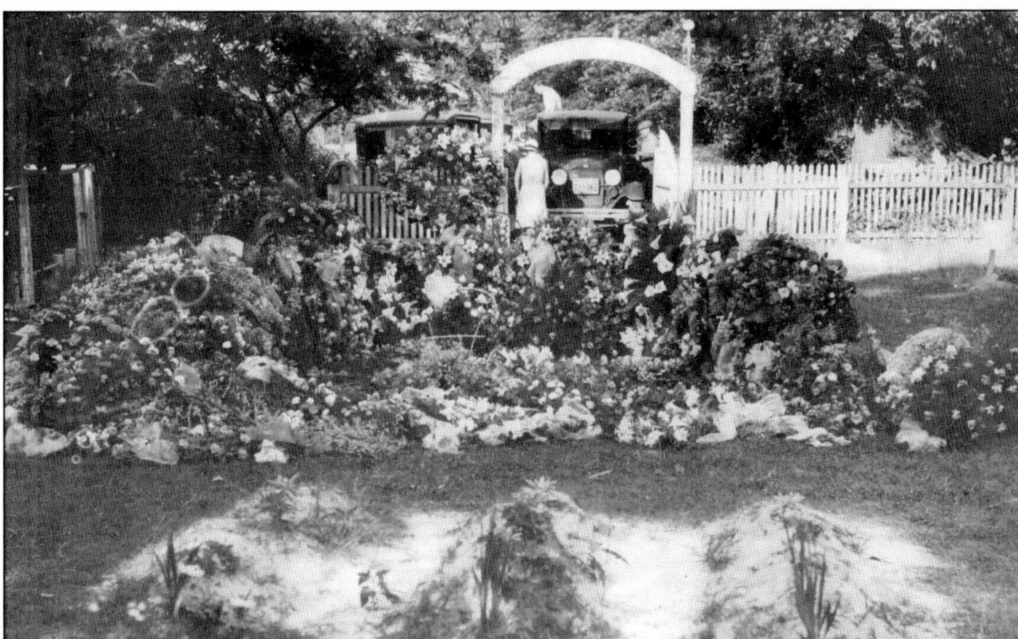

Weston Cemetery, on Poquoson Avenue, is one of the two major cemeteries in Messick. On November 3, 1924, there was an accident involving a passenger bus and a train at Lee's Crossing in Elizabeth City County, near Hampton. A total of 12 people onboard the bus were killed, including one who died a week later from his injuries. Three additional people were injured in the crash. All of the victims, with the exception of one, were residents of York County. Funerals were held in Messick for some of the victims, and their graves at Weston Cemetery are seen here. (Courtesy of Jane Smith White.)

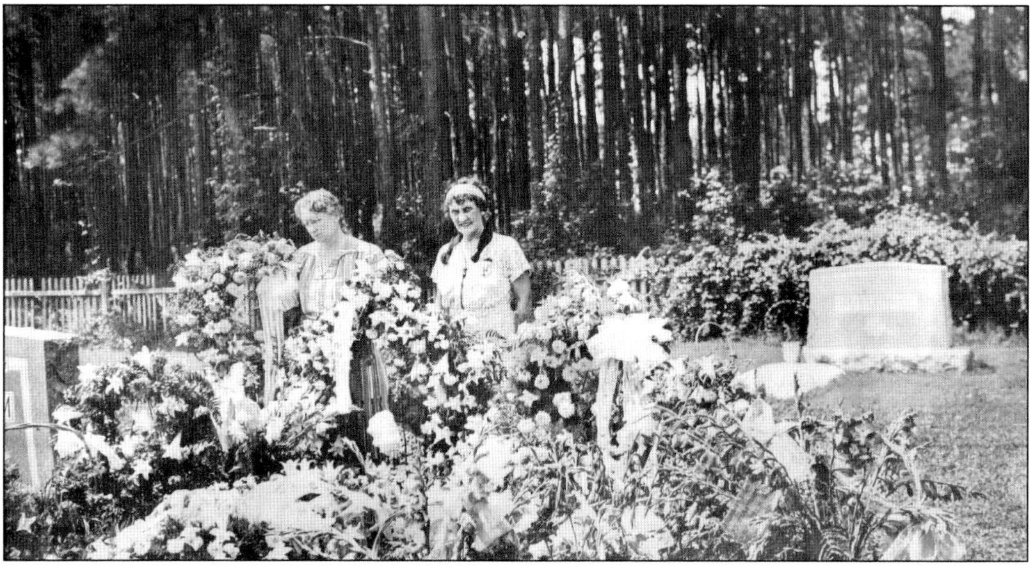

Lola Bradshaw and Anne Bounds look at the flowers on Lemuel Bradshaw's grave in Weston Cemetery. He was born in 1870 and died in Messick in 1939. He was known as Lem by the local residents. It is likely that Bradshaw was a descendent of Richard Bradshaw, who served in the Maryland Militia during the American Revolution. Note the large number of flowers around his grave. (Courtesy of Melissa Forrest Gardy.)

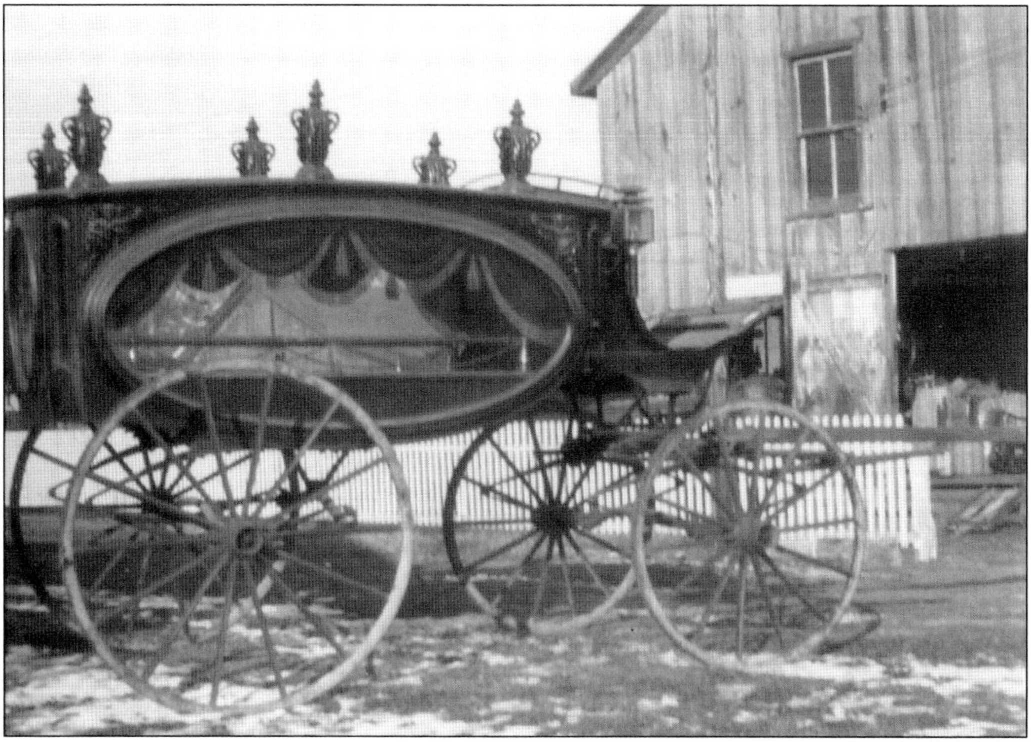

This horse-drawn black hearse was purchased by James Taylor Rollins for his funeral home. It is still well maintained, and it is used as a display at the Poquoson Seafood Festival and during funerals of important residents. (Courtesy of Claytor Rollins Funeral Home.)

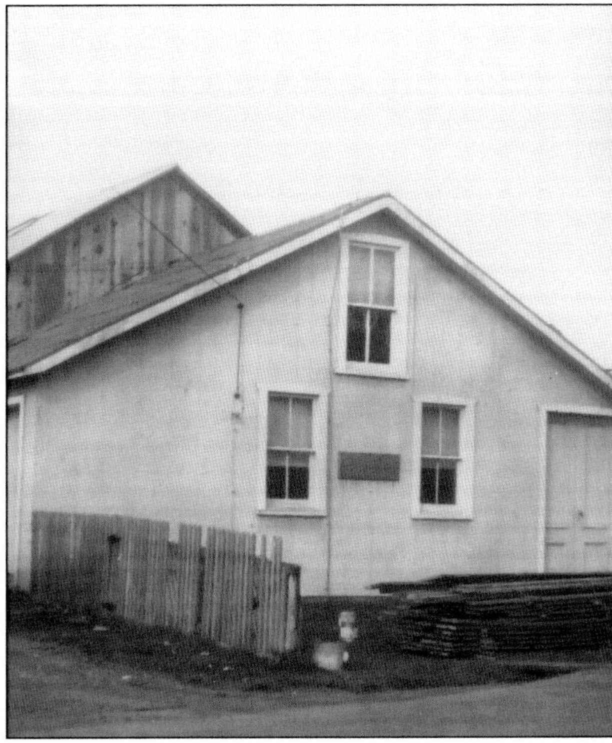

James Taylor Rollins's first funeral home was approximately one block from Trinity United Methodist Church on Poquoson Avenue in Messick. It was a small gray structure with a two-story carpenter shop immediately behind it. It was later replaced by a small brick building, which is still standing. The carpenter shop still stands behind the brick structure. (Courtesy of Claytor Rollins Funeral Home.)

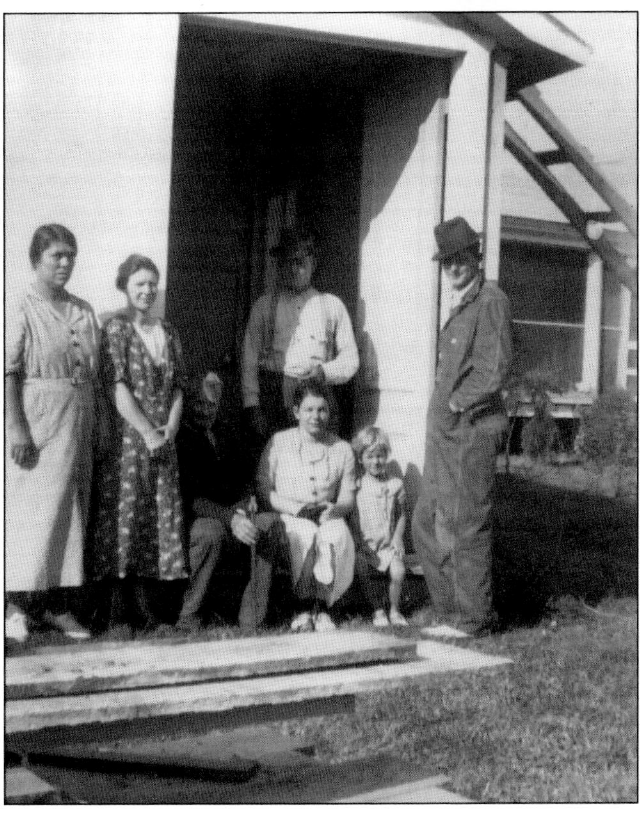

Winnie Eva Evans Rollins, Rebecca Susan Rollins Hopkins, John Franklin Hopkins, Missouri Kathryn Hopkins Krueger, Betty Anne Watkins Forrest, and George Claytor Rollins (standing in the doorway) posed at the door of James Taylor Rollins first funeral home on Poquoson Avenue for a last picture before it was replaced by a new brick structure. (Courtesy of Claytor Rollins Funeral Home.)

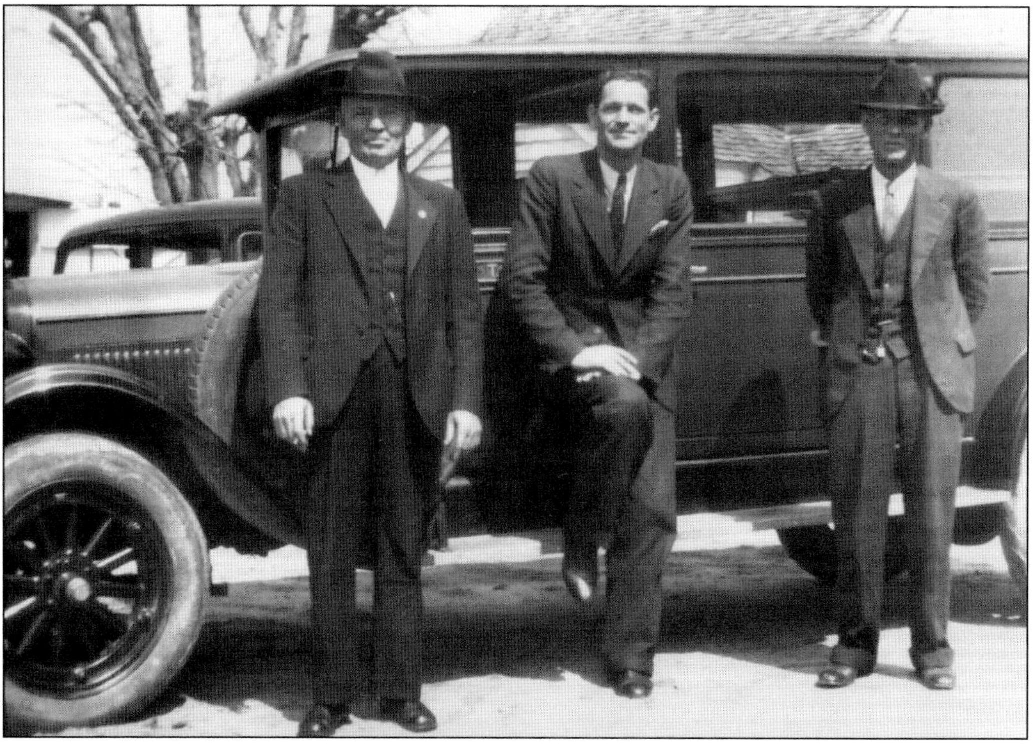

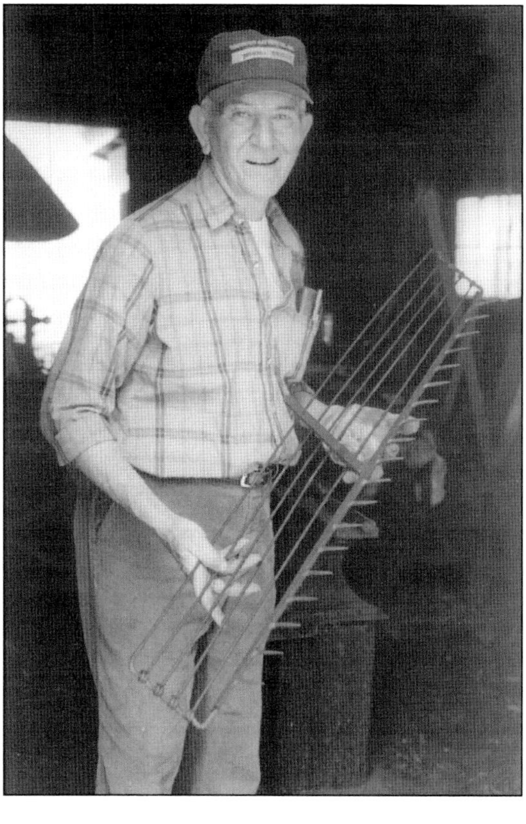

Above, from left to right, George Claytor Rollins, Gladwin Hartley Forrest, and Leroy Franklin Carmines stand in front of Claytor Rollins's first motorized hearse. George Claytor Rollins's father, James Taylor Rollins, established the J.T. Rollins Funeral Home in 1895, which would later become the Claytor Rollins Funeral Home. (Courtesy of Claytor Rollins Funeral Home.)

Bobby Rollins is a blacksmith who took over the old carpenter shop behind the former Claytor Rollins building on Poquoson Avenue in Messick. He is seen here holding a clam rake that he made. He is the son of John King Rollins and Ada Bell Bunting. (Courtesy of Bonnie Karwac.)

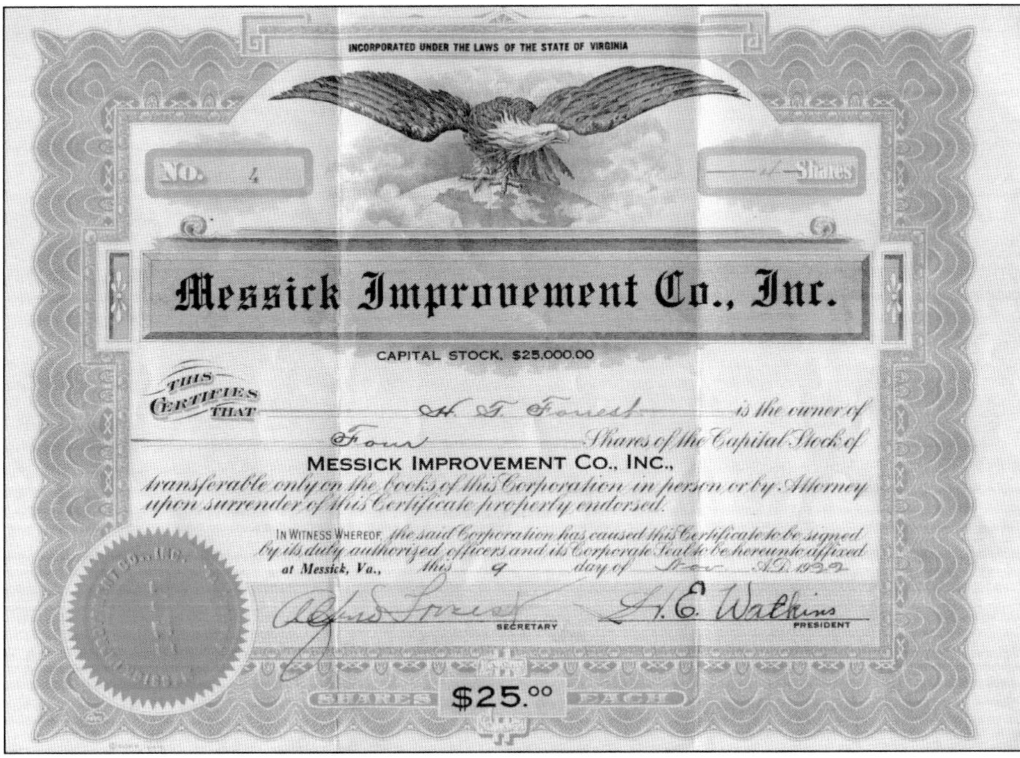

INCORPORATED UNDER THE LAWS OF THE STATE OF VIRGINIA

No. 4 — 4 — Shares

**Messick Improvement Co., Inc.**

CAPITAL STOCK, $25,000.00

This Certifies that H. T. Forest is the owner of Four Shares of the Capital Stock of MESSICK IMPROVEMENT CO., INC., transferable only on the books of this Corporation in person or by Attorney upon surrender of this Certificate properly endorsed.

In Witness Whereof, the said Corporation has caused this Certificate to be signed by its duly authorized officers and its Corporate Seal to be hereunto affixed at Messick, Va., this 9 day of Nov A.D.

Alfred Forest, SECRETARY — H. E. Watkins, PRESIDENT

SHARES $25.00 EACH

The Messick Improvement Co., Inc., was a somewhat mysterious business in the early 1920s. The certificate above is for four shares of stock in the company. While a few residents did purchase stock in the company, it folded and did not leave many clues about its business. (Courtesy of Charles McDaniel.)

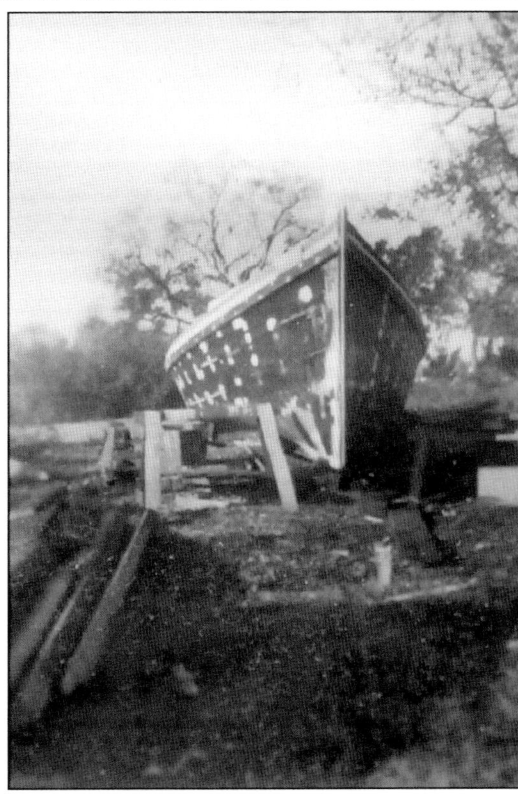

Boatbuilding was both a business and a craft in the area. This boat was in the process of being built at Messick Point by Earnest "Ernie" Franklin Pauls. He was the son of William and Josephine Pauls, and he married Addie Insley on July 21, 1917. She was the daughter of Peter James Insley. (Courtesy of Leroy Wade.)

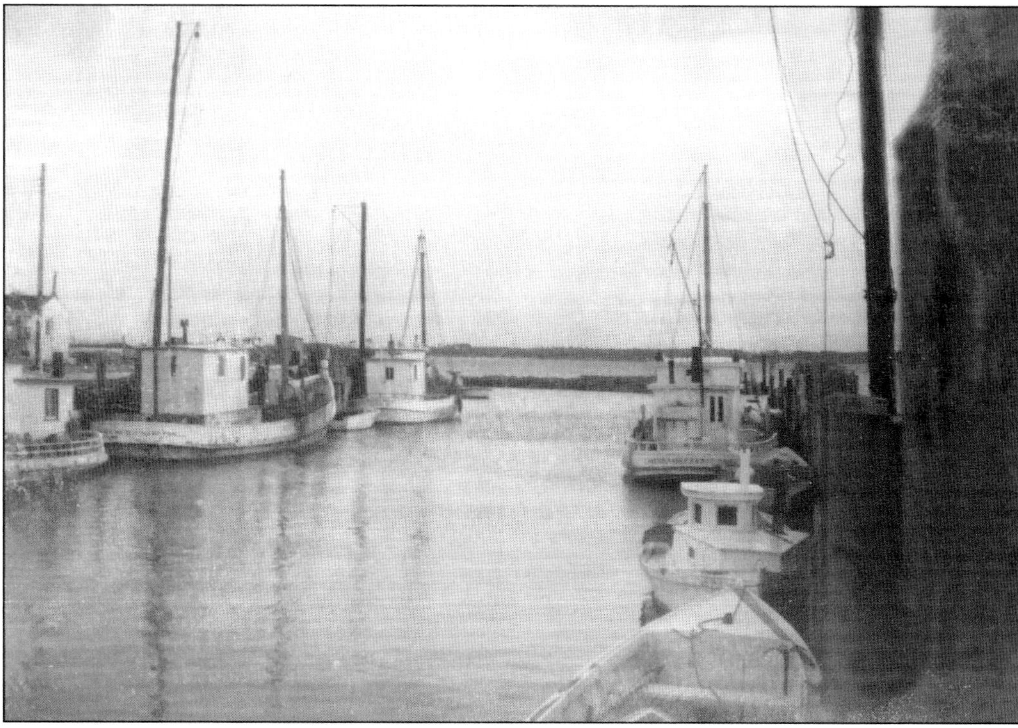

Fishing was one of the primary industries in Poquoson. This early-1950s photograph shows some of the fishing boats tied up at the end of Messick Road at William Garland "Porgie" Evans's dock. "Porgie's Dock" was well known to everyone in Poquoson. Evans was born on April 13, 1908, to Joseph David Evans and Charlotte Belle Firth, and he married Iva Mildred Weston. He died on April 14, 1968. In the 1940s and 1950s, bombers practiced their bombing runs at Plum Tree Island, and one of the B-26 bombers crashed at Messick Point on March 12, 1953, killing the three airmen aboard. The plane crashed on takeoff, sending wreckage through William Garland Evans's car windshield. It also damaged the crab packing plant and the pier that he owned and sunk an oyster boat. (Courtesy of Jane Smith White.)

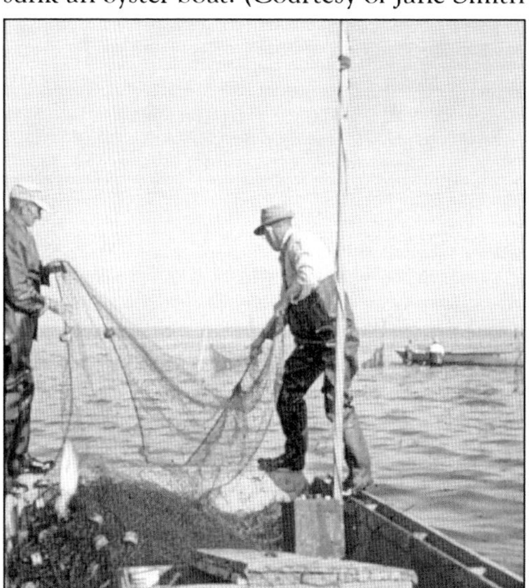

Poquoson fishermen are seen hauling seining, which is the traditional method of net fishing. Alf Huggett (left) and Bill Freeman (right) are taking up the net in this 1956 photograph. (Courtesy of Sonny Isley.)

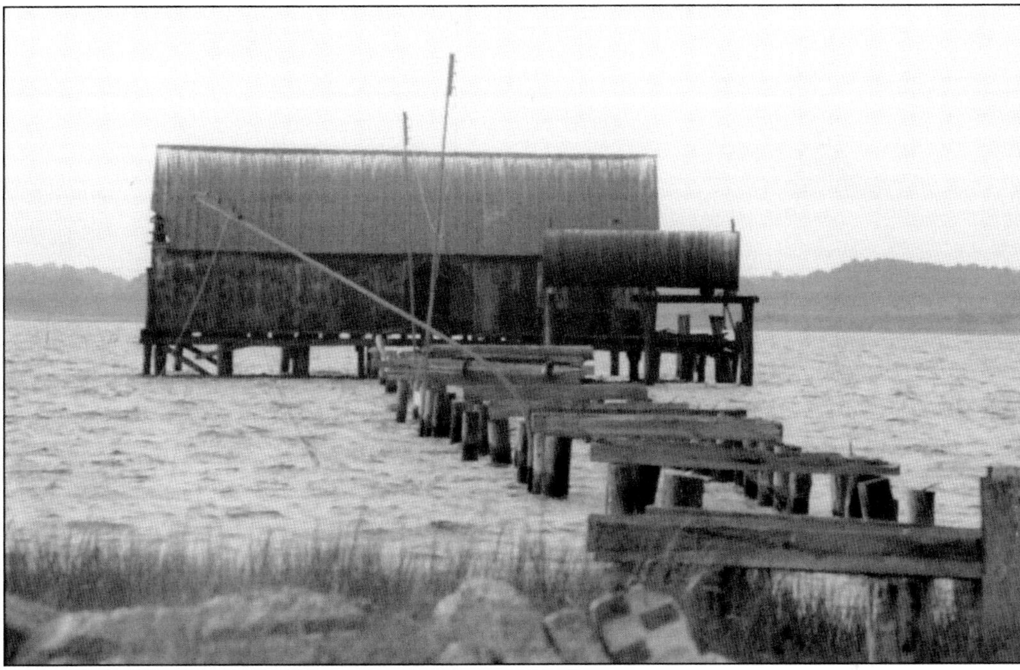

Amory's Wharf was at the southern end of Poquoson Avenue. The Earnest Post Office was in an office at the end of the wharf, in a building on pilings in the Back River. The wharf owners were also the postmasters, George W. Amory and his son-in-law Howard Garland Forrest. (Courtesy of the family of Thomas Clifton Hudgins Jr.)

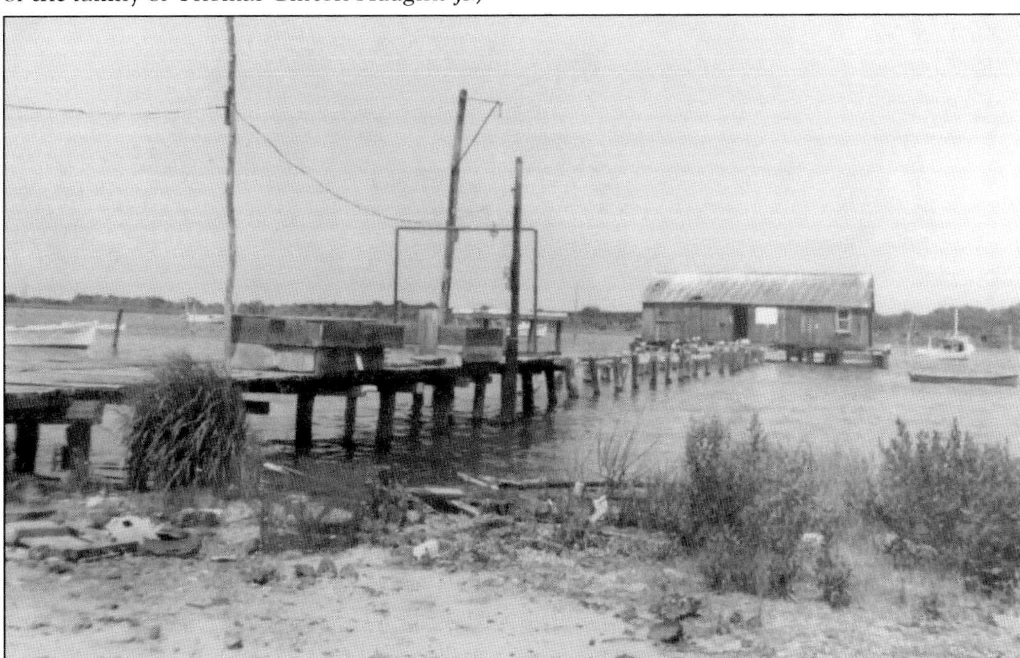

The Forrest family are well-known local watermen and merchants. They are also known for their fresh seafood market. The Forrest Dock was at Messick Point. (Courtesy of the Poquoson Historical Society.)

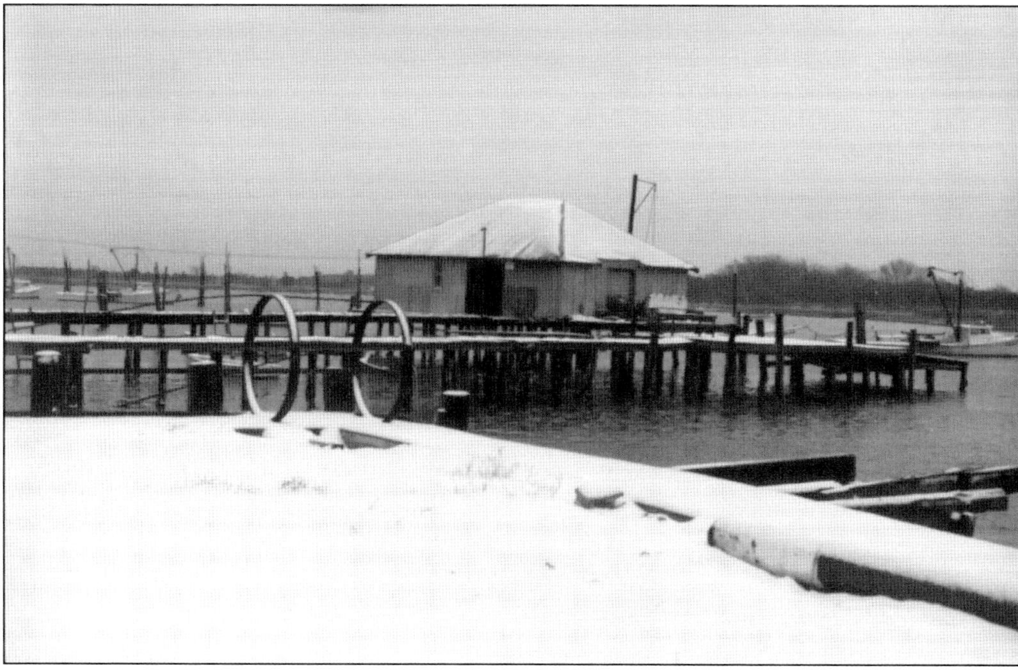

The Diggs Brothers Dock is seen here covered in snow. Seeing a dock covered in snow is very rare in southeastern Virginia, as heavy snowfall does not usually occur in this area. (Courtesy of the family of Thomas C. Hudgins Jr.)

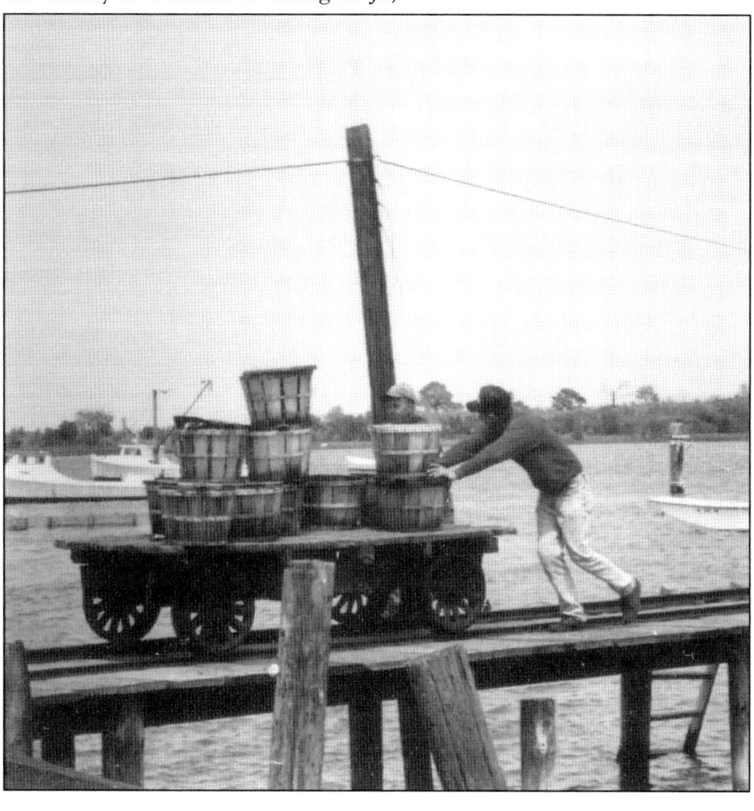

A workman pushes bushel baskets on a dolly down the dock at the Diggs Brothers Dock. After boats were unloaded at the end of the dock, the seafood was iced and loaded into bushel baskets on a dolly to be loaded into trucks. The trucks then distributed the seafood throughout the United States. (Courtesy of Charles McDaniel.)

Capt. George Bradshaw Sr. was a fisherman in Messick for many years. He is seen here working his patent tong rig on the river in the 1970s. The Smith Marine Railway hauled the Bradshaw family boats for many years. Bradshaw worked well into his late 70s or early 80s. (Courtesy of the family of William Bradshaw and Tim Smith.)

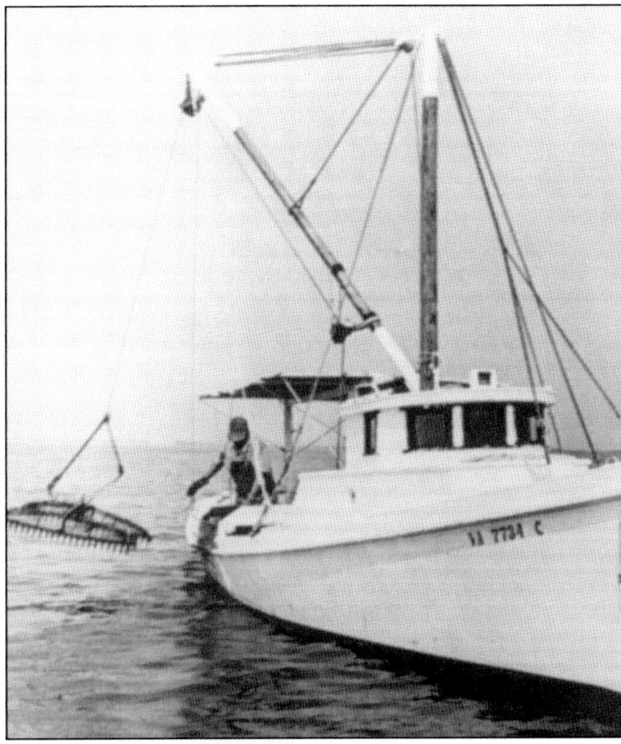

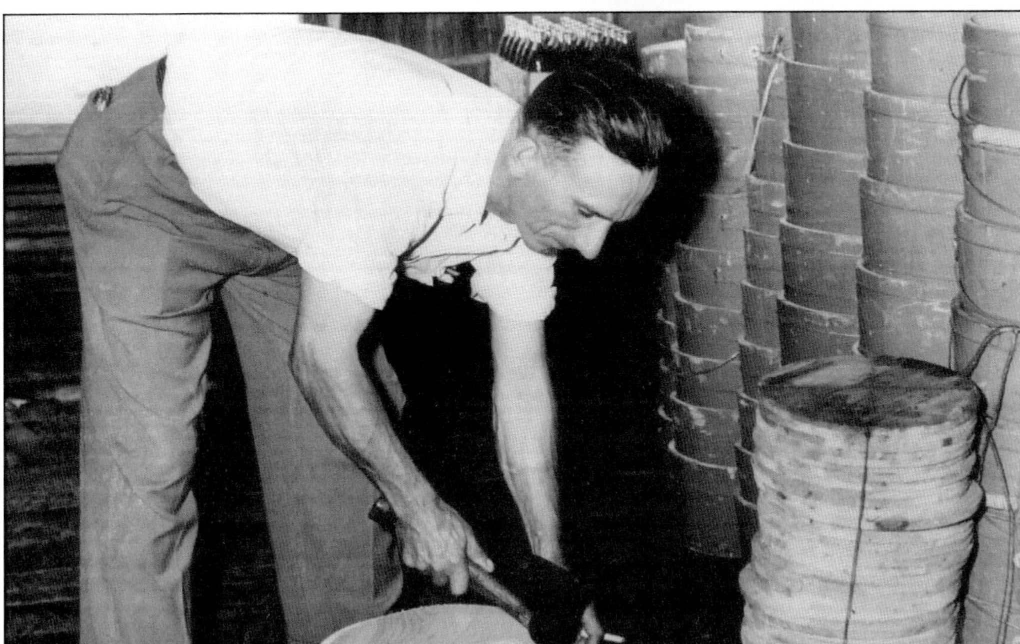

Vernon Edward "Burn" Watkins Sr. owned the Watkins Dock, which was established in 1943 at the end of Lawson Road. Here, he prepares barrels of fish for shipment. On this particular day, he caught so many fish that he had to send his son Vernon Jr. to the icehouse in Hampton to get ice. It took three trips to get all the fish to Fass Brothers in Portsmouth to ship. (Courtesy of V.E. Watkins Jr.)

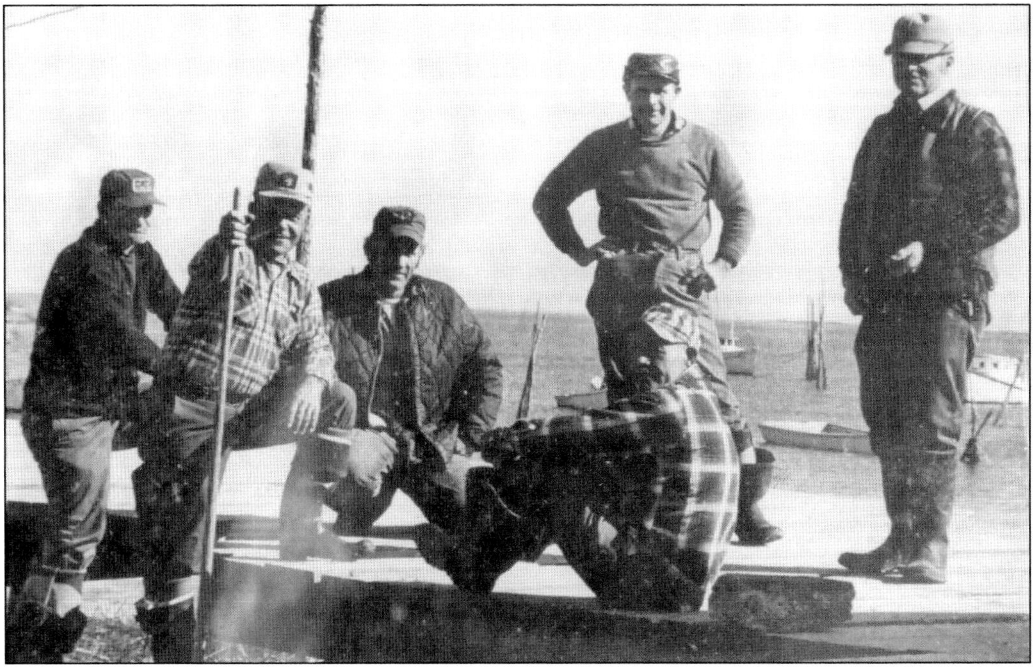

Local watermen talk on the dock after a day of work. They are, from left to right, William Humphrey "Ump" Insley, Robert Holloway, Marvin "Woog" Winder, Ivy Holloway, Norman "Hut" Holloway, and Ned "Nink" Winder. (Courtesy of Carol Ann Winder Mann.)

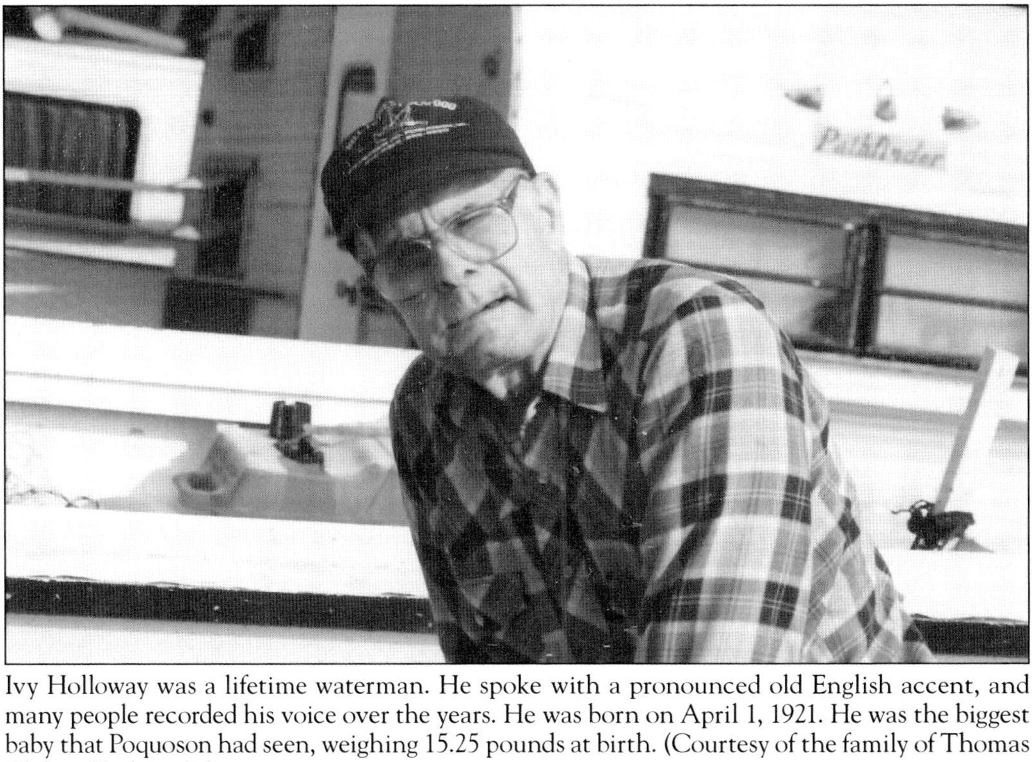


Ivy Holloway was a lifetime waterman. He spoke with a pronounced old English accent, and many people recorded his voice over the years. He was born on April 1, 1921. He was the biggest baby that Poquoson had seen, weighing 15.25 pounds at birth. (Courtesy of the family of Thomas Clifton Hudgins Jr.)

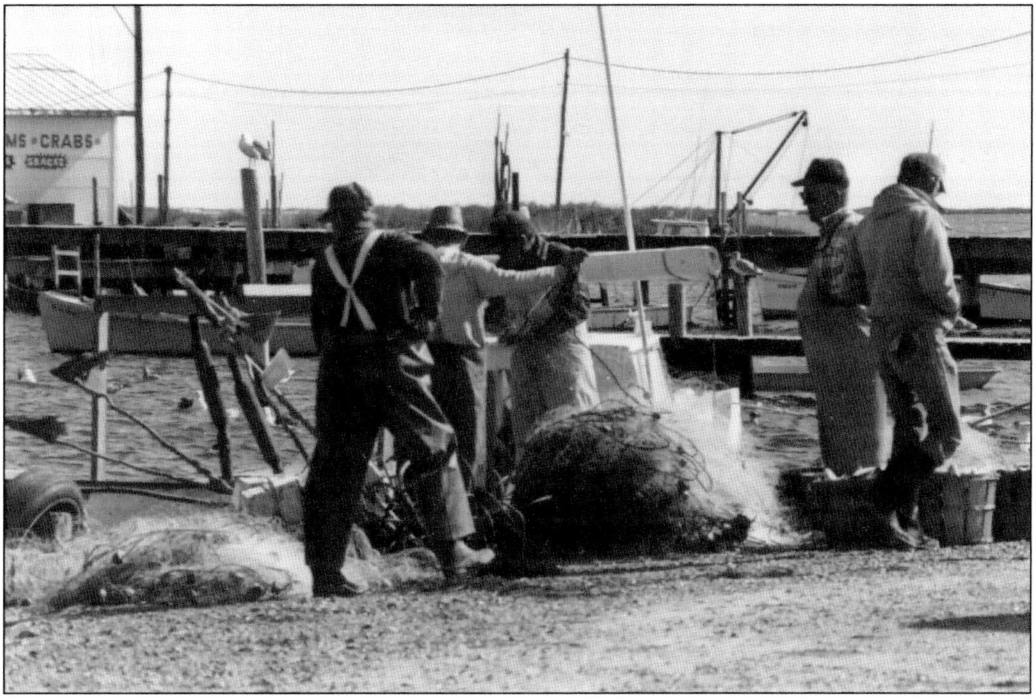

After a day of fishing, the fishermen at Messick Point ready their nets for the next day's work. The nets were checked for any rips, which would have to be mended and then folded to be placed on the boats. (Courtesy of the family of Thomas C. Hudgins Jr.)

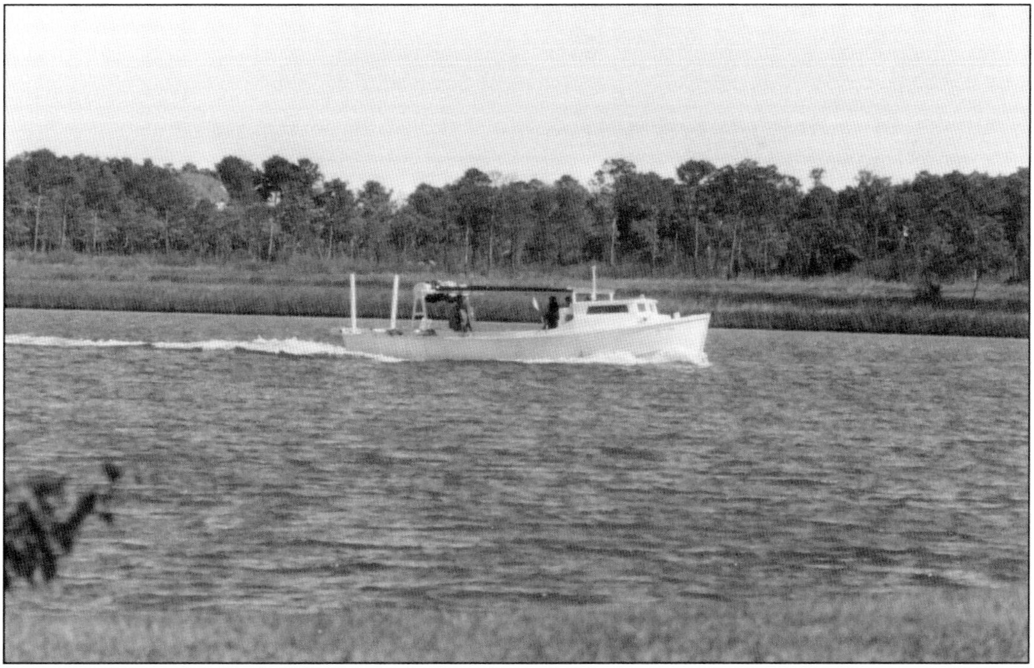

A dead-rise boat heads out for a day of working the water. The fishing boats usually leave early in the morning and return in the afternoon for lunch. The rest of the day was spent preparing the boat for the next day. (Courtesy of the family of Thomas C. Hudgins Jr.)

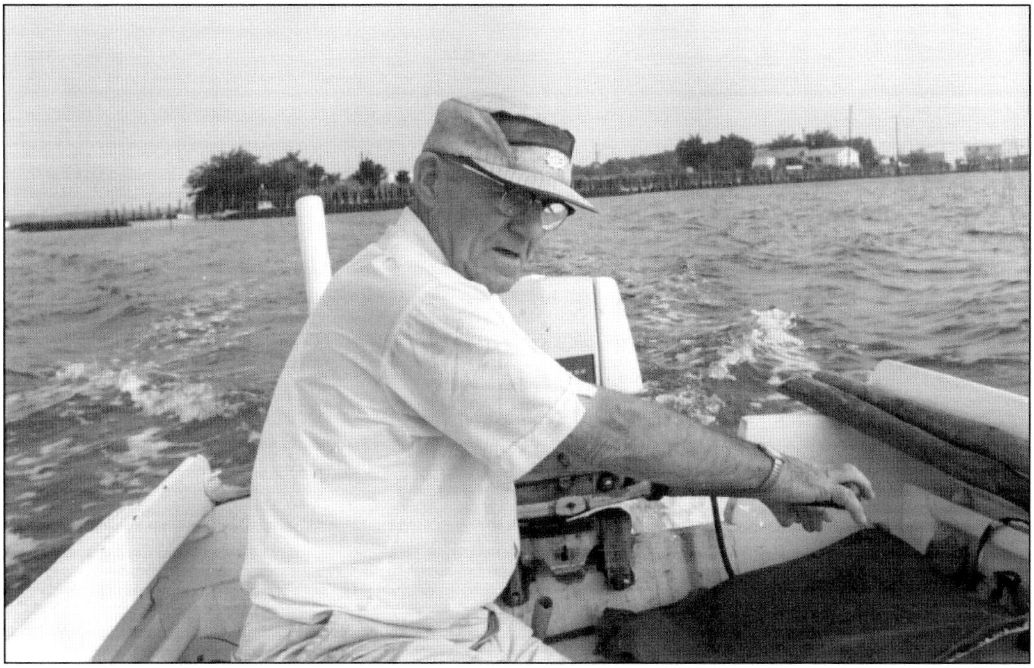

Harry Melvin Evans heads out from the dock at Messick Point in his boat for a day of recreational fishing. He was born in 1899 and married Sallie Martin. His parents were Clarence Evans and Mary Louise Messick, the daughter of early settlers Zaddock Wesley Messick and Indiana Rowe. (Courtesy of Frances Evans Potts.)

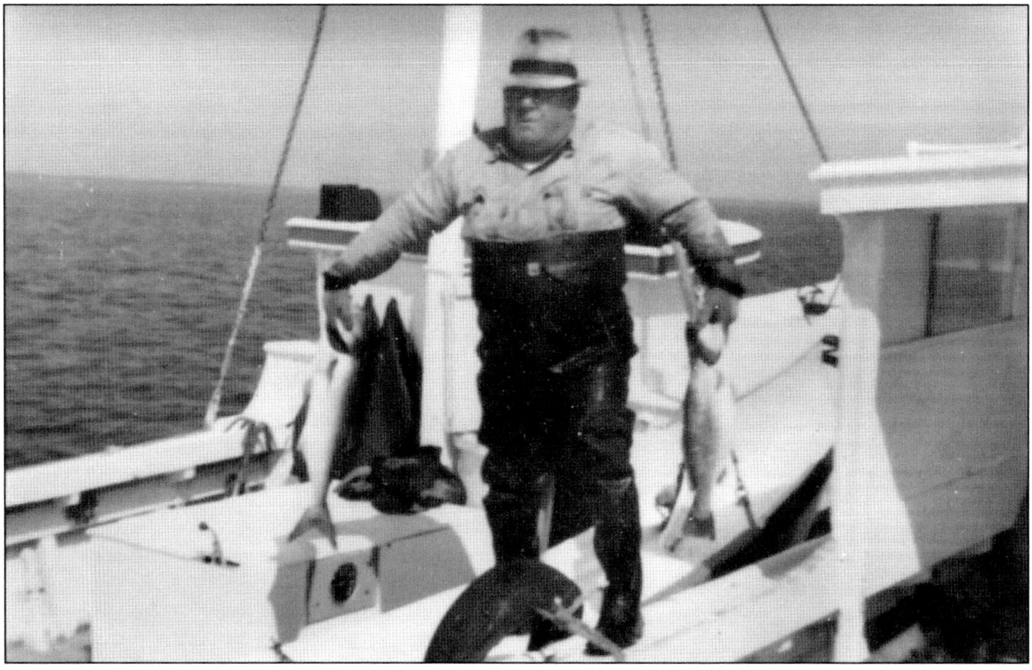

Joseph Allen Evans is seen here showing off the two large fish he just caught. He was one of 11 children, along with Harry Melvin Evans. He was the father of Frances Evans Potts. (Courtesy of Frances Evans Potts.)

Erma Powell Evans examines a dead dolphin on the dock with an unidentified man. She was the wife of Joseph Allen Evans. She was born February 26, 1910, and died on November 16, 1988. She was the mother of Frances Evans Potts. (Courtesy of Frances Evans Potts.)

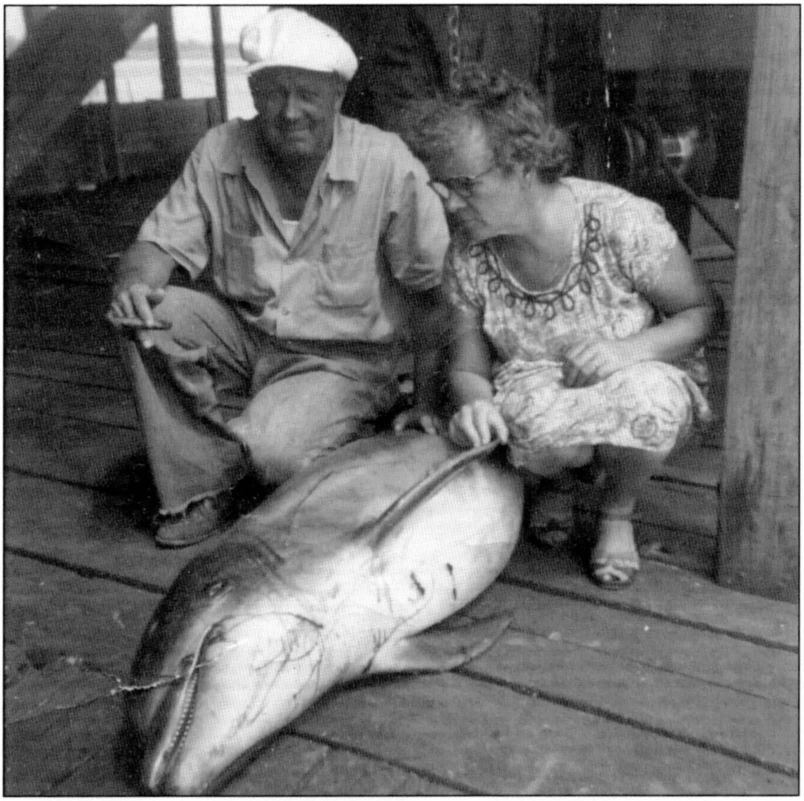

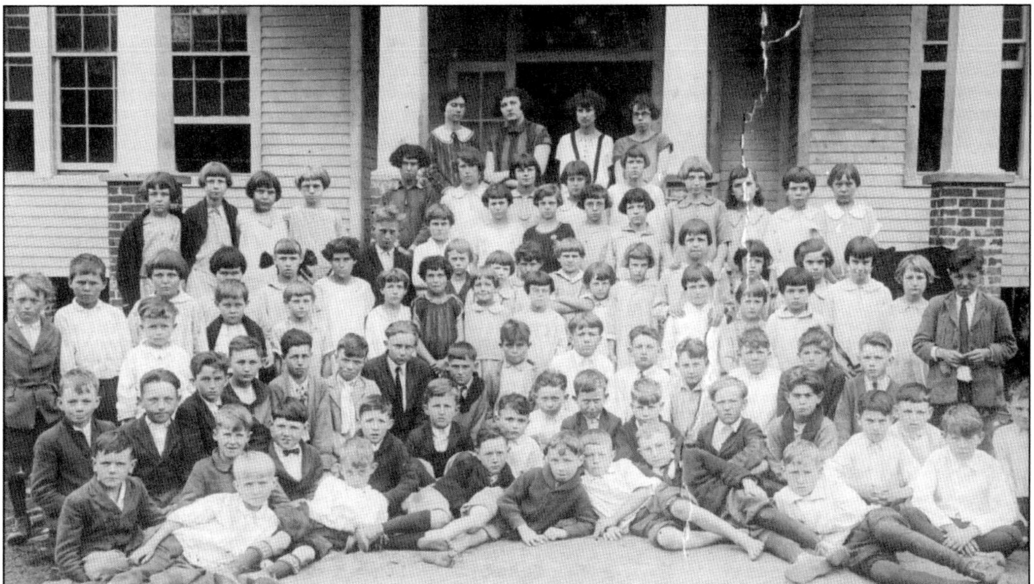

School students from the second East Messick School sit by the front porch in 1924. The teachers standing at the top of the stairs were Betty Forrest White, Helen Amory Holloway, Carrie Freeman Hawkins, and Louise Page Wilson. The school later became a rooming house. (Courtesy of the Poquoson Historical Society.)

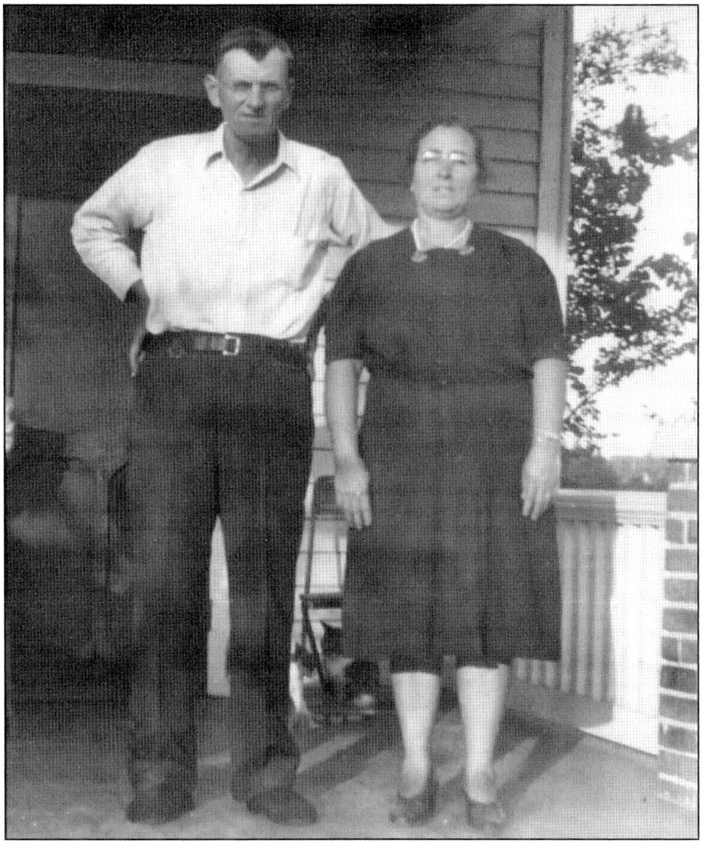

Frank Insley and his wife, Martha Jane Firth, founded a store in the first East Messick School, located on the curve of Messick Road across from the Ridge Road intersection. (Courtesy of Edna Mae Insley Barr.)

Frank Insley's store (below) was a popular meeting place in the 1940s and 1950s. Like many small general stores, it contained all types of merchandise for the community. Many types of penny candy, such as Mary Janes, candy cigarettes, fireballs, and wax lips, could be picked out from behind the candy counter. (Courtesy of Leroy Wade.)

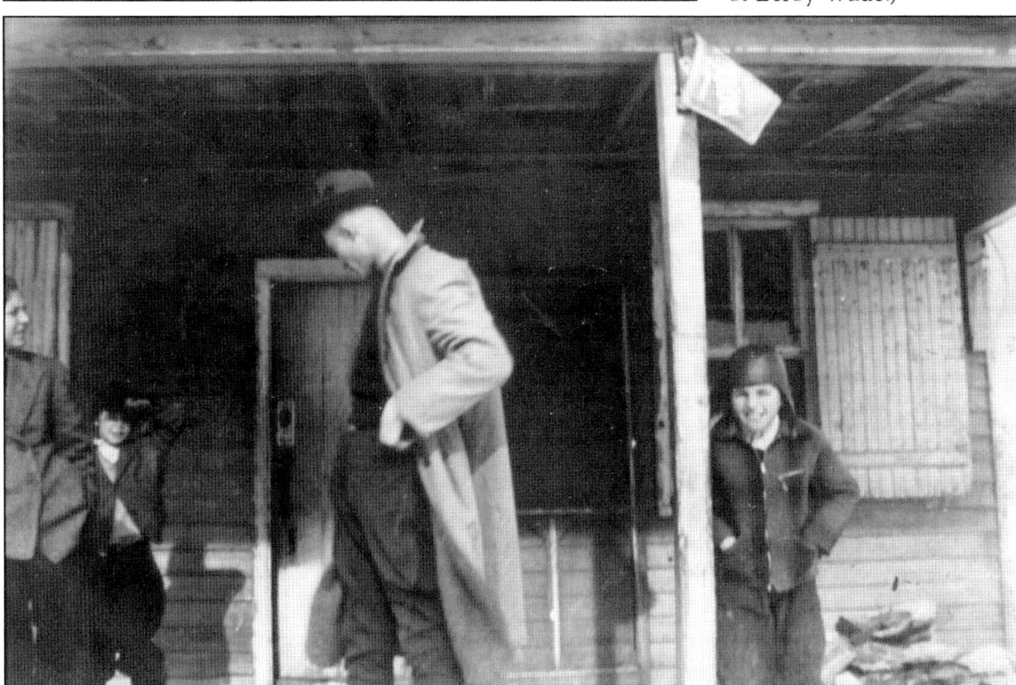

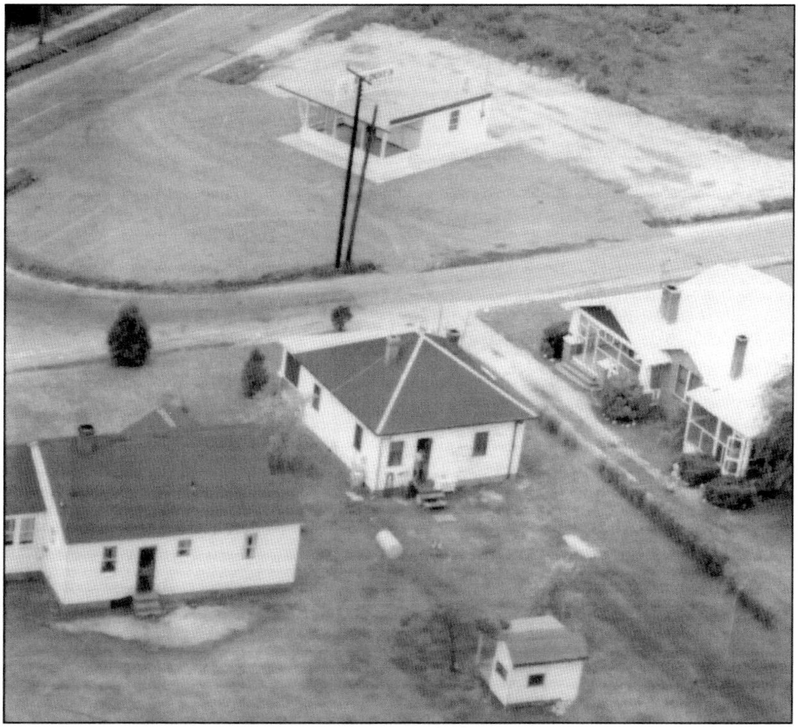

This new soft-serve ice cream business was built at the intersection of Lawson Road and Poquoson Avenue. It was the first of its kind in Poquoson, and would later house other restaurants, including the Crabcake House. (Courtesy of the Poquoson Historical Society.)

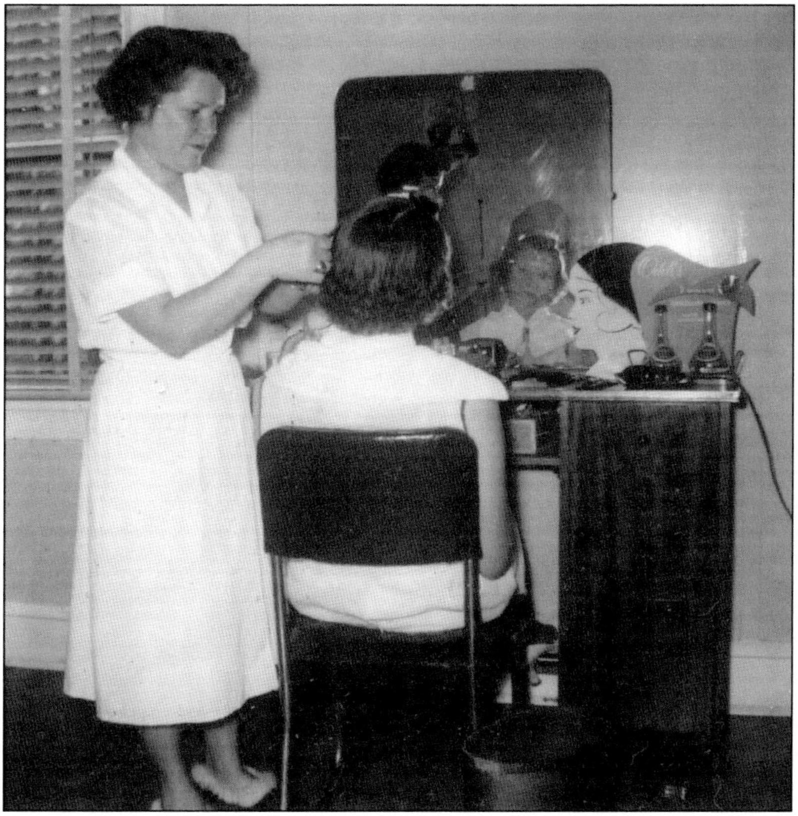

Peachie Hopkins Downs owned a hair salon in the 1950s and 1960s called Lou-Paige Beauty Shoppe. She was well known with a large clientele from the Messick area. (Courtesy of Susan Downs Herring.)

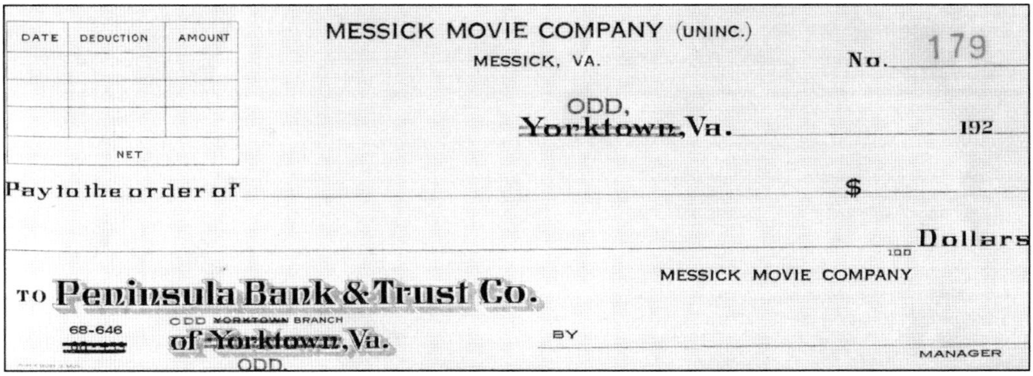

| DATE | DEDUCTION | AMOUNT |
| --- | --- | --- |
| | | |
| | | |
| | | |
| NET | | |

MESSICK MOVIE COMPANY (UNINC.)
MESSICK, VA.

No. 179

ODD,
~~Yorktown~~, Va. 192

Pay to the order of $

Dollars
100

TO Peninsula Bank & Trust Co.
ODD ~~YORKTOWN~~ BRANCH
of ~~Yorktown~~, Va.
ODD.

68-646

MESSICK MOVIE COMPANY

BY

MANAGER

Messick had several movie theaters over the years. This check is from the Messick Movie Company. Note that "Yorktown" was crossed out and "Odd" was printed above it. (Courtesy of the Poquoson Historical Society.)

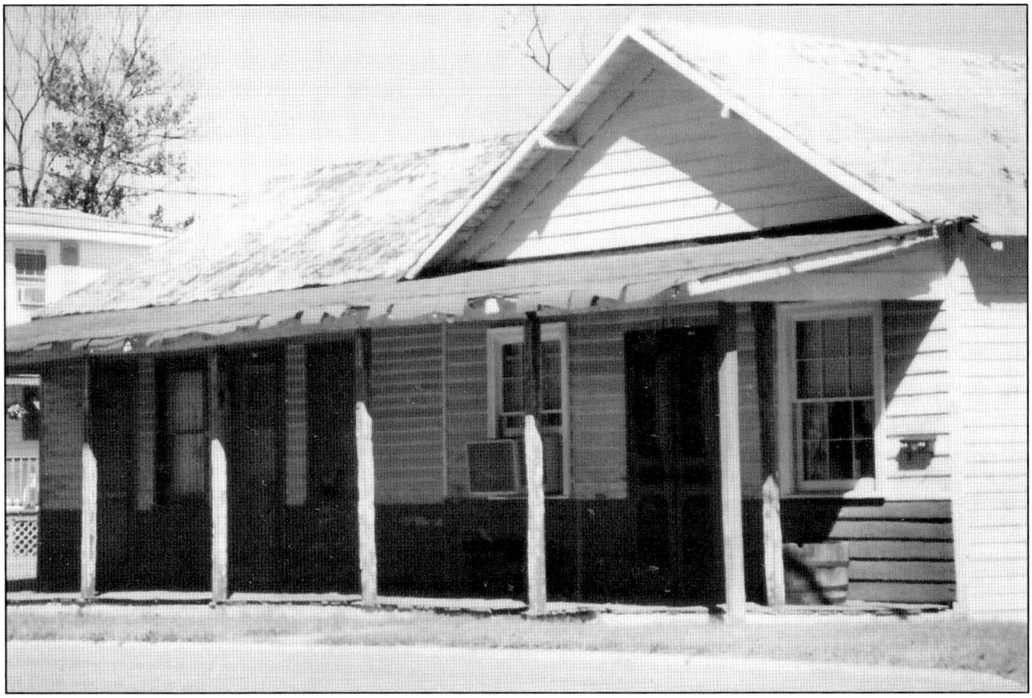

Brownie's was a fixture in Messick for years. This photograph shows the large front porch, which provided a place for people to sit and talk. Inside were pinball machines and a counter to order hamburgers. (Courtesy of Barbara Hudgins Whitlow.)

The Fire Carnival was a fundraiser for the Messick Fire Department. The volunteer organization relied on donations and fundraisers to purchase equipment. Here, at the 1955 Fire Carnival, fire chief Herbert Wiley Downs holds hands with his niece Kathy Krueger. (Courtesy of Susan Downs Herring.)

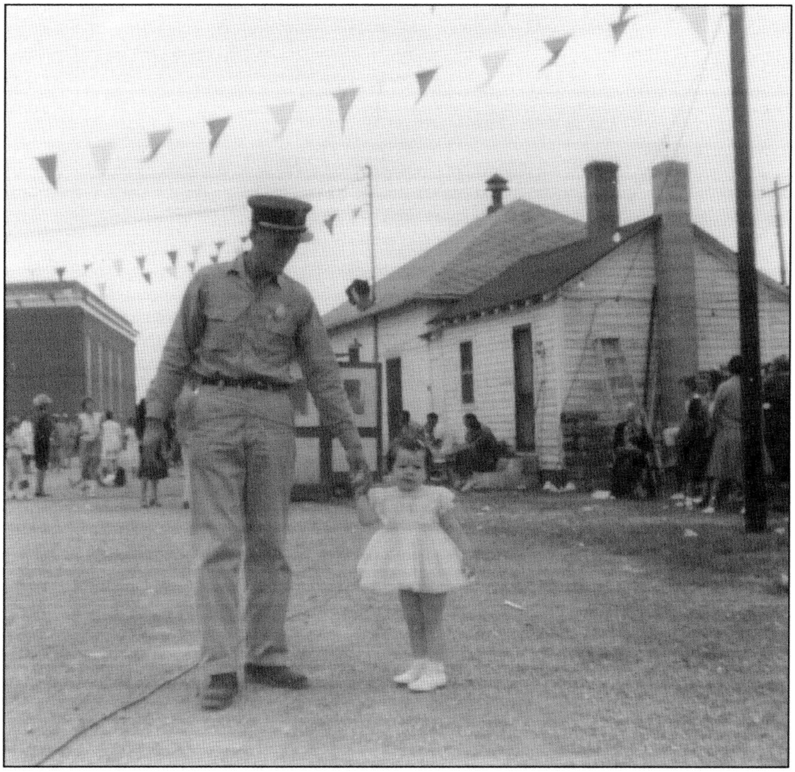

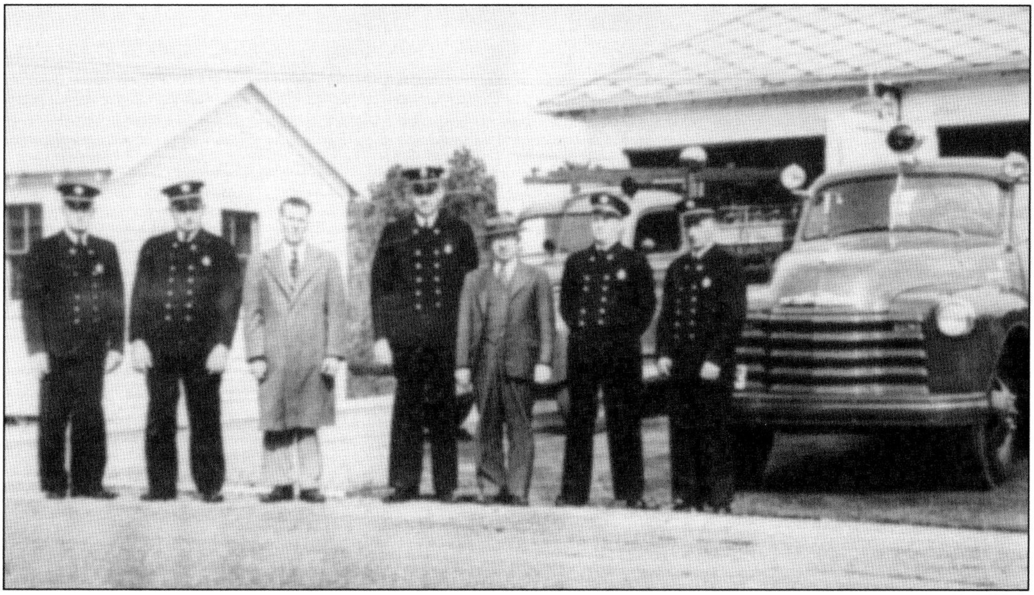

The first fire department was started on October 10, 1941. The Messick Fire Department was a totally volunteer organization that began with just 18 members. The first fire truck was purchased in 1941, and it was stored at the old barrel factory building on Poquoson Avenue until a new structure could be completed in 1943. The volunteer officers were Lorenza Insley, Clarence Evans, Tom Hudgins, Alton White, Henry Hunt, Burgess Lawson, and Vernon Watkins. (Courtesy of the family of Mary Quinn.)

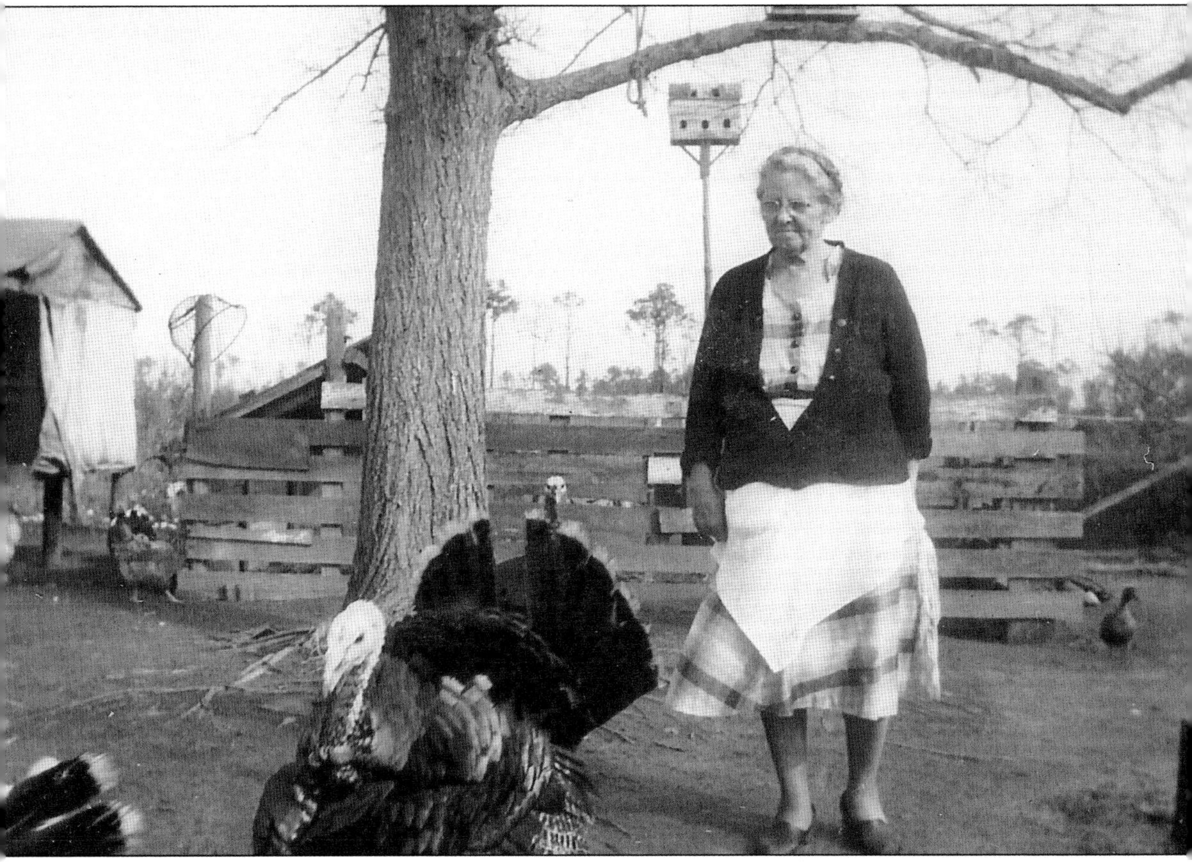

Annie Huggett Forrest is seen here in her poultry yard with a large tom turkey, chickens, and geese. She was born in 1890 to Josiah M. Huggett and Sarah Fiamah Forrest. She married Andrew Ira Forrest, and they lived on North Lawson Road in Messick. (Courtesy of Bethany Forrest Diggs.)

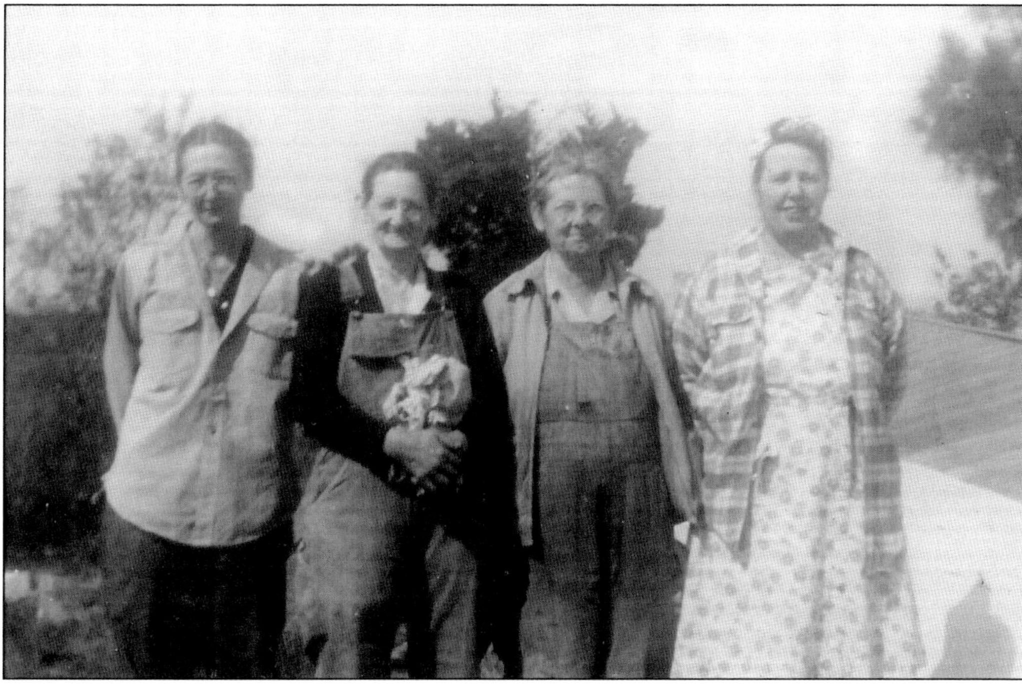

It was a tradition in the area to harvest wild asparagus. Known as the "spargus" women (from left to right), Sadie Huggett, Polly Jordan, Annie Forrest, and Evelyn Diggs went to areas known only to them to harvest asparagus. (Courtesy of Bethany Forrest Diggs.)

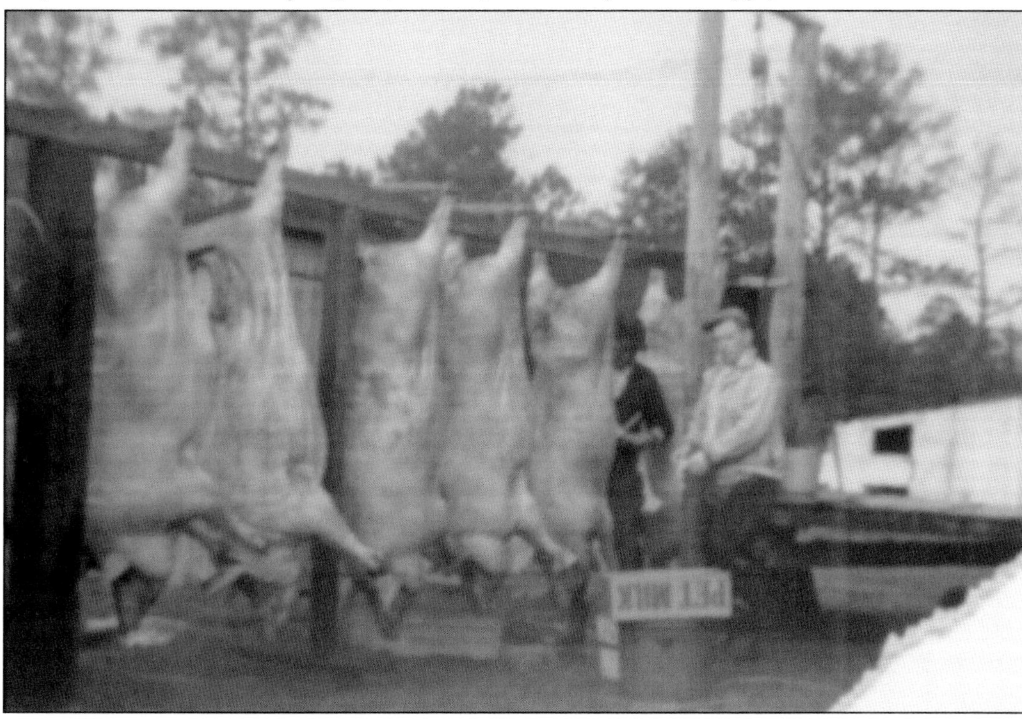

In the 1950s, people still killed their livestock for food. Here, Hartness Insley, left, is gutting a hog with another man. Dolly Boy Pauls was the head man at hog killings. (Courtesy of Sonny Insley.)

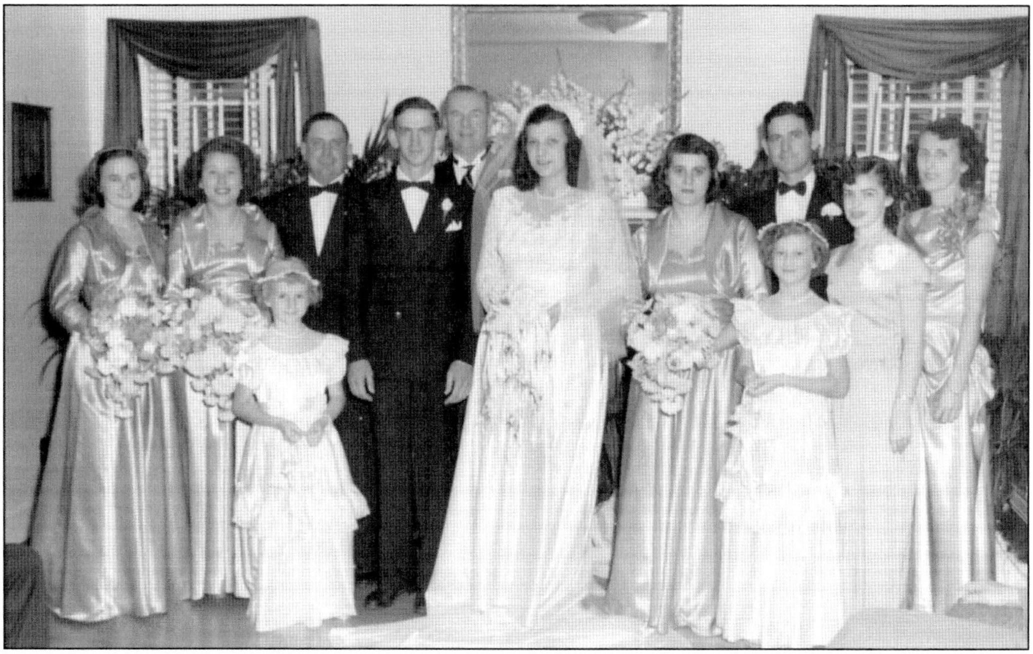

In the early 1950s, while Trinity United Methodist Church was being remodeled, home weddings were commonplace. The wedding of Mack Burcher of York County to Elizabeth Anne Forrest of Messick was held in the home of her parents, John Henry "Buck" and Lavinia Elizabeth Forrest, with Rev. Ralph J. Yow presiding. (Courtesy of Barbara Hudgins Whitlow.)

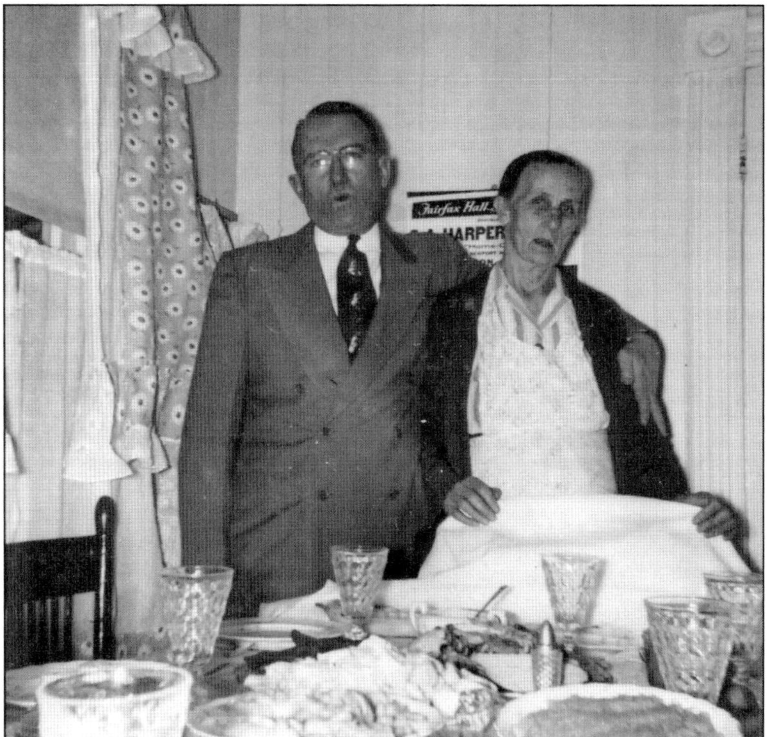

James Thomas Forrest and his mother, Martha Chesser Forrest, get ready for a holiday meal. James Thomas Forrest left Poquoson and established the Forrest Seafood Company in Norfolk. (Courtesy of Barbara Hudgins Whitlow.)

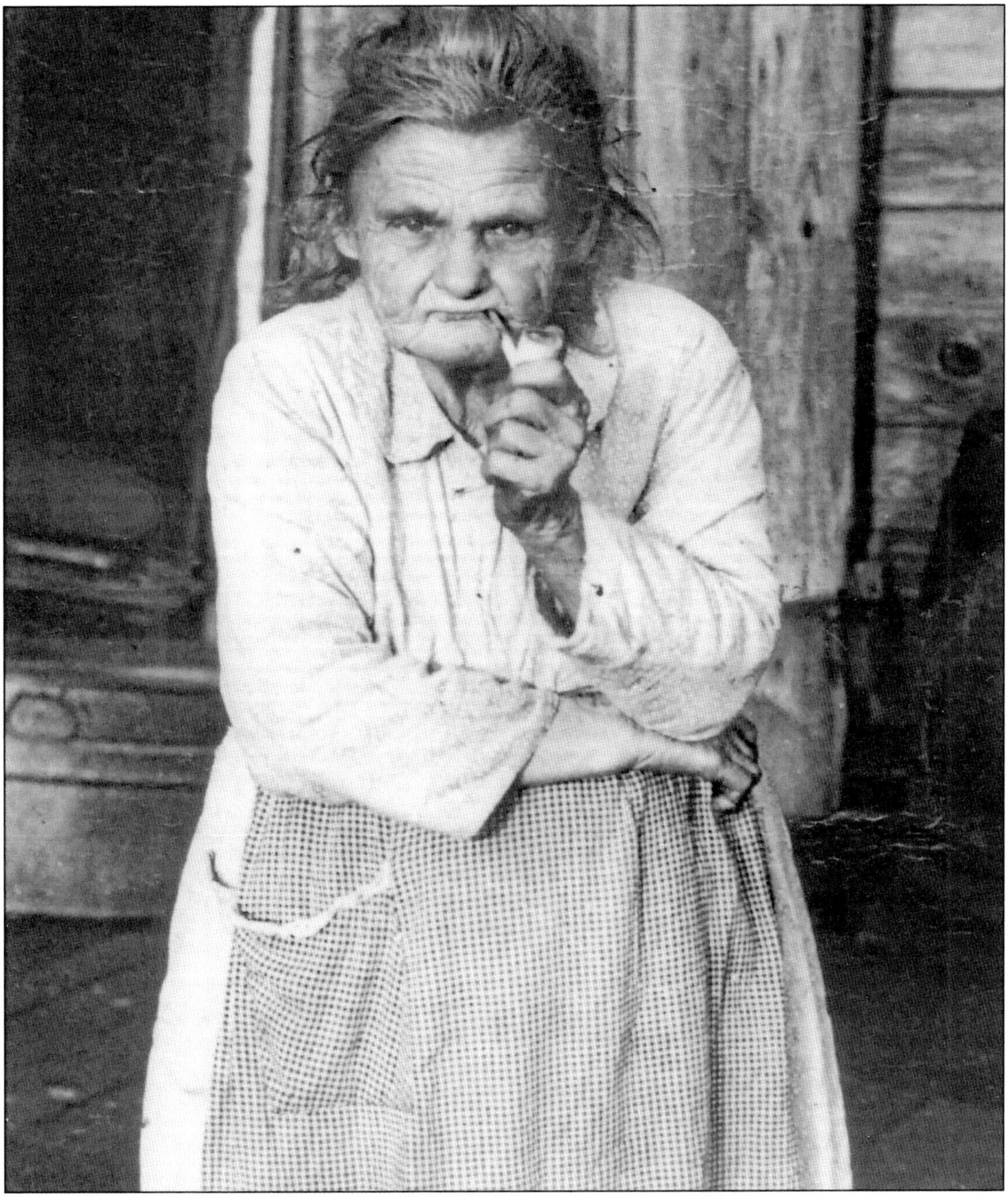

Margaret "Mag" Pauls was born in 1880 and lived to the age of 106. She lived all her life at the end of Messick Point. Note the pipe she is holding in this photograph. Many women in the community smoked pipes, but photographs of them are rare. Many local ladies did not wish to be photographed or even seen in public with their pipes. If visitors came to call, pipes would often be hidden. Sometimes, women would hastily hide a lit pipe in their apron pocket, resulting in burn holes. In one story about a contemporary of Mag Pauls, when an unexpected visitor came to her home, a lady quickly slipped her pipe between chair cushions. Unfortunately, the pipe was lit, burning a hole in the chair cushion. (Courtesy of Phyllis A. Firth and Harold Freeman.)

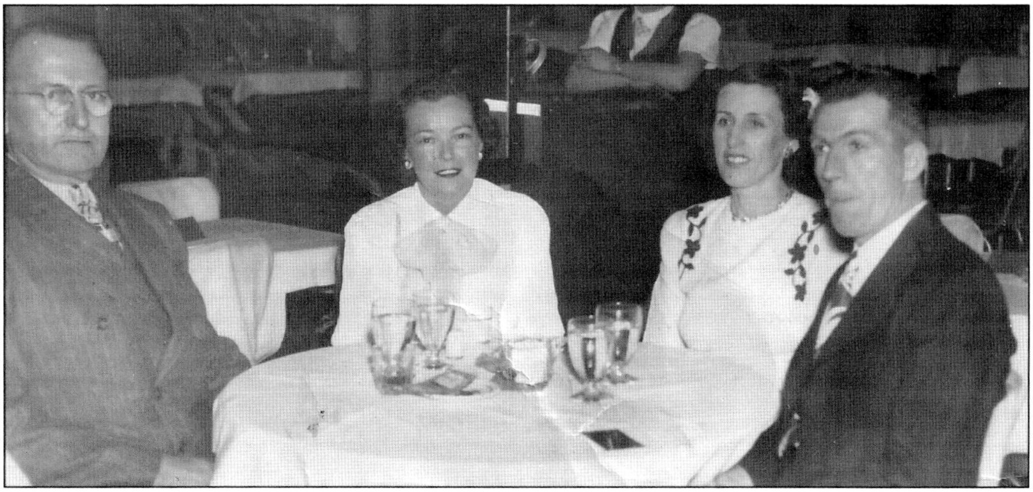

From left to right, James Thomas Forrest, Nina Forrest, Nell Hudgins, and Thomas Hudgins caught a steamer at Old Point Comfort to the Lord Baltimore Hotel for a holiday weekend in Baltimore. James Thomas Forrest was Nell Forrest Hudgins's brother. Outings like this were common in the 1940s and 1950s, before the interstate system, when steamers ran up and down the Chesapeake Bay. It was the quickest method of traveling between Virginia and Maryland. (Courtesy of Barbara Hudgins Whitlow.)

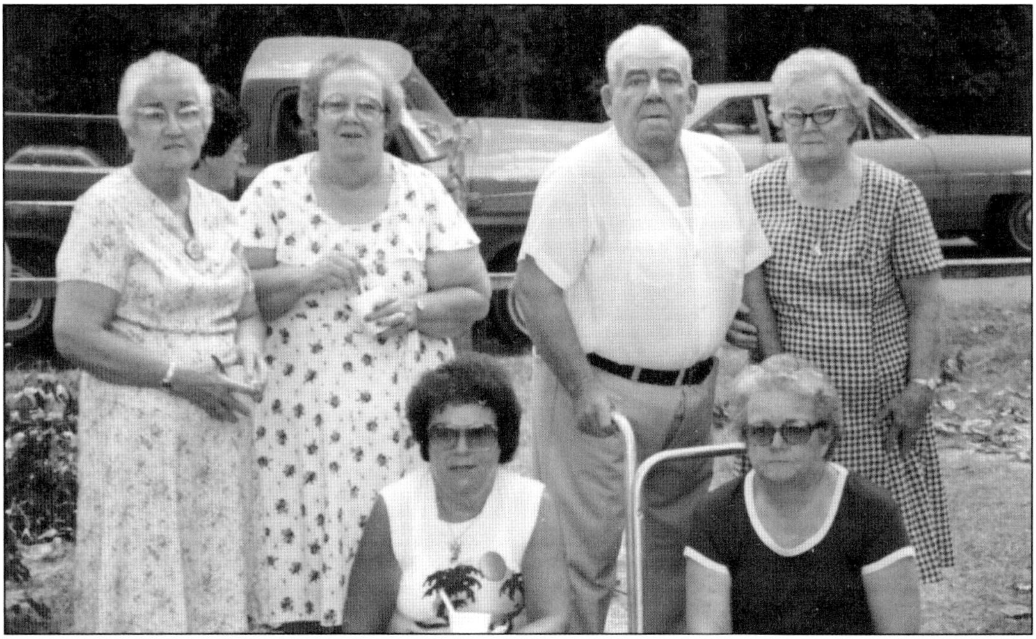

This Evans family reunion photograph includes, from left to right, (sitting) Lottie Evans Hopkins and Matilda Jane Evans Smith; (standing) Viola Evans Bunting, Edna Earline Evans Powell, Joseph Allen Evans, and Katherine Elizabeth Evans Holloway. There were originally 11 Evans children: Harry, Joseph, Will, Honey, Katherine, Louise, Lottie, Matilda, Viola, Edna, and Mary. Lottie Evans Hopkins was the last surviving child of Clarence Melvin Evans and Mary Louise Messick. The parents were married at Trinity United Methodist Church on November 30, 1895. This photograph was taken at one of the last reunions held, when everyone brought their favorite dish to the town park in Poquoson. (Courtesy of Frances Evans Potts.)

*Five*

# POQUOSON

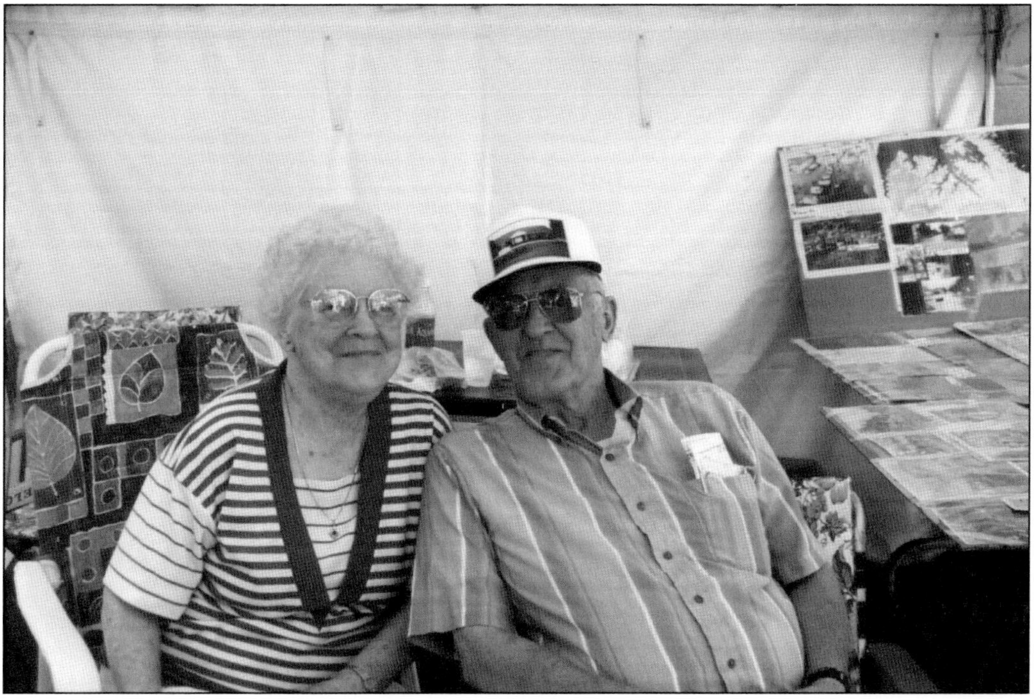

Florence Hopkins Shaw and her husband, Harold, are seen here at the 1997 Poquoson Seafood Festival. Their birthdays usually coincided with the festival when it was held in September, and a celebration was held by the Poquoson Historical Society. (Courtesy of Barbara Hudgins Whitlow.)

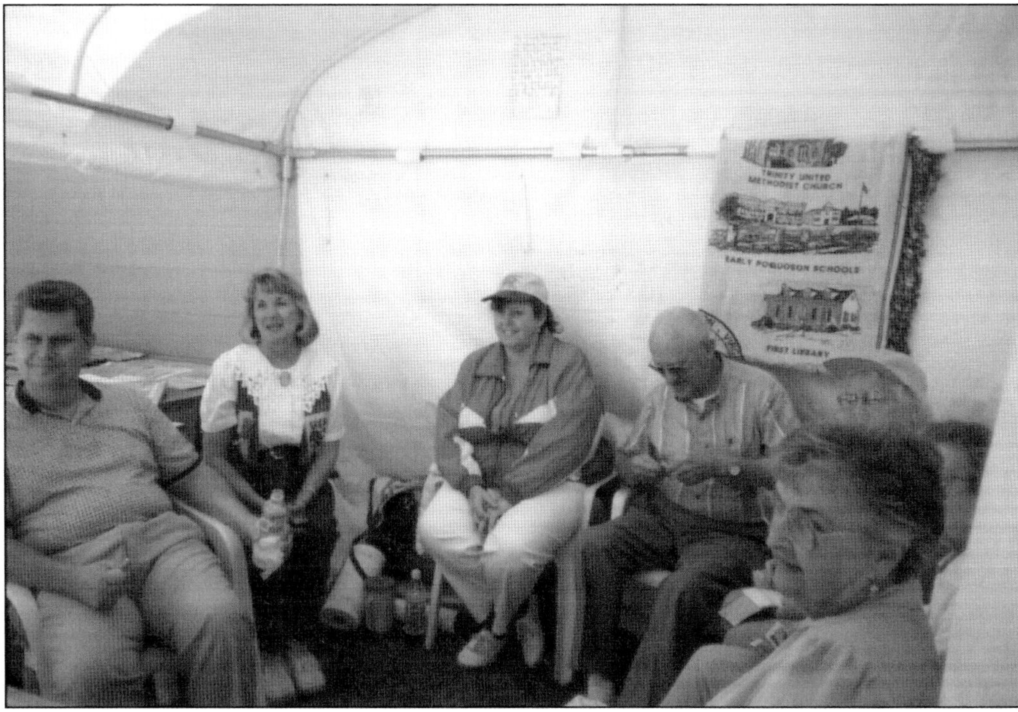


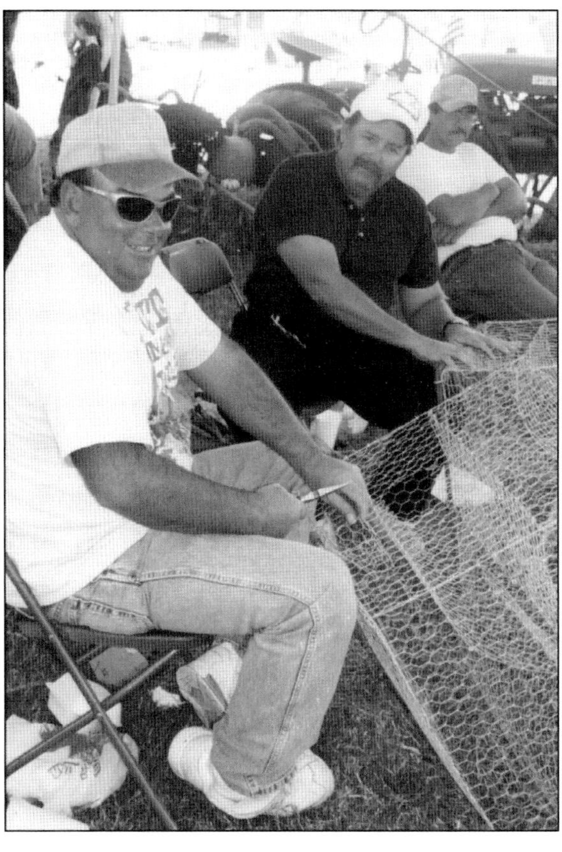

Members of the Poquoson Historical Society are seen above working at the Seafood Festival. They are, from left to right, Robert Holloway, Barbara Hudgins Whitlow, Diane Hudgins Holloway, Harold Shaw, Florence Hopkins Shaw, Emma Watkins, and Jessie Faye Forrest. (Courtesy of Barbara Hudgins Whitlow.)

The Poquoson Seafood Festival began in 1980 as a celebration of the small seaside community. Today, it has grown into a major regional event attended by approximately 50,000 people over the three days. Here, watermen Chet McPherson (left) and Johnny Forrest make crab pots at the festival. (Courtesy of Barbara Hudgins Whitlow.)

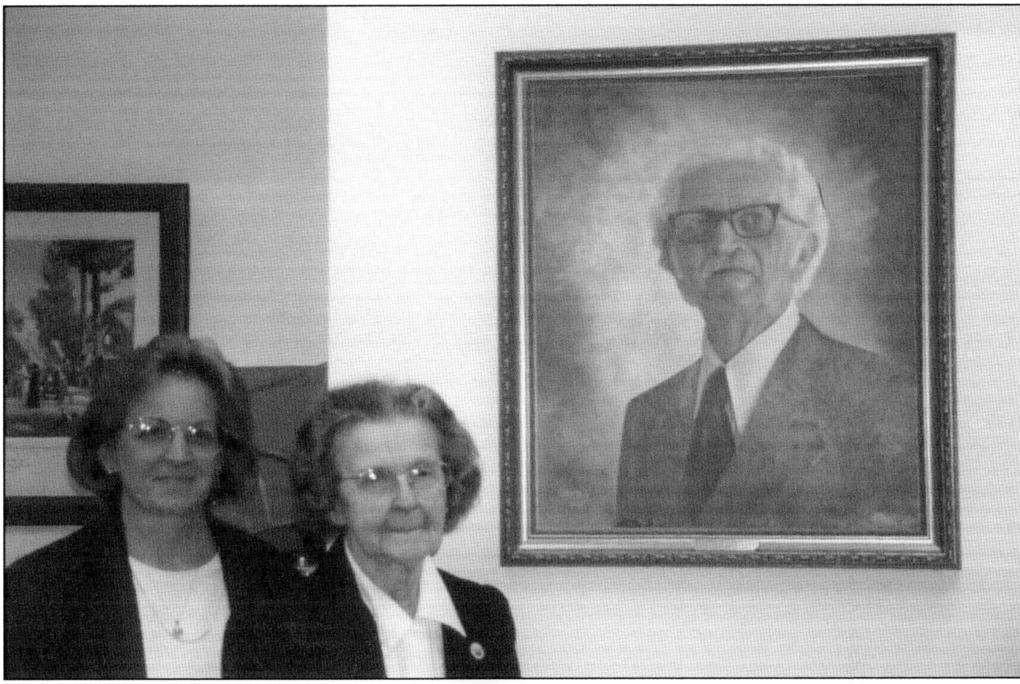

Thomas Vincent Watkins's portrait was dedicated by his wife, Emma Watkins (above, right), and their daughter Carroll Watkins Martin (left) at the Poquoson Public Library Roots Cellar. Watkins was the first historian for the City of Poquoson, and he wrote *A History of Poquoson in Three Parts*, the second edition of which was recently published. (Courtesy of Barbara Hudgins Whitlow.)

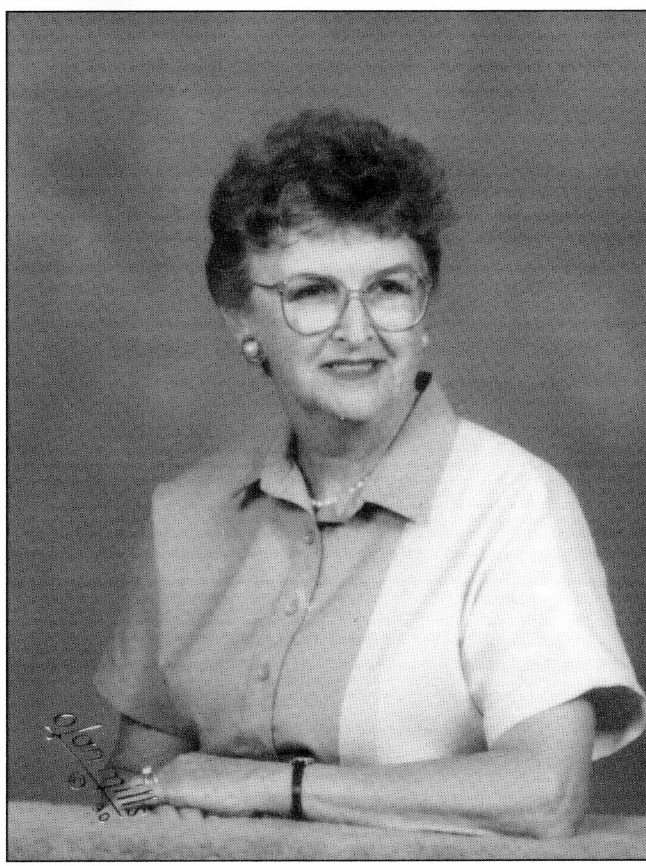

This formal portrait of Jessie Faye Forrest by Olan Mills Studios was hung in the Poquoson Library Root Cellar for many years. Forrest was the wife of the first mayor, Carroll Thomas Forrest, and she was the first female rescue squad director in Poquoson. She was also a founding member of the Poquoson Historical Society, where her portrait now hangs. (Courtesy of Susan Downs Herring.)

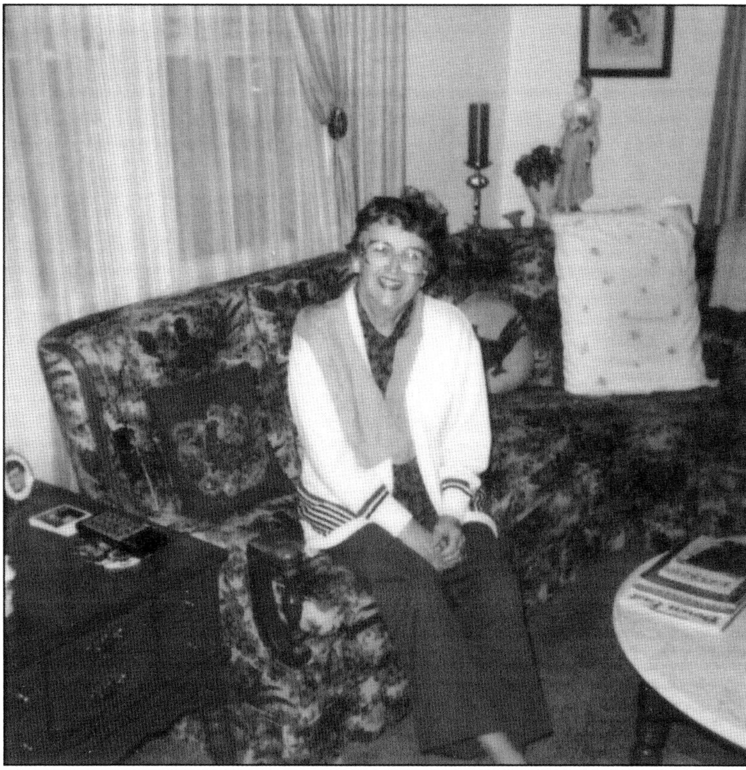

Jessie Faye Forrest relaxes on the sofa during a visit with Florence and Harold Shaw. Forrest had a passion for history and a charismatic personality. She lobbied the City of Poquoson for the establishment of a historical society that would be devoted to the preservation of Poquoson's rich history. Her leadership skills and perseverance paid off in 1986, when the Poquoson Historical Society was commissioned by the city. (Courtesy of Susan Downs Herring.)

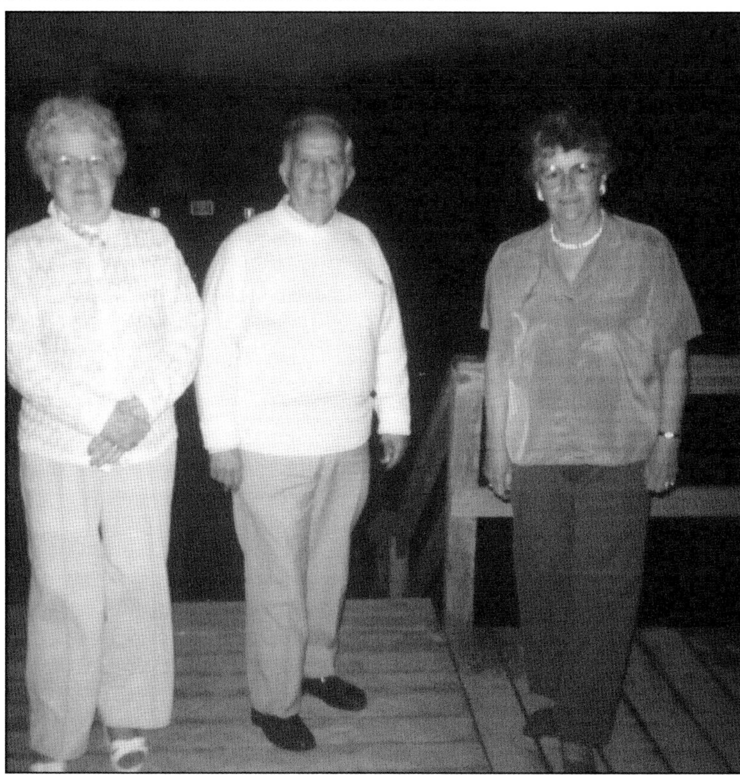

From left to right, original Poquoson Historical Society members Florence Shaw, Floyd Carmines, and Jessie Faye Forrest stand at the end of a pier on Assateague Island during a trip to the Eastern Shore. (Courtesy of Susan Downs Herring.)

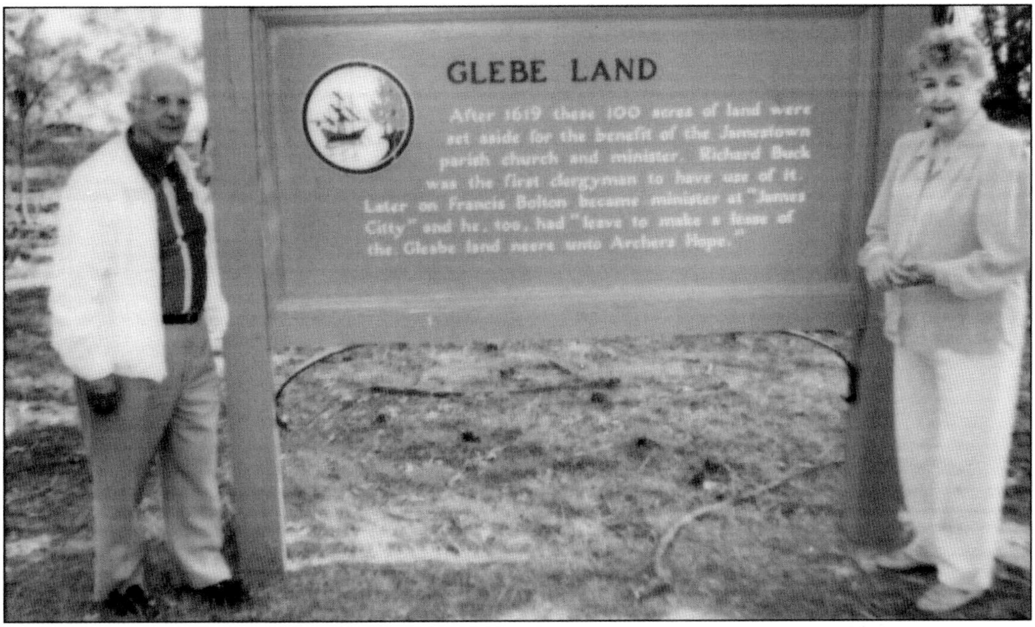


Floyd Carmines and Jessie Faye Forrest are seen here during one of the Poquoson Historical Society's early field trips to Archer's Hope on the James River. Carmines enjoyed traveling and had a large personal library. He was the son of Daniel Horatio Carmines and Bessie Florence Powell Carmines. (Courtesy of Susan Downs Herring.)

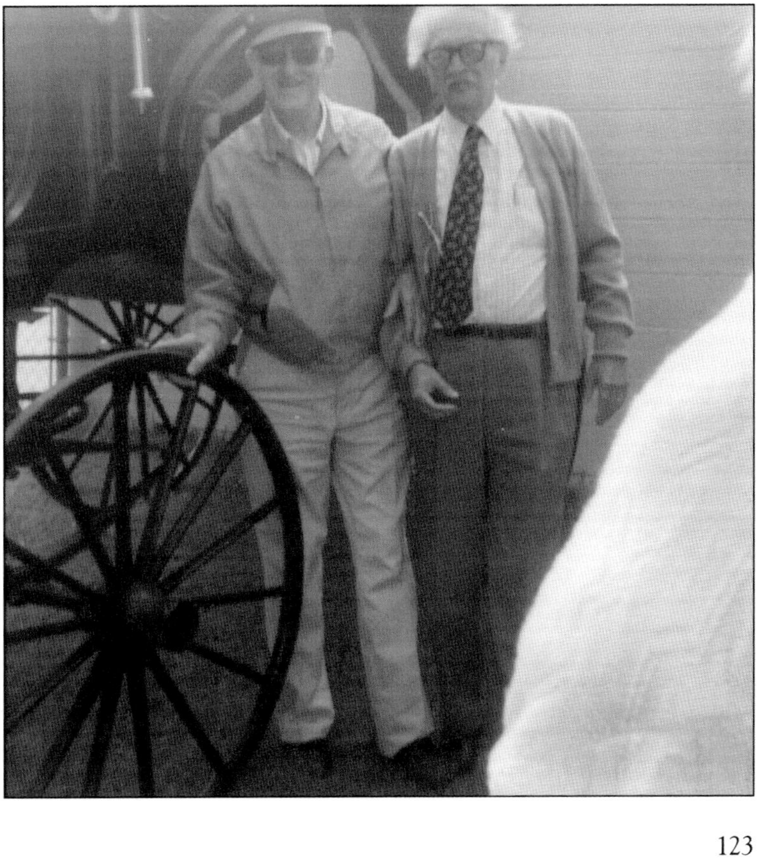

Harold Shaw (left) and local historian Thomas Vincent Watkins pose for a photograph in front of the original Claytor Rollins hearse. Both of the men were original members of the Poquoson Historical Society. Shaw was the treasurer for the organization for more than 20 years. He was 91 years old when he retired from his position. Watkins compiled the first definitive early history of Poquoson, *A History of Poquoson in Three Parts*, which was originally published in 1988. (Courtesy of Susan Downs Herring.)

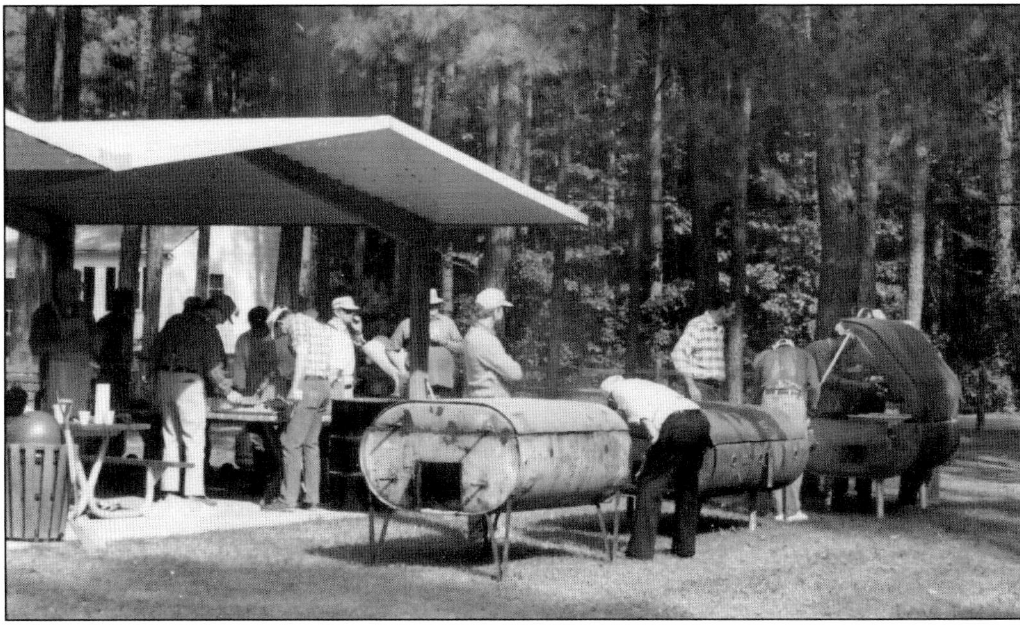

The Kiwanis Club is a very active civic group in Poquoson. They raise money for their budget each year by sponsoring a pig roast. Members of the Kiwanis Club begin cooking the pigs the day before the event. (Courtesy of the Kiwanis Club of Poquoson.)

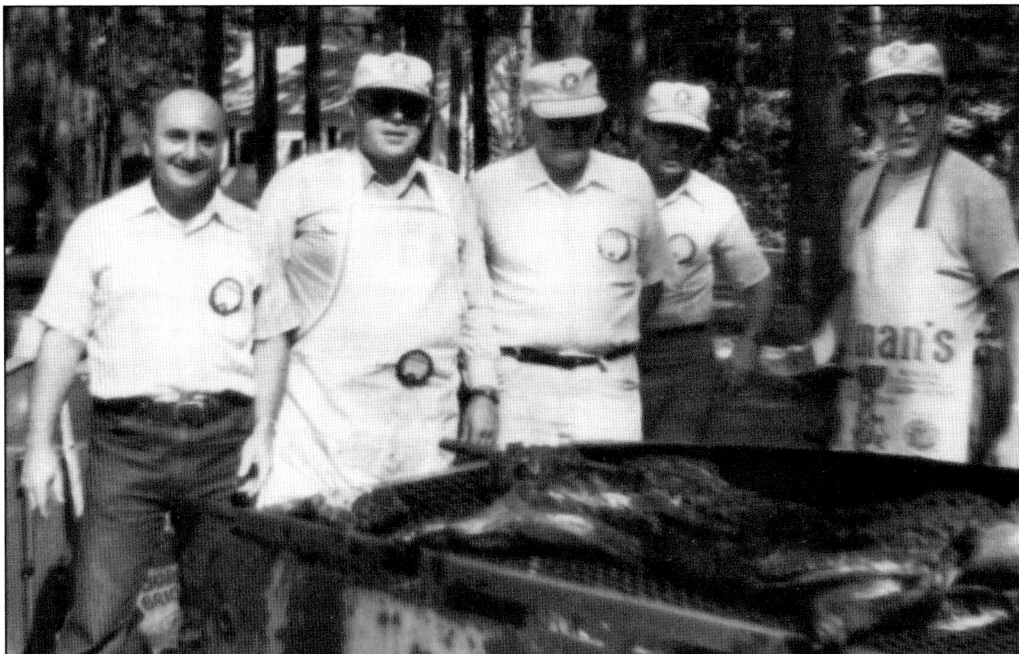

Members of the Kiwanis Club watch a pig roast on the smoker grill. The annual pig roast is a major event in Poquoson. Many people come from other cities to participate in the wonderful fundraiser. The proceeds of the event go to help local youth groups and to fund other important projects. Community is one of the keys to the success of Poquoson, and the Kiwanis Club is one of the groups that brings the community together. (Courtesy of the Kiwanis Club of Poquoson.)

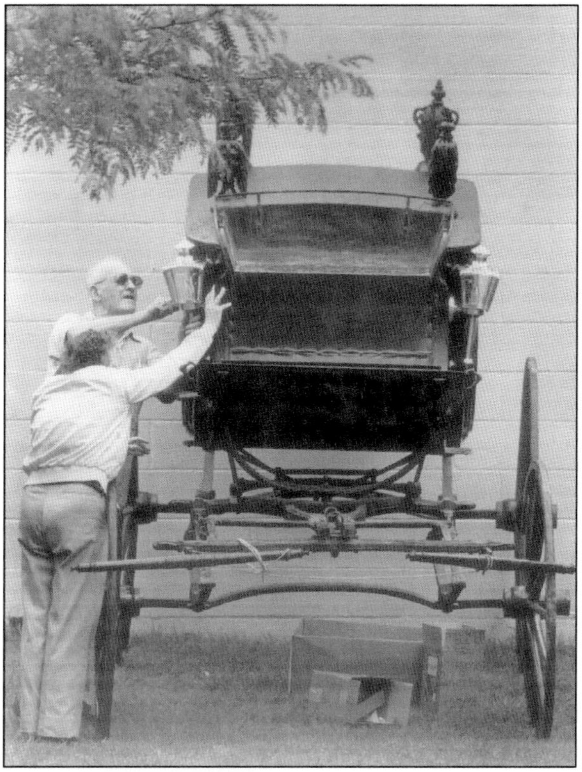

Harold Shaw and Lena Rollins replace the running lanterns on the original Rollins hearse. The hearse is still used for display at the Poquoson Seafood Festival and at funerals of prominent Poquoson residents. (Courtesy of Susan Downs Herring.)

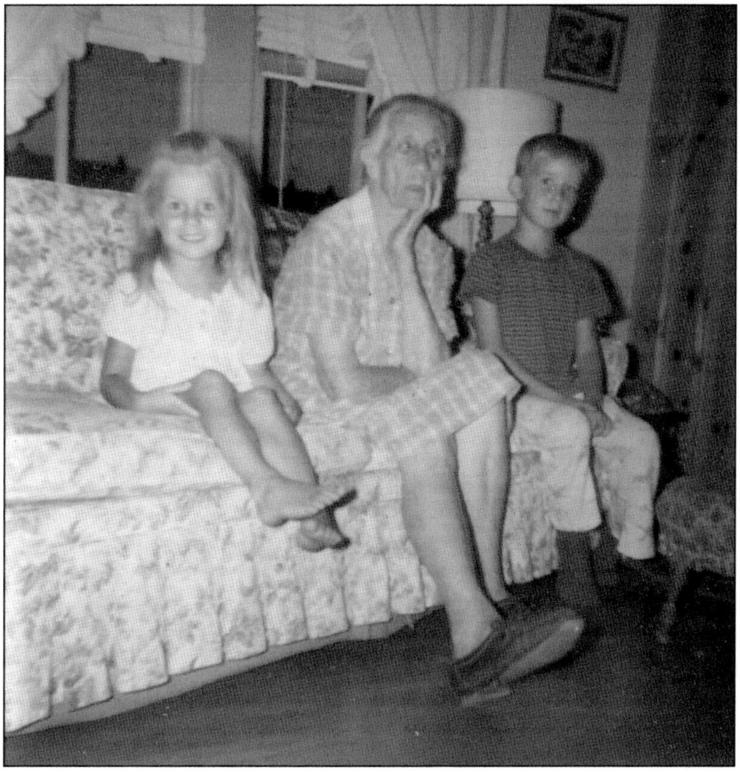

Everyone was excited to see man's first step on the moon on July 20, 1969. Here, Martha Chesser Forrest, at almost 90 years old, watches the television's live coverage of the event at her daughter Nell Forrest Hudgins's home on Messick Road with her great-grandchildren, Kimberly Anne and Tony Whitlow. Forrest was never convinced that the event really happened. (Courtesy of Barbara Hudgins Whitlow.)

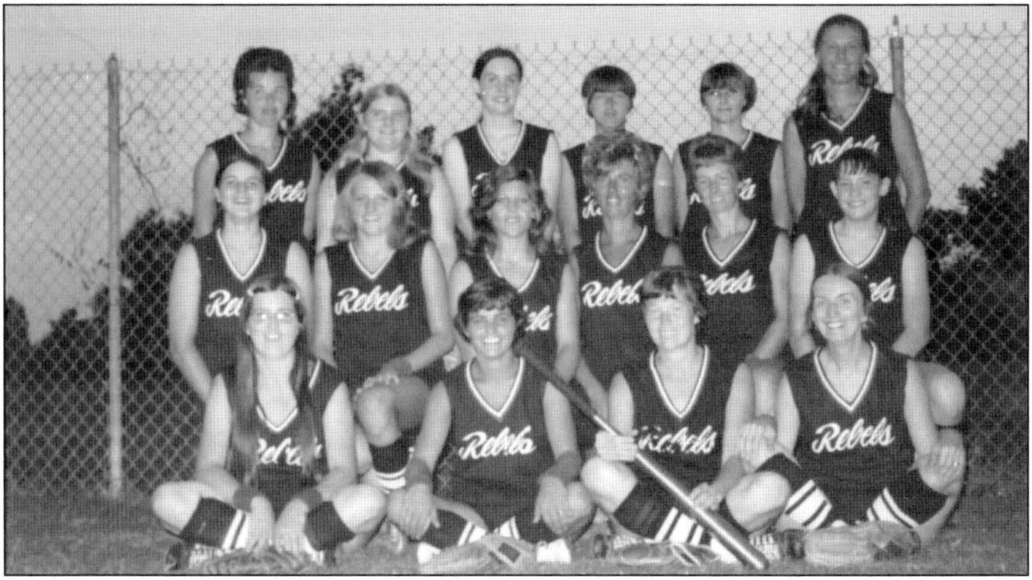


Softball was a popular sport for the young women of Poquoson in the 1970s. This 1973 Rebels softball team included, from left to right, (first row) Mae Richmond White, J.C. Holloway, Pearl Tignor, and Barbara Hudgins Whitlow; (second row) Debbie Guiant, Debbie Ward, Carol Parham, Frances Riggins, Pat Rollins Harris, and Sharon Pauls; (third row) Helen Gibbs Holloway, Debbie Luthie, Becky Phillips, Laura Mae Richmond, Audrey Dryden, and Sandra White Patrick. (Courtesy of Barbara Hudgins Whitlow.)

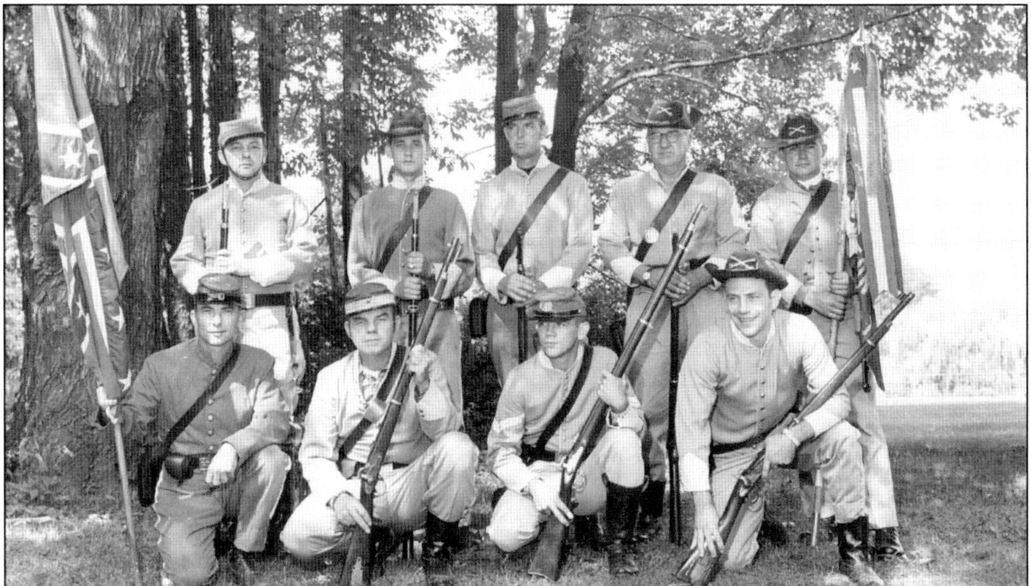

The Old Dominion Dragoons are a North-South Skirmish Association team member. They represent a Civil War unit of the 32nd Virginia Infantry that was made up of men from York County and Hampton. Founded in the late 1950s by Len Eastep and made up of men of Poquoson and the surrounding area, the team participates in the nationals, near Winchester, in October and May with team members using either muskets from the Civil War era or reproductions. (Courtesy of Barbara Hudgins Whitlow.)

# BIBLIOGRAPHY


Forrest, Jessie Faye. *Poquoson Post Offices*. Poquoson, VA: Poquoson Historical Society, 1988.

Trinity United Methodist Church. *A History of Trinity United Methodist Church, 1882–1982*. Poquoson, VA: self published, 1982.

Watkins, Thomas Vincent. *A History of Poquoson in Three Parts (1631–1860)*. Second edition. Richmond, VA: Brandylane Publishers, Inc., 2012.

Willett, Albert James. *Poquoson Watermen*. Easley, SC: Southern Historical Press, Inc., 1988.

———. *Poquoson Families, Volume I: The Forrest Family of the Poquoson District York County Virginia*. Bowie, MD: Heritage Books, 2001.